'If I had only one book to help me understand the Bible, this is the one I would go for. Skilfully edited by Dr Philip Johnston, a group of orthodox scholars not only give a comprehensive survey of all the books in the Bible, but also provide four chapters introducing both the Old and New Testaments (Story, Background, Theology, Interpretation) along with an important chapter "Between the Testaments". The style is clear and accessible, requires no specialist knowledge, and combines sound scholarship with an evident love for the Bible. Students and church members alike will find it invaluable. I commend it wholeheartedly.'

Dr Michael Green, former Principal of St John's College, Nottingham, Professor of Evangelism at Regent College, Vancouver, and Archbishops' Advisor on Evangelism

'This splendid book provides a clear, structured and accessible overview of the whole Bible. Its genius is in blending qualities that might easily cancel each other out. For instance, it provides the essential tools and information to make Bible study illuminating and productive, but does so without readers realizing they are being taught a wide range of literary, historical and theological issues.

Some recent Bible overviews have provided a major motif running like a motorway from Genesis to Revelation, but haven't shown the reader how to navigate the minor roads with profit. This work, by contrast, gives enough detail to explore, and sufficient direction not to get lost. Finally and perhaps most importantly, it blends an academic rigour with a godly humility – essential to hearing God's Word. Brian Rosner conveys this well (p. 183):

> The biggest obstacle to right reading is not a dull mind, nor the absence of specialized knowledge, but a hard heart. As God's word to the world the message of the NT is accessible to all who come to it in faith.

I warmly commend this timely book.'

Richard Cunningham, Director, UCCF

'Both the Bible itself and the field of biblical studies are large and complex. But they are also immensely rich and rewarding. Here is a clear introduction by evangelical scholars who know what they're talking about. It is substantial enough to deliver what it promises without being ponderous and technical. A good introduction for the interested non-specialist. I warmly recommended it.'

Dr Barry Webb, Research Fellow in Old Testament, Moore College, Sydney, Australia

'Anyone who makes a serious effort at reading the Bible soon finds that it is not easy. This book is designed to help by providing both specific information and general perspective for today's readers. It does not assume much prior knowledge, but nor does it "talk down". Be prepared for some demanding reading, as acknowledged experts distil their specialist knowledge into an accessible text. And be prepared too to be led, gently but firmly, out of your "comfort zone": the Bible is not a comfortable book, and this volume does not disguise the fact. But if you are ready to be stretched, welcome to an exciting voyage of discovery that will last a lifetime.'

Dr Dick France, former Principal, Wycliffe Hall, Oxford

The IVP Introduction to the Bible

EDITED BY
Philip S. Johnston

IVP Academic
An imprint of InterVarsity Press
Downers Grove, Illinois

InterVarsity Press
P.O. Box 1400, Downers Grove, IL 60515-1426
Internet: www.ivpress.com
E-mail: email@ivpress.com

InterVarsity Press® is the book-publishing division of InterVarsity Christian Fellowship/USA®, a student movement active on campus at hundreds of universities, colleges and schools of nursing in the United States of America, and a member movement of the International Fellowship of Evangelical Students. For information about local and regional activities, write Public Relations Dept., InterVarsity Christian Fellowship/USA, 6400 Schroeder Rd., P.O. Box 7895, Madison, WI 53707-7895, or visit the IVCF website at <www.intervarsity.org>.

Unless otherwise indicated, Scripture quotations are taken from the Holy Bible, Today's New International Version. Copyright ©2001, 2005 by International Bible Society. All rights reserved.

The Epilogue: "Reading the Bible" is adapted from the article "Reading Plans: How to Approach the Job" by John F. Balchin in The Bible User's Manual (Inter-Varsity Press, 1991).

Cover design: Cindy Kiple

Cover image: King David: Giraudon/Art Resource, NY
The Tribute Money: Detail of two apostles, Jesus and Peter: Erich Lessing/Art Resource, NY
The Tribute Money: Detail of four apostles and St. Peter: Erich Lessing/Art Resource, NY

ISBN 978-0-8308-3940-7

Printed in the United States of America ∞

Library of Congress Cataloging-in-Publication Data

IVP introduction to the Bible/edited by Philip S. Johnston.
    p. cm.
Includes bibliographical references and index.
ISBN 978-0-8308-2828-9 (cloth/casebound: alk. paper)
1. Bible—Introductions. I. Johnston, Philip, 1954- II. Title:
Introduction to the Bible.
BS475.3.I97 2007
220.6'1—dc22

                                                                        2006101782

P   18   17   16   15   14   13   12   11   10   9
Y   26   25   24   23   22   21   20

Contents

Dedicated to all our children –
of flesh and blood or of faith and spirit

List of contributors

Desmond Alexander, Director of Christian Training, Union Theological College, Belfast, Northern Ireland

Jamie Grant, Tutor in Biblical Studies, Highland Theological College, Dingwall, Scotland

Philip Johnston, Director of Studies and Tutor in Old Testament, Wycliffe Hall, Oxford, England

Tremper Longman III, Robert H. Gundry Professor of Biblical Studies, Westmont College, Santa Barbara, USA

Ernest Lucas, Vice-Principal and Tutor in Biblical Studies, Bristol Baptist College, England

Howard Marshall, Honorary Research Professor of New Testament, University of Aberdeen, Scotland

Carl Mosser, Assistant Professor of Biblical Studies, Eastern University, St Davids, USA

Ian Paul, Dean of Studies and Lecturer in New Testament, St John's College, Nottingham, England

Brian Rosner, Senior Lecturer in New Testament and Ethics, Moore Theological College, Sydney, Australia

Mark Strauss, Professor of New Testament, Bethel Seminary, San Diego, USA

Introduction

Philip Johnston (editor)

The Bible and the IVP Introduction to the Bible

The Bible is a truly wonderful book. It leads us to faith in Jesus Christ, nourishes us as we grow in faith, and guides, moulds and corrects that faith throughout our lives. Millions of Christians through the ages and across the world have treasured it as their most valued possession.

Much of the Bible is immediately clear to any reader, like the general storyline in the Old Testament, the ministry of Jesus in the Gospels, and the rapid spread of the early church in Acts. This is why Christians often insist that anyone can read and understand the Bible for themselves.

But many details remain fuzzy until we find out more about their historical or literary setting, like the minor prophets, or specific instructions in the letters. This *IVP Introduction to the Bible* is intended to reduce the fuzziness, in two complementary ways. First, there are four general chapters (1, 2, 7, 8) dealing with overall background issues to the whole Bible and to each testament, as well as filling in the gap between the testaments. Secondly, there are eight chapters (3 – 6, 9 – 12) dealing with all the main sections and each biblical book in turn. So the great biblical panorama is brought to life, first with broad brush strokes and then with fine art work.

This *IVP Introduction* is written by an international and inter-denominational team of evangelical scholars, all involved in teaching Biblical Studies at a theological college, seminary or university, and each writing in their area of specialization. They are all experienced writers and able communicators, and can guide you expertly through the detail so that your understanding of the Bible and its message is enhanced.

Readers of the IVP Introduction to the Bible

Many different readers can benefit from this *IVP Introduction*:

- young Christians, who have a real desire to grow in their faith and to know more about its foundation document;
- older Christians, who have a mature faith but whose knowledge of Scripture is patchy;
- non-Christians, who have a genuine desire to find out more about this book that means so much to their Christian friends.

You can read it in several ways:

- rapidly, right through, to get a thorough overview of the Bible in all its diversity and richness;
- slowly, section by section, reading the text of each biblical book alongside it, to absorb the detail.

Whichever way you choose, you should have a Bible open to check the main references and to follow up as much detail as you can.

You can use any version of the Bible as you read. All quotations are taken from the TNIV, or Today's New International Version, though the authors are aware of different modern versions as well as the original languages. (See ch. 1, E.3, pp. 15–17, for a guide to Bible versions.) Abbreviations are used throughout for Old Testament (OT) and New Testament (NT), and for all the biblical books (see p. xii). Everything else is fully explained.

Further reading

Each chapter concludes with a few suggestions for further reading (cited where possible in British editions). These are helpful resources, with more detailed information and interpretation, and they give further bibliographies for advanced study. Note also:

Reference volumes:

A one-volume commentary and a one-volume dictionary are both extremely useful for further study. We recommend:

New Bible Dictionary, edited by Howard Marshall and others (IVP, 3rd edn 1996).

New Bible Commentary, 21st Century Edition, edited by Don Carson and others (IVP, 1994).

Commentary series:

There are two excellent and inexpensive series of commentaries accessible to everyone, though neither yet covers the whole Bible:
Bible Speaks Today, individually titled *The Message of . . .* (IVP).
New International Biblical Commentary (Paternoster).

There are many other excellent series accessible to everyone, at varying prices, including:
Tyndale Commentary (IVP) – also good value, with more background detail than the two series above.
NIV Application Commentary (Zondervan) – recent and detailed, with emphasis on application.
IVP New Testament Commentary (IVP) – very helpful for the New Testament.

Abbreviations

LXX – Septuagint (Greek version of OT)
MT – Masoretic Text (Hebrew text of OT)
NT – New Testament
OT – Old Testament
p. (pp.) – page(s)
v. (vv.) – verse(s)

Old Testament
Gen. – Genesis
Exod. – Exodus
Lev. – Leviticus
Num. – Numbers
Deut. – Deuteronomy
Josh. – Joshua
Judg. – Judges
1 & 2 Sam. – 1 & 2 Samuel
1 & 2 Kgs – 1 & 2 Kings
1 & 2 Chr. – 1 & 2 Chronicles
Neh. – Nehemiah
Esth. – Esther
Ps. (Pss.) – Psalm (Psalms)
Prov. – Proverbs
Eccl. – Ecclesiastes
Song – Song of Solomon

Isa. – Isaiah
Jer. – Jeremiah
Lam. – Lamentations
Ezek. – Ezekiel
Dan. – Daniel
Hos. – Hosea
Obad. – Obadiah
Jon. – Jonah
Mic. – Micah
Nah. – Nahum
Hab. – Habakkuk
Zeph. – Zephaniah
Hag. – Haggai
Zech. – Zechariah
Mal. – Malachi

New Testament
Matt. – Matthew
Rom. – Romans
1 & 2 Cor. – 1 & 2 Corinthians
Gal. – Galatians
Eph. – Ephesians
Phil. – Philippians
Col. – Colossians
1 & 2 Thess. – 1 & 2 Thessalonians
1 & 2 Tim. – 1 & 2 Timothy
Philm. – Philemon
Heb. – Hebrews
Jas – James
1 & 2 Pet. – 1 & 2 Peter
Rev. – Revelation

1. Introducing the Bible

Mark Strauss

A. *Diversity and unity*

Though 'Bible' (from Greek *biblos*, 'scroll' or 'book') is a singular term, the Bible is not one book but a library, a collection of diverse writings concerning God and his relationship to the world. Perhaps the best way to begin an orientation to the Bible is with the terms *unity* and *diversity*. Diversity means that the Bible is a diverse collection of books written over a period of some 1,500 years by many authors from a wide range of experiences and walks of life. The Bible arose in a variety of historical and cultural contexts and contains an array of literary forms: prose, poetry, genealogies, laws, psalms, proverbs, history, philosophy, prophecy, letters, etc. This diversity may be described as the human side of the Bible, since it encompasses a vast range of human experiences and perspectives.

Side by side with the Bible's diversity is its unity, the claim that despite its many differences the Bible represents one grand story or meta-narrative. This story may be summed up as the actions of God in redeeming the world. This unity was achieved because the Bible is more than a human book. It is the inspired and authoritative Word of God.

B. *Inspiration and authority*

Inspiration means that the Bible is not just a record of religious reflections or human experiences of God, but is God's self-revelation, his meaningful communication to human beings. Scripture claims this inspiration for itself, both implicitly and explicitly. The prophetic literature of the OT carries the sense of 'Thus says the LORD...' and NT writers frequently cite the OT by stating, 'God said...' or 'the Holy Spirit said...' A good example appears in Acts 4:25, where an OT citation from Ps. 2:1–2 is introduced, 'You [the Lord] spoke by the Holy Spirit through the mouth of your servant, our father David'. Here we see the convergence of the human and divine in the inspiration of Scripture. The Lord spoke by means of the Holy Spirit through David his human instrument.

Inspiration is claimed explicitly in 2 Tim. 3:16, traditionally translated: 'All scripture is given by inspiration of God (Greek: *theopneustos*), and is profitable for doctrine, for reproof, for correction, for instruction in righteousness' (AV). The term *theopneustos* was apparently coined by Paul and means 'God-breathed' (as in TNIV). Inspiration means that the Holy Spirit influenced the human writers in such a way that they recorded not just their own words, but God's Word – his divine message. 2 Pet. 1:21 similarly says that 'prophecy never had its origin in the human will, but prophets, though human, spoke from God as they were carried along by the Holy Spirit'.

How this inspiration took place in the minds and hearts of human authors remains a mystery, but certain qualifications can be made:

(1) Inspiration does not mean dictation. While in some cases God may have spoken directly to authors, as in prophetic utterances ('the LORD says...'), in most cases inspiration means that God worked *through the author's own circumstances, thoughts and intentions* to communicate his divine message. This is evident from the unique human styles and personalities which emerge in these writings. Mark, for example, writes in a rather rough Semitic style, while Luke and the author of Hebrews have more polished literary styles.

(2) Nor does inspiration deny the use of written or oral sources. The author of Chronicles drew from passages in Samuel and Kings, as well as non-canonical sources. Luke explicitly refers to written and oral accounts from which he probably borrowed (Luke 1:1–4). Paul at times quotes from pagan poets and philosophers (1 Cor. 15:33; Titus 1:12; cf. Acts 17:28) and the letter of Jude cites the apocryphal work known as 1 Enoch (Jude 14–15).

(3) It follows that inspiration lies not with the sources or traditions behind the text, but with the author and the text produced. The inspired author's selection, editing and composition were guided and 'carried along by the Holy Spirit' (1 Pet. 1:21), so that the result was authoritative Scripture – God's Word.

The terms *plenary* and *verbal* are often used to qualify inspiration. Plenary means 'full' and refers to the fact that all Scripture is equally inspired. Verbal means that the words themselves, not just the ideas, are inspired by God. Here we must be cautious, however, since words are arbitrary signs which indicate conceptual content. It is the *meaning* of these words – the message which they convey – which is ultimately inspired by God. In this way a translation of Scripture which accurately represents the meaning of the text remains God's Word. Another necessary qualification for verbal inspiration is that all language carries a measure of ambiguity and imprecision. Though the Holy Spirit who inspired Scripture may be perfect and precise, the vehicle of transmission (human language) is subject to ambiguity and imprecision. Our comprehension of divine revelation is therefore always partial and incomplete (1 Cor. 13:12).

If the Bible is the inspired Word of God, then it naturally follows that it is *authoritative* for all who worship and serve God. Its theological tenets are to be believed and its commands are to be obeyed. For more specifics on how theology may be gleaned from the text of Scripture and how its truths are to be applied, see the sections 'OT Interpretation' and 'NT Interpretation'.

C. Biblical criticism

The term 'criticism' is not meant to be negative, but refers to a variety of methodologies developed to analyse and interpret the biblical text. In one sense, Jews and Christians have always engaged in biblical criticism, since there has always been a need to identify and interpret the sacred text. Modern biblical criticism arose during the period of the Enlightenment in the eighteenth and nineteenth centuries, when the Bible was placed under the same historical and scientific scrutiny as other works of literature. Though biblical criticism is sometimes viewed as a negative discipline which undermines the authority of Scripture, this is not a necessary conclusion. The human side of this divine–human book makes careful analytic study a necessity. The Bible did not fall from the sky, but arose in the crucible of the challenges and trials of the people of God. The more we understand the settings and situations in which its various books arose, the better we will understand God's revelation to us today.

Biblical criticism can be divided into two broad areas. Historical criticism refers to a variety of methods developed to analyse the history of the text – how it came to be through various compositional phases. Literary criticism refers to the analysis of literary features of the text, apart from its composition history.

1. Historical criticism

Form criticism is the identification and analysis of oral (spoken) traditions which lie behind written documents. Form critics recognize that religious tradition is generally passed down by word of mouth before being codified in written form, and that these 'forms' (or mini-genres) of oral tradition have various functions in religious communities. Forms such as miracle stories, pronouncement stories and parables were analysed to determine their formative context (or *Sitz im Leben*, literally 'setting in life') in the early church. The term *tradition criticism* is sometimes used for the analysis of how these oral traditions changed and developed as they were passed down.

Source criticism seeks to identify the written sources which lay behind biblical texts. NT source criticism has primarily focused on the 'synoptic problem', the literary relationship between the first three Gospels. The most widely held solution is the two-source theory: Mark wrote first; Matthew and Luke (independently) used Mark and another common source ('Q'). The primary competitor to Markan priority is the two-Gospel hypothesis. This is the view that Matthew wrote first, Luke used Matthew as a source, and Mark combined and abridged their two accounts.

Redaction criticism arose in the mid-twentieth century as a reaction against the tendency of form criticism to treat the gospel writers and others as mere compilers, stringing together bits of oral tradition. Building on the results of form and source criticism, redaction critics seek to analyse how the gospel writers edited, arranged and altered their sources to achieve a particular theological purpose (a 'redactor' is an editor).

2. Literary criticism

The term 'literary criticism' has sometimes been used of all methods employed to analyse the biblical text, including those discussed above. More recently, the term is used specifically of methods which examine the biblical documents in their final form, without reference to sources or composition history.

Narrative criticism arose as a correction to the tendency of form and redaction critics to focus on the component parts of the gospels at the expense of their narrative unity. While redaction criticism studies the history of composition of a text, narrative criticism analyses its literary nature, seeking to determine how plot, characters and settings function to produce the desired effect on the reader. Narrative criticism has been particularly helpful in analysing OT narratives, the gospels and the book of Acts.

Rhetorical criticism analyses how authors use literary devices to persuade or influence readers. *Rhetoric* is an ancient art which became the foundation of the educational system of the Greco-Roman world, and treatises on rhetoric were composed by Aristotle, Cicero and others. Modern rhetorical critics utilize these ancient (and some modern) categories to determine the literary strategies of the biblical writers. Rhetorical criticism has proved especially useful in the study of epistolary literature like the letters of Paul, and discourses found in narrative, like the sermons of Jesus and the speeches in Acts.

Canonical criticism, like narrative and rhetorical criticism, focuses on the biblical writings in their final form. Yet it goes beyond these by examining the role these books have played as an authoritative canon in the life of the church (see discussion of the canon below). Some canon critics focus on the history of interpretation, while others on the hermeneutics of canon, that is, how various faith communities read and interpret the Bible as authoritative Scripture.

Structuralism combines insights from linguistics and anthropology, claiming that literature, like language, functions at the level of conventional patterns and rules. Just as there are rules of grammar which govern the way we speak, so there is a 'grammar' of literature which determines how stories operate. While on the surface, stories may have different plots, settings and characters, below this is a 'deep structure' – subconscious for both author or reader – which follows certain universal patterns. By identifying and categorizing these structures (plot movements, character types, kinds of action, etc.), stories can be objectively analysed according to their essential meaning. According to structuralists, meaning does not reside in the author's intention or in a reader's response, but in this deep structure intrinsically encoded in the text.

Reader-response criticism claims that meaning is determined by the reader, not structure of the text or the intention of the author. Reader-centred approaches are diverse, with some claiming there is no 'correct' meaning in the text since each reader creates meaning. Others speak of right or wrong meanings as determined by particular reading communities; still others treat a text's meaning as a dynamic interplay between text and reader. Some reader-response approaches are historically focused, examining how the original readers would have responded to the text. This approach is sometimes called audience criticism.

Liberationist and *feminist* approaches to biblical criticism are closely related to reader-response criticism since they seek to read the text from a particular viewpoint, whether that of women, ethnic minorities, the poor or the oppressed. In general, feminist readings of Scripture assert that the patriarchal character of the Bible is culturally determined rather than divinely sanctioned, and argue for an egalitarian reading which affirms the value, dignity and historical contribution of women.

D. Text and canon

How did we get the Bible we have today? This is the question of text and canon. Textual criticism concerns the preservation of the biblical text. The study of the canon refers to how these particular books came to be viewed as inspired Scripture.

1. Textual criticism

The necessity and goal of textual criticism. How did the books of the Bible come down to us? Before the invention of the printing press, all literature was copied by hand by scribes or copyists. The books of the Bible were copied again and again to disseminate them among God's people and to pass them down to future generations. Of course, when a document is hand-copied, errors inevitably result. Of the thousands of biblical manuscripts, no two are exactly alike. How can we be sure that we have an accurate Bible? The science and art of textual criticism has been developed to reconstruct as accurately as possible the original text of Scripture.

An *autograph* refers to the original document penned by the author. Not surprisingly, considering the ravages of time, no autograph of a biblical book has survived. The goal of textual criticism is to work backwards from the many surviving manuscripts, reconstructing the autograph as closely as possible. This is accomplished by judging where scribes made unintentional errors or intentional changes. Textual criticism is a science, in that there are rules and principles which govern the procedure. It is also an art, in that nuanced decisions must be made from the best available evidence. While one hundred per cent reliability is never possible, there is widespread agreement among scholars today that the text of the Bible has been preserved and restored with a very high degree of reliability.

Old Testament textual evidence. The standard Hebrew text of the OT is called the *Masoretic text* (MT) because it is based on the textual tradition of the Jewish scholars known as the Masoretes, who meticulously standardized and copied the text from the sixth to tenth centuries AD. The Masoretes treated the sacred Scriptures with the highest regard, revering and protecting them. This had a positive and a negative consequence. On the positive side, they did their work with precision and accuracy, thus maintaining a high level of consistency. On the negative side, they tended to destroy old scrolls to protect them from defilement. For this reason our oldest copies of the MT come from the tenth and eleventh centuries, over a thousand years after the last books were written.

Supplementing the MT are both recent finds and ancient translations. The Dead Sea Scrolls (DSS) were discovered from 1947 onwards in caves near the ancient settlement of Qumran on the shores of the Dead Sea. They are important because of the insight they give us into the Jewish community which produced them in the first century BC, and because they contain a wealth of information on the text of the OT. Fragments from almost every book in the OT were discovered. The DSS have pushed back the textual history of the OT almost a thousand years. The greatest find was a magnificent scroll containing almost the entire text of Isaiah.

Another witness to the text of the OT is the Samaritan Pentateuch. When the Samaritans separated from the Jews in the post-exilic period, they came to accept only the Pentateuch, the first five books of the OT, as authoritative Scripture. The value of the Samaritan Pentateuch is disputed among scholars. Some view it as a late revision of the Masoretic text. Others consider it an independent and valuable pre-Masoretic tradition.

Other important witnesses for the OT text are the early translations or 'versions' made from the Hebrew text. The most important of these is the Septuagint, produced by Jews in Egypt beginning in the mid-third century BC. The name comes from the Latin word for 'seventy' (*septuaginta*), a rounded-off reference to the seventy-two scholars who – according to an ancient legend – completed the work in seventy-two days. The Roman numeral LXX is used as an abbreviation. The Septuagint is a valuable witness to the OT, since it represents pre-Masoretic traditions. Other ancient versions utilized by textual critics include the Aramaic Targums (translations with some additions), the Syriac 'Peshitta', Old Latin, the Vulgate and Arabic.

New Testament textual evidence. The manuscript evidence for the NT is much greater than for the OT, including over five thousand manuscripts in Greek. Most of these are fragmentary, containing portions of the NT (e.g. Gospels or epistles). The oldest manuscripts (second to seventh centuries AD) are made of papyri, a paper-like material made from a reed grown in Egypt. There are approximately 100 extant papyri. The majority of manuscripts are made of parchment, or animal skins. These come in two writing styles. The older uncials, similar to capital letters, date from the fourth to the ninth centuries. The later miniscules, cursive letters similar to lower case, date from the ninth century onward. There are approximately 300 uncial and 3,000 miniscule manuscripts. In addition to these, there are over 2,000 lectionaries, church reading books containing selected liturgical readings for the church calendar. These date from the ninth to the fourteenth centuries.

As with the OT, translations of the NT into other languages provide another important textual source, including versions in Latin, Syriac, Coptic, Ethiopic, Armenian, Georgian and Slavonic. Prepared by missionaries to aid in evangelism, these originated in the second and third centuries. Finally, citations of Scripture found in church fathers provide a fourth important source for NT textual critics. These citations, which are many and varied, give insight into the ancient texts available to church leaders at various places and times.

The method of textual criticism. Textual criticism of the OT and NT have tended to be quite different enterprises. For the OT, the standard Masoretic text is widely accepted. Most English versions have tended to follow the MT closely, occasionally introducing variant readings from the LXX or the DSS. NT textual criticism is a more developed discipline because of the wealth of early manuscript evidence and the greater variation among manuscripts.

Contemporary NT textual criticism focuses on two kinds of evidence, external and internal. External evidence relates to the date and value of manuscripts. Based on a comparison of their readings, manuscripts have been grouped into four 'families': Alexandrian, Caesarean, Western and Byzantine. These families are named for the geographical regions in which scholars believe each family arose. The great majority of manuscripts are Byzantine. These are also the latest manuscripts, most from the ninth century onward. The external evidence tends to favour the Alexandrian family, since these are the earliest manuscripts. The two most important Alexandrian manuscripts are Codex Vaticanus and Codex Sinaiticus.

Internal textual evidence refers to the tendencies of copyists and authors. Textual critics have derived certain principles or 'rules' from the kinds of mistakes copyists tended to make. The most basic rule is to choose the reading that best explains how the other readings might have been made. Another common rule is that the shorter reading is usually original, since a copyist was more likely to add a clarifying phrase than to drop one. A third is that the 'harder reading' is usually the original, since a scribe was more likely to smooth over a difficulty than to create one.

Applying these rules of internal evidence to the manuscript evidence results in a text closest to the Alexandrian family. This is not to say that Alexandrian readings are always the best, but in general this family seems to represent the earliest text. Since both the external evidence and the internal evidence favours the Alexandrian family, almost all textual critics consider this to be the earliest and most reliable family.

Textual criticism and modern English versions. The Greek text derived by following the principles of textual criticism is known as the 'critical text'. There are two standard editions, Nestle-Aland (NA, 27th edn) and the United Bible Societies (UBS, 4th edn). Almost all modern English versions utilize the critical text. The exception is the *Revised Authorized Version*, which uses the so-called *Textus Receptus*, the Greek text which lies behind the *Authorized Version* of 1611. The *Textus Receptus* was based on a very limited number of late Byzantine manuscripts available in the sixteenth century.

There are thousands of variant readings throughout the OT and NT, but most are very minor (many in the OT involve spelling), and no doctrine of the Christian faith rests on any of these divergences. Furthermore, the wealth of manuscript evidence and the strong consensus among scholars concerning the practice of textual criticism, together confirm the accuracy and reliability of the text of Scripture.

2. The canon of Scripture

The word canon comes from a Greek word meaning 'measuring rod', and hence a 'rule' or 'standard'. The canon of Scripture are those books recognized by the church as the authoritative Word of God. When did a book become part of the canon? The ultimate answer is when that book was completed by a Spirit-inspired author or authors (2 Tim. 3:16–17; 2 Pet. 1:21). No council or committee made a book part of the canon. Rather, through the centuries the people of God – filled and guided by the Holy Spirit – have recognized those writings which exhibit the power and presence of the Spirit (1 John 2:20, 27).

Nor did formal recognition of the canon occur through a single council or decree. The canon was rather the result of a gradual process of collection, recognition and confirmation. Local canons and collections gradually grew into the widespread affirmation by the church.

The Old Testament canon. The Jewish Scriptures, sometimes called the Tanak, contain the same books as the Christian OT, but ordered differently. TaNaK is an acronym of the Hebrew words Torah (Law), Nevi'im (Prophets), and Kethuvim (Writings). Torah means the five books of Moses (Genesis to Deuteronomy); Nevi'im are the four 'former prophets' (Joshua, Judges, Samuel and Kings) and the four 'latter prophets' (Isaiah, Jeremiah, Ezekiel and the Book of the Twelve, meaning the minor prophets); Kethuvim are the three main books of

The Old Testament
Order in the **Hebrew Bible**

Law (Torah)

Genesis	Exodus	Leviticus	Numbers	Deuteronomy

Prophets (Nevi'im)

Joshua	Judges	Samuel	Kings

Isaiah	Jeremiah	Ezekiel	The Twelve (Hosea–Malachi)

Writings (Kethuvim)

Psalms	Proverbs	Job

Ruth	Song of Songs	Ecclesiastes	Lamentations	Esther

Daniel	Ezra–Nehemiah	Chronicles

Order in the **English Bible**

Pentateuch or Law

Genesis	Exodus	Leviticus	Numbers	Deuteronomy

Historical Books

Joshua	Judges	Ruth	1 & 2 Samuel	1 & 2 Kings	1 & 2 Chronicles	Ezra	Nehemiah	Esther

Poetic Books

Job	Psalms	Proverbs	Ecclesiastes	Song of Songs

Prophetic Books

Isaiah	Jeremiah	Lamentations	Ezekiel	Daniel	Hosea	Joel	Amos	Obadiah	Jonah	Micah	Nahum	Habakkuk	Zephaniah	Haggai	Zechariah	Malachi

poetry (Psalms, Proverbs, Job), the five 'scrolls' (Ruth, Song of Songs, Ecclesiastes, Lamentations and Esther), and three other writings (Daniel, Ezra–Nehemiah and Chronicles). Hence there are twenty-four books in the Jewish canon, which are identical to the thirty-nine books in the Christian OT (see chart).

While one cannot speak definitively of a time or event when the OT canon was 'closed', it seems clear that by the NT period this tripartite division had achieved authoritative status. For instance, Jesus refers once to the 'Law of Moses, the Prophets and the Psalms' (Luke 24:44). Psalms is the first and main book of the Writings, so indicates the whole section. There was also a widespread tradition in Judaism that the prophetic voice of God had ceased after the post-exilic prophets: 'With the death of Haggai, Zechariah and Malachi, the latter prophets, the Holy Spirit ceased out of Israel' (*Tosefta Sotah* 13:2, from the mid-third century AD; cf. Talmud *b. Sanh.* 11a). The so-called 'council' of Jamnia in the decades after the destruction of Jerusalem in AD 70 debated the authority of various books among the Writings, but ultimately affirmed them all. Melito of Sardis writing around AD 170 produced the first known list of all OT books (except Esther).

The New Testament																					
Gospels				Acts	Paul's Letters										Other letters					Reve-lation
Matthew	Mark	Luke	John	Acts	Romans	1& 2 Corinthians	Galatians	Ephesians	Philippians	Colossians	1 & 2 Thessalonians	1 & 2 Timothy	Titus	Philemon	Hebrews	James	1 & 2 Peter	1, 2 & 3 John	Jude	Revelation

The New Testament canon. As with the OT, there is no definitive point at which the NT books received canonical recognition. 2 Pet. 3:15–16 suggests that even in the first century AD Paul's writings were being preserved and read as authoritative Scripture. The early church fathers frequently quote from the NT writings and attribute authoritative status to them. Impetus for formal recognition of the canon arose especially from external challenges, such as when the second-century Gnostic heretic Marcion established his own truncated canon made up of portions of Luke's Gospel and ten letters of Paul (c. AD 140). The church responded with discussions and lists of its own. The Muratorian fragment, dated about AD 170, contains a list which contains our NT with some minor variations. In the fourth century Eusebius categorized books under four headings: accepted, disputed, rejected and heretical. Those 'accepted' contain all our NT books except James, Jude, 2 Peter and 2 and 3 John, which are identified as disputed. Eusebius also identifies Revelation as accepted by some but rejected by others. The first list which is identical to the twenty-seven NT books was produced by Athanasius of Alexandria in his Easter letter of AD 367.

Apocryphal Books

Roman Catholic Deuterocanonical Books

Tobit · Judith · 1 & 2 Maccabees · Wisdom of Solomon · Ecclesiasticus · Baruch · Additions to Esther · Additions to Daniel

Other Books

1 & 2 Esdras · 3 & 4 Maccabees · Prayer of Manasseh · Psalm 151

The Apocrypha. The most significant canonical debate among Christians concerns the books of the Apocrypha, a group of Jewish works mostly written between the times of the OT and the NT. These are included in our earliest complete copies of the LXX (fourth century AD), produced by Christians, but we do not know when they were first included with the OT. The canonicity of the Apocrypha was rejected by Martin Luther and the Protestant Reformers, following the tradition of Jerome (translator of the Vulgate). Roman Catholics accept the Apocrypha as 'deuterocanonical'. This does not mean it is less inspired than the proto-canonical books, but rather a 'second canon' beside the first. Catholics claim that the Apocrypha has been read and cherished by Jews and Christians from antiquity, and was included in the Septuagint. Protestants counter that these books were not part of the Hebrew Scriptures as recognized by Jesus, that they contain historical and doctrinal errors, and that they lack the prophetic power of inspired Scripture.

Historical tests of canonicity. For the OT, its acceptance as Scripture by Jesus and his apostles has been sufficient authority for Christians.

For the NT, we can discern certain tests which the people of God applied to writings to test their authority and canonicity.

(1) *Apostolic origin.* Does the book show evidence of divine authority? Jesus commissioned his apostles to pass down the authoritative message. When judging books for canonicity, the early church placed great emphasis on apostolic authority. Even those books that were not written directly by an apostle (e.g. Mark, Luke) bore the stamp of apostolic authority because their authors were closely associated with the apostles.

(2) *Theological consistency with the rest of Scripture: the rule of faith.* Since God is a god of truth, new revelation will not contradict earlier revelation, but will conform to the body of tradition passed down by the authentic community of faith.

(3) *Recognition by the Spirit-filled community.* Although this test does not reject differences of opinion or debates about canonicity, in time the church has recognized the presence of the Spirit in truly inspired writings.

(4) *Transforming power.* Has the work demonstrated the power of God to change lives? God's Word is recognizable by its living and dynamic capacity to renew and restore people's lives (Heb. 4:12).

Is the canon of Scripture closed? There is no explicit evidence for this in the Bible, but that is not surprising, since no NT author wrote with the intention of establishing the NT canon. Yet two thousand years of church history have confirmed that God's people have all they need in these sixty-six books to know God's nature, purpose and plan for the world.

E. Translating the Bible

Most people in the world do not read the Bible in its original languages, but in translation. The history of Bible translation begins in the third century BC and continues today, as scholars and linguists around the world labour to make God's Word understandable to people everywhere.

1. The languages of the Bible

The Bible was originally written in three languages: Hebrew, Aramaic and Greek. Most of the OT was written in Hebrew, the ancient language of the Jews. A few passages were written in Aramaic, a related Semitic language which served as the trade language for the ancient Near East. By the first century, most Jews in Israel spoke Aramaic as their native tongue. Hebrew was restricted to religious contexts (rather like Latin in the Middle Ages). Since the conquests of Alexander the Great in the third century BC, Greek had replaced Aramaic as the common trade language of the eastern Mediterranean. Jews engaged in commerce and administration with non-Jews (Gentiles) needed to speak Greek. Jesus was probably trilingual, speaking and teaching primarily in Aramaic, reading Hebrew in the synagogue and conversing with non-Jews in Greek. As Christians began proclaiming the gospel outside Palestine, they spoke and wrote mainly in Greek. The whole NT was written in Greek, except for a few of Jesus' words recorded in Aramaic (e.g. Mark 5:41; 7:34; 14:36).

2. The history of Bible translation

Ancient versions. By the third century BC, the Jews of Egypt were speaking Greek instead of Hebrew and the need arose for a Greek version of the Hebrew Scriptures. The result was the Septuagint (LXX; discussed above). By the first century the Septuagint was the primary Bible for Jews of the *diaspora* (or 'dispersion'), i.e. those living outside of Israel. A similar need arose in Israel since most Jews now spoke Aramaic rather than Hebrew. After the Hebrew text was read in a synagogue service, an Aramaic paraphrase or explanation, called Targum, would be given so the people could understand. These Targums were eventually put down in written form.

The need for translation also arose in the early church, as Christian missionaries began spreading the gospel beyond Greek-speaking regions. Versions in Latin and Syriac were produced in the second century, and many more followed: Coptic (the language of Egypt), Armenian, Georgian, Slavic, Ethiopic and others. The most enduring of ancient versions was the Latin Vulgate, produced by the early church father Jerome in the late fourth century. Commissioned by Pope Damasus I, the Vulgate was intended to replace the Old Latin version. Jerome's magnificent translation became the standard Bible of the Catholic church for over a thousand years. 'Vulgate' comes from the Latin word for 'common' and refers to the vernacular, the everyday language of the people.

Early English versions. Although the Vulgate was intended to be a common language translation, by the Middle Ages its Latin was understood only by the elite. Fearing the potential for heresy if everyone interpreted the Bible for themselves, the church placed strict limits on the production of vernacular versions. Yet people like Oxford theologian John Wycliffe believed that God's Word was meant for everyone. In 1382 Wycliffe and his associates produced the first English translation of the entire Bible.

With the invention of the printing press by Johannes Gutenberg in 1450, and the Protestant Reformation in the early sixteenth century, Bible publication flourished. In 1526 William Tyndale produced the first printed version of the NT in English. Tyndale's excellent translation, the first English version rendered directly from the Greek, set the standard for accuracy and style and became the model for all subsequent English versions. Yet vernacular translations were still illegal in England, and Tyndale was forced to flee to continental Europe to finish his work. He was eventually kidnapped, imprisoned and executed. Tyndale's legacy lives on today as international Bible translators suffer hardship and even martyrdom to take God's Word to the remotest parts of the world.

The Authorized or King James Version. The changing political climate of Britain as well as the popularity of Tyndale's work resulted in an easing of restrictions and the proliferation of English versions. The *Authorized Version*, known in North America as the *King James Version* (KJV), was commissioned by James I of England in 1604 as a compromise between two competing versions, the *Bishop's Bible* (1568), the official Bible of the Church of England, and the *Geneva Bible* (1560) favoured by the Puritans. The translation work was completed in seven years by forty-seven of the leading biblical scholars in Britain and published in 1611. Though – like all new versions – the AV was initially rejected by some, it quickly became the most widely used English version of its day and, eventually, the most popular English Bible of all time.

Revisions of the Authorized Version. Though the AV remained the pre-eminent English Bible for over 300 years, changes in the English language, advances in biblical scholarship, and the discovery of older and more reliable manuscripts resulted in the need for revision. In 1870 the Church of England commissioned the *Revised Version* (RV, 1881–85). A separate revision, the *American Standard Version* (ASV) was published in 1901 to reflect the preferences of North American scholars. Though neither of these versions challenged the popular dominance of the AV, they launched an era of translation and revision which continued throughout the twentieth and into the twenty-first centuries.

3. Contemporary versions and modern translation principles

English Bible versions today can be categorized in a variety of ways. One distinction is between those versions which are in a direct line of revision from the AV and its predecessors, and those which are 'new' versions translated directly from the Hebrew and Greek. Some of those in the AV tradition include the *Revised Standard Version* (RSV, 1952), the *New American Standard Bible* (NASB, 1971), the *Revised Authorized Version*

(RAV, 1982), the *New Revised Standard Version* (NRSV, 1990), and the *English Standard Version* (ESV, 2001). New versions without direct link to the AV include the *New English Bible* (NEB, 1970), *Good News Bible* (GNB, 1976), *New International Version* (NIV, 1978), *New Century Version* (NCV, 1986), *Revised English Bible* (REB, 1989), *Contemporary English Version* (CEV, 1995), *New Living Translation* (NLT, 1996), and *Today's New International Version* (TNIV, 2005). Most of these would be categorized as 'Protestant' versions, since their translation teams were primarily Protestant. Recent versions which are predominantly Roman Catholic include the *Jerusalem Bible* (JB, 1966), the *New American Bible* (NAB, 1970), and the *New Jerusalem Bible* (NJB, 1985). In 1985 the Jewish Publication Society released the *Tanakh*, a modern Jewish translation of the Hebrew Scriptures.

Another more significant distinction between modern Bible versions is their translation philosophy. *Formal equivalent* versions, also called 'literal' or 'word-for-word' versions, seek as much as possible to follow the lexical and grammatical form of the original Hebrew or Greek. *Functional equivalent* versions, also known as dynamic equivalent or idiomatic versions, seek first to translate according to the *meaning* of the text, regardless of the form. For example, the RSV renders Acts 11:22 quite literally: 'News of this reached the ears of the church at Jerusalem...' Recognizing that 'the ears of the church' is a Greek idiom rather than an English one, the GNB translates 'The news about this reached the church in Jerusalem'. While the RSV reproduces more closely the form of the Greek, the GNB captures the meaning in natural, idiomatic English.

There are no pure versions of either translation philosophy. Since no two languages are the same, all versions must frequently introduce idiomatic renderings in order to make sense. The difference is how much freedom translators take to alter the form in order to produce natural-sounding English. All Bible versions lie on a spectrum between form and meaning. Some recent versions which are generally formal equivalent include RSV, NASB, RAV, NRSV and ESV. Functional equivalent versions include GNB, CEV, NCV and NLT. Versions somewhere in between are the NIV, REB, NAB, NJB and TNIV, and many Christians use one of these as their 'all-purpose' Bible. (Most quotations in this *IVP Introduction* are taken from the TNIV.)

There are strengths and weaknesses of both formal and functional translations, and students of the Word should be encouraged to use a variety of versions from across the translation spectrum. Both kinds of translations have an important place in Bible study. Formal equivalent versions are helpful for examining the formal structure of the original text, identifying Hebrew or Greek idioms, locating ambiguities in the text, and tracing formal verbal allusions and recurrent words. Functional equivalent versions are more helpful for communicating accurately the meaning of the text, and for providing clarity, readability, and natural-sounding language. The weakness of functional equivalence is the danger of misinterpreting the original and so misleading the reader. The weakness of formal equivalence is producing obscure and awkward English when the text was clear and natural to its original readers.

Bible translation continues to be a critical concern of the church. God's Word was meant to be for all people everywhere, yet there are ethnic groups around the world which do not yet have Scripture in their native tongue. There is also the continual need for updating existing versions. Language changes over time, requiring periodic revision to keep up with contemporary idiom and to eliminate archaic language (e.g. the AV's archaic use of 'pitiful' in the sense of 'compassionate' in Jas 5:11). Advances in biblical scholarship and archaeological discoveries also create the need for ongoing assessment and improvement of existing versions. While no Bile version is perfect, the steadfast goal remains to communicate the meaning of the sacred text with accuracy and clarity.

Further reading

On inspiration and authority:

Howard Marshall, *Biblical Inspiration* (Paternoster, 1995) – well-written standard summary.

Howard Marshall, *Beyond the Bible: Moving from Scripture to Theology* (Baker, 2004) – helpful reflections in accessible lectures.

Richard Bauckham, S*cripture and Authority Today* (Grove, 1999) – thoughtful, booklet response to postmodernism.

Tom [N. T.] Wright, *Scripture and the Authority of God* (SPCK, 2005) – very readable, with helpful application to church life. Published in the USA as *The Last Word* (HarperCollins, 2006).

On text, canon and translations:

F. F. Bruce, *The Books and the Parchments* (Zondervan, 1991) – very readable survey of all the issues.

David Dewey, *Which Bible? A Guide to English Translations* (IVP, 2004) – now the best straightforward introduction available.

Dick [R. T.] France, *Translating the Bible: Choosing and Using an English Version* (Grove, 1997) – excellent booklet introduction, though it pre-dates the TNIV.

Bruce Metzger, *The Bible in Translation: Ancient and English Versions* (Baker, 2001) – another good survey, with more detail on the ancient versions.

2. Introducing the Old Testament

Desmond Alexander, Jamie Grant, Philip Johnston

OLD TESTAMENT STORY

One of the most remarkable features of the Bible is the way in which this library of sixty-six books forms an overarching story or meta-narrative that begins in Genesis with an account of the divine creation of the earth and ends in Revelation by describing the coming of a new earth. Between these two events the Bible paints a picture of human history that quickly moves from a 'good' creation (Gen. 1 – 2) to a state of imperfection due to the rebellion of Adam and Eve against the Creator (Gen. 3). Thereafter, the Bible provides a detailed, but selectively focused, account of how the Creator sets about redeeming and restoring the whole of creation. Central to this is the coming of Jesus Christ who, as the perfect God-man, atones for human sin, setting in place the means by which individuals may be both justified and sanctified.

As the first three-quarters of the biblical meta-narrative, the OT plays an indispensable role in illuminating how Jesus Christ stands at the heart of God's redemptive activity in the world. Explaining the origin and nature of the human predicament, the OT prepares for Christ's coming by detailing how he is both the fulfilment of divine promises

Sections in this chapter were written as follows – Desmond Alexander: Old Testament Story; Jamie Grant: Old Testament Background, Old Testament Interpretation; Philip Johnston: Old Testament Theology.

given centuries earlier and the means by which the consequences of human sin will be addressed.

Recognizing that the OT story is just part of a larger meta-narrative, it is nevertheless helpful to consider its content and presentation. Undoubtedly, the books of Genesis to Kings form the backbone of the OT story. Viewed together these books are, in certain respects, like a modern novel. Read from beginning to end they provide a progressive account, with later books presupposing and building upon what has been told in the preceding sections. A significant part of the Genesis–Kings story is repeated with additions and modifications in the book of Chronicles. The author of Chronicles produces another version of the history of the Davidic dynasty with its own distinctive emphases. The OT story, which contributes to the biblical meta-narrative, must incorporate the distinctive features of both versions.

The OT story extends well beyond Kings and Chronicles, taking in the return of the Judean exiles from Babylon, the rebuilding of Jerusalem and the temple (as described in the books of Ezra and Nehemiah) and the story of Esther. These events, as we shall see, introduce a further dimension to the OT story. Finally, other books which might not be viewed as forming part of the 'historical' narrative contribute to the OT story. To varying degrees the prophetic and wisdom books, as well as the Psalms, enrich the OT part of the biblical meta-narrative, adding important elements that look forward to the coming of Jesus Christ.

While the distinctive shape of the OT story is provided largely by the so-called historical books of the Bible, we need to recognize that these books are not 'historical' in the modern sense of the term. Unlike contemporary historical works, the biblical writings are not governed by Enlightenment presuppositions regarding the relationship between God and the universe. Specifically, the biblical writers readily acknowledge the possibility of divine activity influencing the outcome of human affairs. This stands in sharp contrast to many Enlightenment thinkers who favour a mechanistic view of the universe, concluding that every event in history can be explained without recourse to divine intervention. Not surprisingly, because they work with a very different set of presuppositions, the authors of the Bible's 'historical' books frequently affirm the role of God in shaping world events. Indeed, for them human history can only be accurately comprehended when the activity of God is fully recognized. Consequently, the OT story is in large measure an account of the interface between divine and human activity, especially as it relates to God's redemptive plan for all creation.

The OT story moves through a number of distinctive stages which are clearly marked by chronological and geographical factors. While these stages provide one way of setting out the OT story, there is a continuity to the story that bridges and unites these different elements. These stages may be outlined as follows:

A. *Primeval era*

The opening eleven chapters of Genesis provide a brief overview of the early history of humanity from creation up to about 2000 BC. By focusing on a small number of highly significant episodes, the dominant perception in these chapters is of the deep alienation that exists between God and humanity, resulting in a world that is marred by all kinds of divisions. Yet, while divine punishment is meted out in a variety of ways, a thread of hope runs throughout the narrative that through a righteous line of Adam's descendants, associated with the descendants of first Seth (Gen. 5) and then Shem (Gen. 11), the consequences of Adam and Eve's actions will be reversed. Linear genealogies are used to establish the identity of Eve's offspring who will eventually crush the serpent's head (Gen. 3:15).

B. *Patriarchal period*

The line of special descendants introduced in Gen. 1 – 11 leads to Abraham. He and selected members of his immediate family dominate the rest of Genesis. Divided by genealogies, Gen. 11:27 – 50:26 falls into three main sections that focus principally on Abraham (Gen. 12 – 25), Isaac and his son Jacob (Gen. 25 – 36), and Joseph (Gen. 37 – 50).

At the start of the patriarchal period, God makes various promises to Abraham that will eventually result in two important outcomes. First, although initially childless and landless, Abraham is promised that his descendants will become a great nation. Second, through a future royal descendant of Abraham, all the nations of the earth will be divinely blessed. These promises, which are articulated by God in a variety of forms to Abraham, Isaac and Jacob, reveal that the divine redemption of humanity will be dependent upon a royal line traced from Abraham (cf. Matt. 1:1–17).

Within the patriarchal narratives the principle of primogeniture (preference for the first-born son) is often overturned, with a younger brother receiving the patriarchal blessing (cf. Gen. 27:27–29). Consequently, Genesis concludes by portraying Joseph as the heir to the royal line, which in turn will be continued through his younger son, Ephraim (Gen. 48). As 'father to Pharaoh', Joseph's administration of Egypt brings blessing to many nations when a period of famine envelops the entire region. In this he prefigures the much greater blessing associated with the special line in Genesis. Later, Joseph's lineage includes Joshua, under whose leadership the Israelites take possession of the land of Canaan.

Although Joseph is clearly presented as the one through whom the royal lineage will be initially traced, Gen. 37 – 50 draws attention to an alternative lineage linked to Judah. The insertion into the main Joseph story of Gen. 38, which focuses on Tamar's extraordinary actions in raising up an heir for Judah, gives the impression that Judah's line may yet have a role to play in the fulfilment of God's purposes. This expectation is heightened through the bizarre events associated with the birth of twin boys to Tamar. While the midwife attaches a scarlet thread to Zerah's arm in order to identify him as the first-born, it is Peres who breaks out first. As the larger OT story reveals, the line of Judah through Peres leads to King David. His dynasty is especially important as regards the fulfilment of God's promise to bless the nations of the earth.

C. The life of Moses

The books of Exodus to Deuteronomy are bound together by events that take place during the lifetime of Moses – except for Exod. 1, his birth and death frame everything recorded in these books. Within this framework, the events move geographically from Egypt, via Mount Sinai, to the eastern bank of the River Jordan in the land of Moab. Between these locations the Israelites spend periods of time wandering in the desert of the Sinai Peninsula. Chronologically, most attention is given to the relatively short period that the Israelites spent at Mount Sinai; the account of this twelve-month sojourn runs from Exod. 19 to Num. 10. In a comparable way, the book of Deuteronomy, which consists mainly of two speeches made by Moses to the people, covers a very short period of time.

The account of the Israelites' time in Egypt centres on their remarkable deliverance from bondage to Pharaoh. With Moses as his spokesperson, God challenges Pharaoh by sending a series of punitive signs and wonders. As these come with increasing severity, the Egyptians gradually acknowledge the sovereign power of the Lord (Exod. 7 – 10). Nevertheless, Pharaoh's stubborn resistance continues until God punishes the Egyptians by putting to death all their first-born males. This occasion, which requires the Israelites to distinguish their homes by sprinkling blood on the door-frames, is designated the Passover (Exod. 11 – 12). This is the decisive moment in God's deliverance of the Israelites from Egypt, and becomes the focal point for later annual celebrations as the Israelites remember their exodus from Egypt on the 14th day of the month of Abib. In Israelite thinking the Passover becomes a major paradigm for the concept of divine salvation.

While the death of the Egyptian first-born sons at last persuades Pharaoh to let the Israelites leave Egypt, a further change of heart causes him to lead out his best chariots and horsemen against the fleeing slaves. In one final display of power, God parts the waters of the Red Sea, enabling the Israelites to cross over in safety. When the Egyptians attempt to follow, God causes the waters to return, drowning the entire army.

About seventy days after the Passover, the Israelites arrive at Mount Sinai. Here, following suitable preparations, the Lord comes to the people in a theophany (divine appearance), pronouncing in their hearing the principal obligations of the covenant that he wants to make with them (Exod. 19 – 20). We know these as the Ten Commandments. Further obligations and instructions are mediated to the people through Moses before a special ceremony confirms the unique relationship established between God and the Israelites (Exod. 21 – 24).

By submitting to the Lord's authority, the Israelites, formerly slaves to Pharaoh, become servants of God. To confirm this new relationship the Lord gives Moses instructions for the manufacture of a very distinctive tent and its furnishings. Known as the tabernacle, this tent of regal design, becomes God's dwelling place, enabling him to live in the very midst of the Israelite camp. God also instructs Moses to set apart Aaron and his sons to be priests responsible for the oversight of the tabernacle and the rituals associated with it. When the tabernacle is finished God comes to dwell in it, confirming by his presence his unique relationship with the Israelites (Exod. 25 – 31, 35 – 40).

By living among them, God sanctifies the people, making them a 'holy nation'. This holy status, however, needs to be maintained in the face of various influences that make the people 'unclean'. For this reason, the book of Leviticus sets out in detail the steps necessary to promote holy living and to atone for uncleanness.

As the Israelites move on towards the promised land, their trust in God falters when they hear reports of the strength of the enemy nations facing them in Canaan. Although Caleb and Joshua speak positively about taking the land, their opinions are drowned out by the voices of others. This causes the Israelites to rebel against God. Consequently, the Israelites are condemned to remain in the Sinai wilderness for a period of forty years, until the death of all those who doubted God's power to overcome all opposition. Only Caleb and Joshua are permitted to enter the promised land (Num. 13 – 14).

At the end of forty years, Moses leads a new generation of Israelites to the eastern side of the river Jordan just north of the Dead Sea (Num. 20 – 21). In a valedictory speech making up most of Deuteronomy, Moses reminds the people of all that has happened and invites them to renew their commitment to God. Moses' lengthy speech sets out afresh the teaching or 'torah' that should guide the people as they take possession of the land of Canaan.

D. Possessing the land of Canaan

When Moses eventually dies, his place as leader is taken by Joshua, an Ephraimite. Various references to Joshua throughout Exodus to Deuteronomy indicate that he is especially well placed to assume Moses' position as national leader. Indeed, the book of Joshua subtly presents him as a second Moses. Joshua guides the Israelites into the land of Canaan, enabling them to overcome successfully various alliances of local kings (Josh. 1 – 12). While much of the land still remained outside Israelite control, by the end of Joshua's life the tribes of Ephraim and Judah are settled in the territories allocated to them. Although they still need to take possession of it, the rest of the land is allocated to the other tribes. Under Joshua, the Israelites made good progress towards occupying all of the land previously promised by God to Abraham (Josh. 13 – 24).

In contrast to the positive steps taken under Joshua, the book of Judges describes how the Israelites are attacked by surrounding nations and live under constant threat. The blame for this unwelcome transition is placed on the Israelites themselves; contrary to their covenant obligations they adopt the religious customs of the nations of Canaan and worship their gods. Consequently, God permits the Israelites' enemies to overcome them. When they cry to the Lord for help, he raises up leaders, known as judges, who bring temporary relief by repelling the oppressors and promoting justice in the land (Judg. 2).

The book of Judges, however, portrays the judges as becoming less and less effective due to the increasing spiritual and moral corruption of the Israelites. As the book's epilogue (Judg. 17 – 21) clearly demonstrates, within a few generations God's people have abandoned the covenant obligations set before them by Moses and upheld by Joshua. Significantly, Judges contains subtle criticisms that reveal how the tribe of Ephraim progressively fails to follow Joshua's example by providing positive leadership for all the Israelites (e.g. 1:29; 8:1–2; 12:1–6; 17:1–5). This has an important bearing upon the rise of the monarchy in ancient Israel.

E. The early monarchy

The books of Samuel describe the transition in ancient Israel from tribal government to monarchy, with two closely related developments. First, leadership of the nation moves from Samuel, the last of the judges, to David, the youngest of the sons of Jesse (1 Sam. 16). As the book of Ruth highlights (Ruth 4), David's family belongs to the tribe of Judah. Second, the throne of God, as symbolized by the ark of the covenant, is moved from Shiloh in the territory of Ephraim to Jerusalem, the city of David (2 Sam. 6). Neither of these transitions is straightforward. However, the eventual outcomes are highly significant. As Ps. 78 reveals, these changes are due to God's rejection of the lineage of Joseph and of Shiloh in the region of Ephraim, and to his decision instead to choose David and Jerusalem (Zion), both associated with the tribe of Judah.

By bringing the ark of the covenant to Jerusalem, David confirms his status as God's chosen king over Israel. When David subsequently desires to construct a temple for God in Jerusalem, the Lord promises him that his dynasty will last for ever (2 Sam. 7). This promise establishes between God and the Davidic dynasty a special relationship that will have an important bearing upon the future history of Israel. The construction of the temple, however, is deferred until the reign of David's son, Solomon.

While the reign of Solomon (1 Kgs 1 – 11) contains many positive features, including the building and dedication of the Jerusalem temple, his failure to adhere faithfully to the instructions for kings detailed in Deut. 17 results in divine punishment. The outcome of this is the division of Solomon's kingdom into two parts following his death (1 Kgs 12).

F. The divided kingdoms

While the reigns of David and Solomon were marked by tribal unity and national prosperity, this changes dramatically after Solomon's death about 930 BC. Ten of the twelve tribes disown Solomon's son, Rehoboam, and opt rather to be governed by Jeroboam, an Ephraimite. They form a kingdom in the north that retains the designation 'Israel'. Two tribes remain loyal to Solomon's son Rehoboam, and establish the kingdom of Judah in the south. Over the next two centuries the relationship between the two nations blows hot and cold, until the northern kingdom is decimated by the Assyrians in 72 BC. After a long siege Sargon II captures Samaria, the capital city of the northern kingdom, and deports its leading citizens to Mesopotamia.

While the book of Kings attributes the fall of the northern kingdom to God's displeasure with the people living there (2 Kgs 17), the behaviour of those in the southern kingdom is little better. In due course a similar fate befalls Judah and its capital Jerusalem. This time the invading force comes from Babylon, who become the major power after defeating the Assyrians in 612 BC.

Babylonian supremacy does not lead to the immediate destruction of Jerusalem. An invasion of Judah by the Babylonians in 598/7 BC results in some Judeans being taken off to Mesopotamia. Then about twelve years later, an ill-fated attempt by Zedekiah the king of Judah to get the support of Egypt against Babylon leads to the destruction of Jerusalem in 587/6 BC. This included the demolition of the temple and the removal of the Davidic dynasty from royal office. These dramatic events herald the start of the Babylonian exile.

G. The Babylonian exile

Like earlier Assyrian kings, the Babylonian king Nebuchadnezzar II (605–562 BC) follows a policy of relocating subjugated peoples from one part of his empire to another. As a result, many of the leading citizens of Judah are exiled to Mesopotamia. The first of these deportations may have occurred as early as 605 BC (see Dan. 1:1), with larger deportations occurring in 598/7 BC and especially 587/6 BC. These events mark the beginning of a period of extreme uncertainty for the Judean exiles as they struggle to comprehend the theological significance of their removal from the promised land, the destruction of the Jerusalem temple and the demise of the Davidic dynasty. For the author of Kings, the loss of land, temple and kingship is due to the failure of the people of Judah, especially their leaders, to keep the obligations of their covenant with the Lord (2 Kgs 22:10–17).

H. The restoration

The overthrow of the Babylonian empire by the Persians in 539 BC leads to a major reversal of fortunes for the Judean exiles. As head of the Persian empire, Cyrus facilitates the return of Jews to Jerusalem with the specific objective of rebuilding the temple. While progress towards the completion of the project is slow, temple worship eventually recommences in 516/5 BC (Ezra 1 – 6). Later, under the leadership of Ezra (from 458 BC) and Nehemiah (from 445 BC), the walls of Jerusalem are repaired, bringing greater security to the population of Judah.

While these positive developments reflect an important change in God's attitude towards his chosen people, with punishment giving way to mercy, one important element continues to be missing from the picture; a Davidic king is not restored to the throne. However, post-exilic biblical writings exhibit a clear expectation that the fulfilment of God's redemptive purposes will include the re-establishment of the Davidic dynasty. In this way the earlier divine commitment to bless all the nations of the earth through a royal descendant of Abraham will be fulfilled.

Although the OT story looks forward with anticipation to the outworking of these divinely-given expectations, they only begin to be realized with the advent of Jesus Christ. What the OT story promises, the NT story fulfils.

OLD TESTAMENT BACKGROUND

The story of Israel is a fascinating account of God's committed love for a chosen people. God's plan from the outset was to reach sinful humanity through the agency of a single people (Gen. 12:1–3). So a small Middle-Eastern nation has had a significance in world history that far outweighs its numerical size and political stature. This significance can lead us to treat Israel as a special case, beyond the norms of historical investigation. However, divine salvation actually broke into human reality – the 'really real'. Israel was an historical people, like any other, and to understand the OT we must learn something about the background of the Hebrews, the people of Israel.

A. National identity

The earliest archaeological reference to Israel as a nation is found on the Egyptian Merneptah Stele dating from c. 1210 BC, but the roots of Israel's nationhood go back much further than that. The OT points to a self-identity beginning in the prehistoric period. Israel's creation story bears clear points of contact with those of her neighbours, but is also markedly distinctive. Rather than resulting from conflict between the gods (as in Mesopotamian stories), the earth was created by the word of a personal God, who seeks relationship with those created in his image. Although the term covenant is nowhere used in the Genesis creation accounts, there are clear hints of this central OT tenet from the very beginning: the God of Israel is a covenant God, committed to his people. This is important because the idea of divine covenant shapes the formation of Israel's national identity and touches every area of her life and culture.

The implications of covenant are first seen in the calling of Abraham (Gen. 12:1–3). This begins the account of God's dealings with the patriarchs, which are foundational to the later formation of the nation Israel. The call of Abraham (early second millennium BC), is significant in that the origin of a nation lies in the obedience of an individual. Abraham enters into relationship with the covenant God. The purpose of that relationship was to bring blessing to him, to his descendants and ultimately to 'all the families of the earth' (NRSV). The choice of this one family would lead to blessing on a nation and then the whole world. Abraham's grandson Jacob (later renamed Israel) had twelve sons and from these sons the twelve tribes developed.

Exod. 1 highlights an interesting dynamic. In the opening verse 'the sons of Israel' refers to the twelve physical sons of Jacob. But when Pharaoh uses the same phrase in v. 9, he refers to a people large enough to threaten Egypt. The text indicates massive population growth, and with that comes the beginning of nationhood. It is in the events of Israel's release from slavery in Egypt, and their climactic meeting with God at Sinai (Exod. 19 – 20), that national identity is truly formed. The exodus experience came to define a nation. Further, God is now known by his personal name 'Yahweh' (usually translated in English Bibles as 'the LORD', in small capitals; cf. Exod. 3:14–15).

At Sinai the Israelites not only came to know more fully the God of their forefathers, they also received a calling to be 'a kingdom of priests and a holy nation' (Exod. 19:6). National identity was expressed in terms of divine calling. Israel was to be shaped by the ways of Yahweh (as holy) and was to be an intermediary between God and the other nations (as priests). Also significant was their calling, not only out of Egypt but also into Canaan. With the grant of land, a people group became a settled nation. The land was given as a trust to Israel, confirming their divine calling. The early chapters of Deuteronomy (4, 7, 9) make clear that Israel did not become God's 'treasured possession' because they were more powerful or righteous than other nations. Their calling was to become a light to the other nations, attracting them to the true God, Yahweh. Should Israel fail to follow this call to be God's witnesses, they too could be removed from the land.

Israel continued as a single nation through several centuries under the judges and early kings. It reached its political zenith under Solomon, but due to his unwise government and personal apostasy, inter-tribal tensions arose, leading to civil unrest and the ultimate division of Israel into two states: the larger part, still called Israel, in the north, and the smaller Judah in the south (1 Kgs 11 – 12). The formation of two nation states clearly threatened the identity of a single people with the same calling. Geographic and political factors meant that northern Israel was distanced from the Jerusalem temple, so it established alternative unauthorized worship sites. Judah maintained an official worship of Yahweh, although as a nation often strayed from true faith. Israel ultimately fell to the Assyrian empire in 722 BC, while Judah was protected by God for another century before falling to the rising superpower Babylon in 586 BC. However, the OT cites not political developments but the rejection of Yahweh as the cause of exile. Many key people from both states ultimately ended up in exile in Babylon, with only the poor remaining in the land.

Nevertheless, rather than destroying a sense of identity, the exile seemed to renew awareness of Israel's calling, resulting in the rebuilding of the temple and the restoration of Jerusalem once the exile was over. Israel remained a puppet state of one eastern power or another, but the sense of national identity remained strong, based on the call to follow the ways of Yahweh.

B. Political governance

Israel was key to God's plan to restore relationship between himself and sinful humanity and, because of this, the nation was meant to be unique. The people were not meant to follow the patterns of those who had lost the land because of their offensive acts. Israel at every level was meant to be different – from commoners to kings. The reason for Israel's uniqueness was her unique relationship with Yahweh. The covenant impacted every area of society, including political governance.

Prior to nationhood, classic ancient Near Eastern patterns of patriarchal rule governed the lives of the Abrahamic clan and their descendants. The head of the family was 'elder' (ruler) of the extended family group. Some of the patriarchal narratives demonstrate that this was not always a straightforward question of unchallenged leadership (e.g. Gen. 27), but the traditional pattern was significant for the formation of political structures within Israel. The population expansion that occurred in Egypt was to stretch these traditional paradigms, however. One son had become twelve, and the families had become tribes, yet they were still organized according to the pattern of clan eldership (Exod. 3:16; 4:29). The arrival of Moses on the scene was to significantly change authority structures amongst the Israelites. First, he himself became the divinely appointed ruler over this newborn nation (Exod. 3), a new phenomenon for Israel and in some ways a prototype of kingship. Secondly, elders were appointed on a meritocratic basis because of gifts and abilities, not simply family pecking order

(Exod. 18). The clan structure, however, continued in force throughout the wilderness years and into the early post-conquest era.

Joshua followed Moses as leader of Israel, but there was no succession beyond that second generation, which led to a breakdown of leadership. Israel still functioned as a federation of clans, each with its own land and autonomy. This worked fine in terms of local administration, but was more problematic in the face of military challenge on a national scale. The book of Judges tells of the repeated subjugation of the clans by foreign powers and of Yahweh raising up a series of leaders who focused Israelite opposition to bring a period of release. Again, however, there was no succession between these leaders, and the interim periods saw foreign nations grabbing their chance to invade or oppress Israel. Two significant features are emphasized in Judges: first, Israel's oppression in the land resulted directly from her rejection of Yahweh's rule (13:1); and, secondly, Israel's moral decline was associated with the lack of kingly leadership (21:25). The implication is that kingship would have a profound effect on the obedience of the people.

The law code in Deuteronomy contains a section addressing the key governing offices in Israel (Deut. 16:18 – 18:22). Interestingly, the law concerning judges takes priority over the law of the king, perhaps implying that justice takes ultimate precedence in a godly society. This section also defines the functions of priests, Levites and prophets within Israel. How these offices actually functioned in reality, and how closely office-bearers stuck to the Deuteronomic ideal, is far from clear. Nevertheless, this section provides for an equitable ordered society with clear division of powers and responsibilities. This included kingship, which became a reality in Israel fairly late in the day compared to other ancient Near Eastern nations.

There is much debate about whether the OT history books are pro- or anti-kingship. The account of the origins of kingship (1 Sam. 8 – 12) seems to speak both for and against the institution. Yet, since kingship was permitted in the societal order indicated in Deuteronomy, and given the pivotal, symbolic importance of Yahweh's covenant with David, it appears that monarchy was not alien to God's plan for Israel. The crucial issue regarding Israelite kingship is not whether it should have existed or not, but rather the type of kingship that Israel should have. In asking for a king 'such as all the other nations have' (1 Sam. 8:5), the people sought the wrong leadership – Israel's king should be *different* from those of the nations. They sought a strong ruler and military leader, but in covenant terms the king was only ever meant to be a vice-regent subject to the rule of Yahweh. He was to be the archetypal OT believer, to trust in God and follow his rules. Yahweh himself would protect the people. The OT history books record that when the king followed the Lord so did the people, but when he did not they did not.

Kings governed the Israelites for almost 450 years, but few of them followed their call to model Yahwistic faith for their people. Hence, after the glory years of David and Solomon, Israel and Judah often fell under the control of one or other of the superpowers. Still notionally independent, they had to pay tribute to a larger protectorate state (e.g. 2 Kgs 18:13–18). Ultimately, both king and people were removed from the land by being taken into Babylonian exile. The land grant was removed because of their rejection of Yahweh and his messengers, the prophets, who had called for repentance. Following the return to the land after exile, Israel was ruled by governors and high priests under the control of a succession of military powers (Persians, Ptolemies in Egypt, Seleucids in Syria, and Romans). It was during this time – following a series of monarchic failures prior to the exile and long years of external rule – that the expectation of a renewed Davidic king really came to the fore in the faith of Israel.

C. Religious experience

The national and political experience of Israel cannot be separated from her faith. National identity was formed in covenant with God, and all political rule in Israel was subject to his ultimate authority. The religious experience of Israel began in the patriarchal roots of nationhood (the call of Abraham) and extends through the whole history of the nation (including the exile). Everything has a 'religious' cause or effect.

From Genesis onwards, the OT highlights the call to 'walk with God'. The image is implied in Eden (Gen. 3:8) and runs like a thread through the accounts of God's dealings with his people. Abraham was called to 'walk before me faithfully and be blameless' (Gen. 17:1) and Israel as a community was called to do the same (Lev. 26:3, 12). Israel was to make a whole life response to Yahweh, giving themselves (individually and corporately) over to God. This is expressed in the central command of OT faith: to 'love [Yahweh] your God with all your heart and with all your soul and with all your strength' (Deut. 6:5).

Such devotion to God was to be demonstrated by keeping God's law (Deut. 10:13; Ps. 1); offering sacrifices for sin (Lev. 1 – 6); giving regularly to support the priests and the poor (Deut. 26); praying and fasting (both are presented as 'good practice' throughout the OT); keeping a Sabbath day of rest; and attending communal festivals of worship three times each year (Exod. 23:14–17).

However, the OT makes it abundantly clear that there is to be no separation of the religious and the secular in Israel. Following Yahweh must be formative in every area of life. It should impact family relationships, business practices, bringing up children, use of time and wealth, care for others and every area of work or leisure. This is reflected repeatedly as 'doing what is right and just' (Gen. 18:19; Prov. 21:3; Isa. 56:1). The prophet Micah sums up the essence of Israel's religious experience in this simple verse: 'And what does the LORD require of you? To act justly [or: do justice] and to love mercy and to walk humbly with your God' (Mic. 6:8).

D. Daily life and society

A snapshot of life in Israel would, of course, vary depending upon when that photograph was taken. Genesis presents the patriarchal clan as pastoral – a nomadic community with livestock (Gen. 47:1–6). Abraham and his line were tent-dwellers, who would wander with their flocks to find appropriate grazing land. Clearly Abraham was a wealthy and powerful man (note his frequent interaction with kings), yet he and his family were often confronted by the common difficulties of transient communities (Gen. 21:22–34). This type of lifestyle continued until Jacob and his clan went to live in Egypt, following a severe famine throughout the Near East (Gen. 46 – 50). There the clan grew into a nation and, for a while at least, lived as a landed people around Goshen because of Pharaoh's land grant (Gen. 47).

However, the Egyptian rulers later grew fearful of having what was effectively a foreign nation in their midst (Exod. 1). So they began a brutal programme of enforced labour and infanticide. Such atrocities were far from uncommon in the ancient Near East, where the young men of defeated nations were often taken as slave labour by the victors. The biblical accounts suggest a period of great hardship in the later years in Egypt, yet the Israelites also grew to appreciate the benefits of landed status. Following the exodus from Egypt, the return to nomadic life for forty years was clearly difficult to accept (Exod. 16:3; Num. 11:5), yet during that period the people were to learn to trust completely in Yahweh for every provision in their daily lives. This was later celebrated annually in the Feast of Tabernacles.

Life in Canaan brought great benefits, but also challenges. The Israelite community was able to enjoy the fruits of the land and the stability of settled homes. However, the great challenge of material stability was not to forget to trust in God as their provider (Deut. 6:10–25). Israel's was a predominantly agrarian society. Most people would make their living off the land, either as landowner farmers or as agricultural workers (the book of Ruth gives insight into post-conquest social life), although skilled trades of all kinds would also have been practised (stonemasonry, carpentry, etc.). The life of labourers would often be precarious, as they received their wages daily. Not working, for whatever reason, would leave a family without provision and with no social security system to fall back on. In such circumstances the nuclear family would depend on the support of the wider family and clan (Lev. 25:25–55).

Education, both spiritual and general, would normally have happened in the home (Deut. 6:6–7). The royal court in Jerusalem would have been a place where young men in training for civil service would be schooled in languages and statesmanship. As in every society, there would have been an educated class in Israel that filled the influential offices of state and religion. From the time of the early monarchy on, a standing army (as opposed to ad hoc conscription) was in place, providing a source of employment other than agriculture and the skilled trades, an option often popular amongst the poor of the land.

E. Conclusion

Israel as a nation was to be characterized by what we could call a holistic Yahwism. Every skill, gift and ability could be (and was to be) used for the glory of their covenant God (Exod. 31:1–11). This is why the OT laws address each area of human life and societal existence. One key idea of Israelite society was to live in 'fear of the LORD'. Basically, this means that Yahweh made a claim on every aspect of his people's lives, and they should respond by seeking to please God in all of life. Many times Israel strayed from the ways of her Lord. But theirs was to be a life lived – individually and corporately – in constant awareness of the presence of God, and with the deep desire to demonstrate love for him in every aspect of life.

OLD TESTAMENT THEOLOGY

A. A centre?

The NT is clearly centred on the person and work of Jesus of Nazareth. The Gospels give accounts of his life, death and resurrection, Acts and the letters spell out his significance for believers, and Revelation looks forward to his return. So the whole collection of books – and indeed Christian faith in general – has an obvious centre.

By contrast, the OT has no such centre, no single person or period around which this larger and more diverse collection of books revolves.

Various twentieth-century scholars wrestled with this issue and proposed single, dual or multiple themes as representing the core of the OT,
but without reaching consensus.

A moment's reflection reveals many more contrasts between the two
testaments. The NT covers a few decades, the OT several millennia. The
NT presents a change of era, the OT recounts the ebb and flow of history.
The NT presents one generation of a new movement, in the socio-
political context of one empire; the OT covers dozens of generations, in
many different socio-political contexts, countries and empires. So it is no
wonder that the OT seems more diffuse, and less easy to interpret
coherently.

Nevertheless, the 'problem' of no theological centre is more apparent
than real. If the OT is taken on its own terms, rather than in comparison
to the NT, then it clearly does have a core theme which underlies its
presentation of people, events and history from one end to the other. And
that theme is God and his people. Whether in the historical development
from creation to the patriarchs, slavery, promised land, monarchy, exile
and beyond, or in the literary diversity of law, history, poetry and
prophecy, the central theme is the nature of God and of human relationship with him.

B. The Mosaic heart

For most of the OT, the Mosaic law provides the basis for this relationship between God and humanity. The foundational period in the OT is
the half-century covering the exodus from Egypt and entry into Canaan,
and the key body of teaching is the law of Moses originating from then.
So the books of Exodus to Deuteronomy present the theological heart of
the OT, the nearest equivalent to a centre. The term 'law' is often used
as a handy summary of all this material, but this term can hide from
view other, equally important, aspects of these books.

First, God delivered his people from slavery in Egypt, forcing their
release by bringing increasingly calamitous plagues, and sealing their
escape at the Sea of Reeds (traditionally called the Red Sea; Exod. 1 – 15).
This event is repeatedly recalled in the Psalms and prophets, in
celebration and warning. Deliverance from Egypt precedes the giving
of the law at Sinai; so obedience to the law was to be a response to
salvation, not the reason for it.

Secondly, God revealed himself in several ways. This occurred
initially to Moses with a new name, 'Yahweh' (Exod. 3:13–14; 6:2–3).
Yahweh means 'he is' (same root as 'I am'), in the sense not so much that
God exists, but rather that he is present with his people. It is relational

more than existential. Yahweh's presence was to be crucial to the Israelites' deliverance and vital to their faith. (Most English translations follow the ancient Jewish practice of not using the name Yahweh, but instead substituting the term LORD, in small caps. This makes the OT more accessible to many readers, though it loses the intimacy of a personal name.) God then revealed himself to the Israelites in awe-inspiring thunder, lightning, smoke, trumpet blast and earthquake (Exod. 19:16–19). This intense physical manifestation was a clear indication of God's holiness, and ample reminder that any relationship with him required a proper basis. The visible reminder of God's presence continued throughout the wilderness period as a fiery cloud over the tabernacle (Exod. 40:36–38). And God revealed himself most comprehensively in the law given to Moses, setting out the detailed requirements for holy worship and godly life.

Thirdly, God established his covenant with Israel (Exod. 19:5–6). God had already made a covenant with Abraham and his descendants (Gen. 12; 15; 17); here it is re-affirmed in new circumstances and with much more content. It is important to remember that the law is set in a covenantal context: the first section of law (Exod. 20 – 23) is actually called 'the Book of the Covenant' (24:7). The term 'covenant' simply means contract, treaty, alliance, and implies that there are obligations on both parties. It was regularly used in secular contexts for agreements between individuals or treaties between states, both in ancient Near Eastern documents and in the OT itself. And it is not just the term that is borrowed from everyday life: the very structure of Deuteronomy reflects the pattern of ancient international treaties. Israel's religion was distinctive in the ancient world in using this secular concept of mutual obligation for a people's relationship with their God. Yahweh committed himself unmistakably to Israel.

Fourthly, God gave Moses the ten commandments and the rest of the law at Sinai. This complex body of material comes both in small sections interspersed among narrative (in Exodus and Numbers) and in large coherent blocks of text (in Leviticus and Deuteronomy). Throughout there is a mixture of different types of law, sometimes described as ceremonial, civil and moral. This type of categorization is useful in helping Christians work out their implications for today: ceremonial law is largely fulfilled in Jesus Christ; civil law applies to a theocratic (i.e. God-governed) state which is no longer the case for us, even if some of the principles are still relevant; and moral or criminal law identifies activities which are still unacceptable today, even if our penalties may differ. However, the OT texts do not make these distinctions, since all the law applied to Israel. Another element of complexity is that the same laws are sometimes repeated with variations. Even the ten command-ments have two different explanations of the Sabbath law (Exod. 20:11; Deut. 5:15). This implies that the laws were passed down for generations in oral form and occasionally adapted to new circumstances. Later forms were then incorporated in the final text, without detracting from the sense of Mosaic origin – just as a modern law-code or student textbook can be emended or re-edited while retaining the name of its originator (e.g. *Gray's Anatomy*, first published in 1858, retains the same name 150 years later in its much expanded and modified 39th edition).

Fifthly, the ancient practice of sacrifice is institutionalized. While Noah and Abraham apparently built open-air altars and offered sacrifice themselves, now there is to be an enclosed portable shrine or tabernacle (later replaced by the temple), with an ordained priesthood and a regulated sacrificial system. Priests, sacrifices, people, campsite and all of life are classified on a 'holiness spectrum', ranging from holy to clean to unclean. Sin and other forms of pollution lead down the spectrum; purification and sacrifice lead back up it. Holiness has traditionally been understood as separateness, and God's otherness is certainly evident in the OT. But it also includes completeness, perfection and (for humans) consecration to God. These positive aspects complement the austerity of the traditional view, giving us a richer understanding of holiness.

Finally, the Mosaic material notes that God's interest reaches beyond Israel. They were to be 'a kingdom of priests' (Exod. 19:6): just as priests were intermediaries between ordinary Israelites and God, so the people of Israel should be intermediaries between God and other nations. Deut. 4:6–8 similarly notes that Israel's obedience to Yahweh would be a witness to the nations. Thus this theme, which stretches from Genesis (12:3) to Malachi (1:11), is also present in the heart of the OT. While it became a minor OT motif, due to Israel's disobedience, it nonetheless remains important.

C. Pre-Mosaic faith

Though 'Mosaic Yahwism' is the main and dominant form of OT religion, the Bible begins with a whole book recounting events and people before Moses. Chs. 1 – 2 give two different portrayals of creation, though both highlight the uniqueness of God and his creation of humanity as male and female. Ch. 3 presents human disobedience and resultant loss of God's immediate presence and of their potential immortality (though the link between individual sin and death is seldom noted later in the OT). In this, as in much more, the Genesis texts are distinct from other ancient creation accounts. The following chapters recount the spread of sin, leading first to the flood, and then the disruption of humanity into different language groups and the scattering of the nations. This brief section is theologically crucial, since it presents the backdrop for God's intervention through a specific family.

Chs. 12 – 50 present this divine response, through the 'patriarchal history' of Abraham, Jacob and Joseph. God makes a covenant with Abraham which will lead to innumerable descendants, national territory and worldwide blessing (12:1–3; 13:14–16). But the immediate issue was his own childlessness, and most of the patriarchal story concerns individual descendants and family survival.

Interestingly, patriarchal religion is significantly different from later Mosaic practice, lacking priests and enclosed altar, commandments and laws, Sabbath and festivals. Further, Abraham co-existed happily with his Canaanite neighbours in a way later prohibited to Israel. Also, most of the names for God in direct speech are compounds of the widespread term El (a generic term meaning 'god'), not Yahweh. The narrator often refers to Yahweh, but this probably reflects later writing, after his name became known. In fact, patriarchal religion is so different from Mosaic practice that a book title calls this early period *The Old Testament of the Old Testament* (R. W. L. Moberly, Fortress, 1992). Nevertheless, Abraham's faith was genuine, and in the NT Paul uses this to underline that the foundational aspect of OT religion was faith, not keeping the law (Rom. 4).

D. Post-Mosaic developments

1. Monarchy

Settlement in the land brought no new theological developments. On the contrary, as time progressed the Israelites slipped into ever greater apostasy, worshipping local Baal deities and adopting Canaanite practices. According to the book of Judges, they only survived because God raised up deliverer-judges who kept their enemies at bay.

The monarchy, however, brought several new elements. First there was David's capture of Jerusalem, and Solomon's construction of the temple there. So this city became the religious as well as the political capital of the nation, and came to be seen as the place of God's dwelling on earth. Secondly, for all his well-known faults, David was 'a man after [God's] own heart' (1 Sam. 13:14), and his reign was idealized in later imagination. He became the standard against which biblical historians judged successive kings (mostly negatively), and the model by which prophets presented a future deliverer. Thirdly, the king became the agent for divine blessing or the cause of divine punishment. Ps. 72 epitomizes the positive side of this theology, with the king now the protector of the vulnerable and the agent of international blessing.

2. Prophecy

Prophets were essentially intermediaries between the divine and human realms, mostly delivering God's word to the people and occasionally representing them to him. Moses fulfilled both aspects, and Abraham the second, so they could be called prophets (Deut. 18:15; Gen. 20:7). However, the term is mostly used for later figures, named and unnamed, male and female (cf. Judg. 4:4; 2 Kgs 22:14), who fulfilled this task throughout the periods of the judges and kings, the exile and beyond. The best known of these are Samuel, Nathan, Elijah, Elisha, and those with books named after them, traditionally known as classical or writing prophets.

The prophets are rightly described as 'covenant enforcers'. They reminded individual kings and the general populace of God's standards, and often proclaimed his judgment for their failure to keep them. This came to the fore in the eighth century BC, with the ministry of Amos and Hosea in northern Israel, and Isaiah and Micah in southern Judah. It is perhaps surprising that these prophets rarely use the term covenant. However, this need not mean (as some have argued) that covenant only emerged later as a theological concept, and that the Pentateuchal texts were then edited accordingly. On the contrary, the writings of these eighth-century prophets have many allusions to law and covenant, e.g. Hosea mentions half of the ten commandments in one verse (4:2), and Isa. 1:2–3 uses the language of covenant treaties (witnesses summoned, father–child relationship, the verbs 'rebel' and 'know'). Throughout, the prophets assume a relationship of mutual obligation between God and his people, and castigate the latter for failing to keep their side.

As punishment threatens and then falls, with the exile of Israel to Assyria and later of Judah to Babylon, the prophets look beyond to restoration. Even prophets who warn of imminent catastrophe give glimmers of hope. Amos urges Israel to seek God and live (Amos 5:4, 6, 14), and glimpses restoration (9:11–15). Hosea also sees beyond judgment to a return (Hos. 1:10–11). Similarly Jeremiah a century later repeatedly warns of exile, yet looks beyond it (e.g. 3:14–18). These and other passages often envisage a restored monarchy with a new King David who will shepherd the gathered flock (e.g. Isa. 11:1; Mic. 5:2; Jer. 23:5–6; Ezek. 34:23–24). They also speak of a new community, with a new relationship with God (e.g. Jer. 31, which predicts a new covenant).

This strand of prophecy moves beyond the Mosaic theology of blessing for obedience and punishment for disobedience (e.g. Lev. 26; Deut. 28), and portrays God's willingness to forgive and restore.

3. Exile and restoration

The exile was a theological catastrophe. Ps. 89 is a glorious, lengthy celebration of God's power demonstrated in creation and his love shown in covenant with David, until the dramatic change of v. 38: 'But you have rejected, you have spurned, you have been very angry ... you have renounced the covenant...'. The emotional trauma of Jerusalem's destruction is portrayed most poignantly in the book of Lamentations, five poetic laments full of pathos and sorrow, which end with barely flickering faith: 'You, LORD, reign for ever ... Restore us ... unless you have utterly rejected us...' (Lam. 5:19–22).

Some fifty years later, Cyrus defeated Babylon and the restoration began. In the early decades governor Zerubbabel and high priest Joshua are spoken of in glowing terms (Hag. 2:23; Zech. 3 – 4). Zerubbabel was a grandson of Judah's last king (1 Chr. 3:17–19), so may have seemed to fulfil the earlier prophecies. But kingship was not restored, and the province was ruled by a governor as part of the Persian empire. Indeed, another oracle addressing this context seems to 'democratize' or broaden to the whole community the Davidic covenant: 'I will make an ever-lasting covenant with you [plural], my faithful love promised to David' (Isa. 55:3). As in the past the king mediated God's blessing to the people (see D.1 above), so now the people would mediate God's blessing to the nations. God's universal purpose would be fulfilled.

Over time, the small province of Judah settled into routine under the Persians and then the Ptolemies. But persecution in the second century BC by the Seleucids led to renewed hope for political independence and national revival under a new David. This hope for restoration under a 'messiah' (literally 'anointed one') led to a proliferation of apocalyptic writing and contributed to the growth of parties within Judaism. The grandiose visions of renewal in the prophets, which had only been partly fulfilled in the return from exile, were revisited, and the Davidic figure awaited with new zeal. Jewish life and religion followed the old frame-work, but anticipated its renewal.

E. Life and death

One important aspect of OT life and faith not mentioned so far is that of life, death and the afterlife. Christians are familiar with the NT perspective of different fates after death for believers and unbelievers, and may mistakenly read this back into the OT. However, 2 Tim. 1:10 affirms that 'Christ Jesus ... brought life and immortality to light through the gospel', which implies that before then the afterlife was in the dark, or at least in the shadows. This fits with the OT evidence.

The perspective of the OT is largely limited to this present life on earth, and it repeatedly emphasizes that this is the arena for relating to God (cf. Deut. 30:15, 19). There is no other, and the OT shows little interest in death and its realm. The only post-mortem fate envisaged is the underworld, called 'Sheol' (usually translated 'grave' in TNIV), a dreary place of minimal activity whose occupants are cut off from God (Ps. 6:5). Many Israelites probably believed that everyone went to Sheol, and that relating to God would be continued by their descendants rather than themselves.

Nevertheless, there is an imbalance in the way the term Sheol is used. Passages which speak of going down to Sheol predominantly refer to the ungodly, whereas the death of the righteous is usually recounted in other terms. There are a few exceptions: Jacob, King Hezekiah, Job and a psalmist all seem to envisage Sheol (Gen. 37:35; Isa. 38:10; Job 14:13; Ps. 88:4). But they do so when in great trouble, and there is a noticeable contrast when the trouble is resolved (as in the accounts of Jacob's actual death). Further, a few psalms seem to glimpse an alternative of continued communion with God, though its form remains unspecified (Pss. 16:10; 49:15). This imbalance leaves an unresolved tension in the OT.

Finally, two eschatological passages (i.e. envisaging the future or end-time) speak of resurrection. Isa. 26:19 affirms that 'your dead will live, LORD' (but not ungodly rulers, v. 14). And Dan. 12:2 predicts: 'Multitudes ... will awake: some to everlasting life, others to shame and everlasting contempt.' These are the first rays of the hope which was developed in the NT. However, it is important to note that the concept of resurrection lies at the margins of the OT. Other books reflecting the exile and restoration maintain the traditional OT view that this life is the arena of faith. Here, as elsewhere in Israelite theology, it is the coming of Jesus which gives a new perspective.

OLD TESTAMENT INTERPRETATION

It should be clearly stated from the outset that the task of interpreting the OT is essentially no different from that of interpreting the NT. In fact, the basic principles of hermeneutics remain the same whether we are reading a passage from the Gospels or the sacrificial laws in

Leviticus. Contrary to popular opinion, there is no special, secret knowledge required for the interpretation of the OT. It is not the preserve of the learned few. The OT is much neglected today because of the misapprehension that it is beyond the grasp of the ordinary reader. Many Christians see it as being far removed from their reality and generally unintelligible, so they do not go anywhere near it. The church is *much* the poorer as a result. Without the OT, we have an incomplete picture of God, a partial comprehension of the divine plan of salvation, and a fragmentary understanding of who Jesus was and what he came to do. Simply put, we cannot really know God without the OT.

A. *Bridging the gap*

Key to interpreting the OT is the task of bridging the gap that exists between life in the ancient Near East at the time the OT books were written and our life now. The revelation of God in the OT was written and received in a specific context. Often we treat the OT (and the Bible in general) as a special case, as a book that is different from all others, and, of course, there is a sense in which that is absolutely right. The Bible is unique in that the living God speaks through its pages. However, we must remember that this revelation came first to a specific group of people living in the Near East centuries before the rise of the Roman Empire. It meant something first to an ancient people group known as the *ibrîm* – the Hebrews. To understand what the OT means today, we must first make the effort to understand what it meant to them in their day. This is because, with a few exceptions, the OT cannot mean something today that it could not mean then. Hence, we must ask what it *meant* then, in order to understand what it *means* now.

Several barriers to understanding need to be overcome if we are going to interpret and apply the OT properly. Primarily these are barriers of history, culture and world-view. At first glance, these barriers may seem intimidating, and place non-specialists entirely in the hands of apparent experts. However, in reality, there is a great deal that every Christian can do to overcome these challenges by careful reading of the text.

1. *Read broadly*

Is it possible to know how an ancient and distant people viewed the world around them? What was their 'take' on religion, family, law, education, art, recreation, commerce, politics and all the other things that come together to shape a nation's culture? How was their understanding of these matters shaped by the revelation that they gradually received, as now recorded in the OT?

In reality, learning the culture, history and mindset of the OT community is not as hard as it may seem. There is a simple key: *read the OT often and in large chunks*. The best way – the only way – to really understand the background and outlook of the ancient people of God is to take time to read their stories, to examine their history, to trace the themes and common threads that weave their way throughout all their interactions with the same God that we worship today. Part of our problem regarding OT interpretation is that we tend to atomize our Bible reading. We read short passages or even single verses, but this does not help our comprehension of the macro-themes of the OT's history, prophecy and poetry. To really grasp the significance of the OT for us today we must read the text for what it is: a story of God's amazing dealings with his people. Of course, this 'story' takes many different literary forms – narrative, law, history, poetry, philosophy – however, it is all part of one great, overarching story of God and his love for his people. Our task is to let the story captivate us, draw us in and shape us. As this process occurs, we will learn lessons of history and culture unconsciously, as if by osmosis.

2. Read inquisitively

Understanding also comes from asking questions as we read. The task of the reader is to place the text being read into *context*, because context aids understanding. For instance, when reading a passage from the prophet Isaiah, we gain deeper insight by placing his words in their historical and theological context. We should ask, 'What do we know about Judah during the reigns of Ahaz and Hezekiah?' And that question sends us to the books of Kings and Chronicles to find out more about the situations, challenges and dilemmas faced by God's people at that time. So we must read the OT broadly and inquisitively – cross-referencing, asking questions.

3. Read guide books

However much we read the text itself, there will be some issues which remain unclear without some further research. Classic novels often include an explanatory introduction, because their historical backdrop is unknown to later readers. A richer understanding of the story is opened up by this background research. The same principle applies to the OT, and pays huge dividends.

Various aids provide easy access to information that helps us grasp more fully the meaning of the OT. If you are baffled by the military manoeuvres of Dan. 11, a *Study Bible* will outline the machinations of the Ptolemies and the Seleucids in the second century BC. If you are working your way through Isaiah and get weary of all the 'woes', then an accessible *commentary* can provide insight to their context then and their application now. If you get lost in the detail of a particular biblical book and forget how it fits into the broader narrative, then *Bible guides* like this one can be very useful. There are many good aids that enable us to see both the wood and the trees.

B. *Understanding genre*

The next challenge – and in some ways, the greatest – is to be able to discern the essential from the peripheral. Vital to proper OT interpretation is the ability to differentiate between the indispensable, lasting truth of the text and the historical context that merely provided the setting. How do we set about this task without running the risk of 'explaining away' the plain meaning of the text?

Understanding *genre* is crucial if we are to grasp the Bible's message. The OT is not all written in simple prose. The complete text is not made up of propositional statements that are immediately clear and unambiguous. Rather, we encounter epic stories that cover many centuries with vivid ease; we find poetry that moves us to cry out in despair and to rejoice with exuberance; we are faced with philosophical deliberations that would have us question everything while retaining a vibrant faith. So we need to understand what type of text we are dealing with in order to get at the heart of its message. Straightforward statements do occur and we should treat them as such. Israel was charged to 'love the LORD your God with all your heart and with all your soul and with all your strength' (Deut. 6:5), and Christians today have every reason to accept this exhortation as our own. It is a simple truth with a very direct application in our lives (Matt. 22:37). However, this is not always the case.

We do not read English *poetry* in the same way that we read a newspaper. We expect something different in poems – pictorial language, unusual sentence structure, vivid imagery, etc. It is the same in the OT, and lessons from the poetic books are derived in a different way. Ps. 95:7 tells us that we are the 'people of his pasture, the flock under his care'. Clearly, a literal interpretation does not apply here. So we look for the essential truth that is conveyed through this literary form. Brief examination of the content of Ps. 95 shows that this verse is speaking about God's care for his people as they listen and obey. So the 'essence' is to respond in obedience to God's ways, knowing that he cares for us.

It is, perhaps, easy to acknowledge that poetry involves metaphor, and metaphor speaks indirectly rather than directly. What about the obscure *laws* that seem to dominate the OT? How are we to deal with the law of the 'goring ox', for example (Exod. 21:28–32)? Not many of us keep oxen (goring or otherwise) these days, so where does the 'didactic essence' lie in this law? If we pause for a moment, it is easy to see that this law refers to the sanctity of life and the importance of taking all reasonable action to preserve life – the responsibility lies with us to do everything we can to protect the lives of those around about us. We may not keep oxen, but we do drive cars. So the 'essence' of the law requires that we drive in a way as not to put ourselves or others at risk. This is just one example, showing that it is not really difficult to cut through the details and arrive at the essence. Ask yourself the questions, 'What is the bigger picture? Why is this law here? What does it teach?'

What about all the stories? Much of the OT is made up of lengthy *narratives* that recite the major events of Israel's history. Is this all just background, filling in the story until Christ comes? Or are we meant to learn how to live from these stories? While legal texts point to the minimum required standards, narrative passages provide us with both positive examples to emulate and negative examples to avoid. The issue of their interpretation is complicated, however, because often these stories are recorded without explicit approbation or condemnation from the narrator. So how are we to know what to think about them?

We should look for clues elsewhere – either in legal texts or in narrative passages where explicit judgment *is* passed in similar circumstances. Take the example of King Solomon. He is presented as a ruler of outstanding wisdom in 1 Kgs 1 – 11, yet at the same time the narrator subtly raises question marks. He tells us, for example, about Solomon's great wealth (10:14–21) and the requirements of his court, the fact that he accumulated chariots and horses from Egypt (4:26–29). It is well known that Solomon's many wives were ultimately a major cause of his demise and he is roundly condemned for this failure (11:9–13). But what about these other factors – what are we meant to think about them? The kingship law (Deut. 17:14–20) presents the paradigm for kingship in Israel, and that short text teaches that the king is not to accumulate for himself vast wealth or many horses or many wives. These events of Solomon's life pass without comment in 1 Kgs 1 – 11 because *we already know* what to think about them. The narrator is giving us subtle clues – great king he may be, but the warning signs are present. The narrative is telling us not to follow Solomon's example of disregarding God's word and ways, despite otherwise being greatly gifted.

So we must look for the essence of the message in the various texts that we read in the OT. Not all of the detail speaks directly to our circumstances, so we seek out the message of the broader text that speaks to every believer through all generations. Each text has a didactic purpose; our task is to ask the question, 'What is this passage trying to teach us?'

C. The Old Testament and the law

Sometimes Christians avoid the OT because they think that the law is no longer binding upon the church. Such confusion can lead to a real lack of confidence in the OT. There is one absolute point that we should always remember: When Paul writes, 'All Scripture is God-breathed and is useful for teaching, rebuking, correcting and training in righteousness' (2 Tim. 3:16), the 'Scripture' to which he refers is the OT! Is this how you view the OT *in its entirety*? God-breathed, useful for teaching, rebuking, correcting, training? Certainly, we should not allow concerns about the continuance of the law to discourage us, because it is *all* designed to teach us the ways of the Lord.

With regard to the question of the continuance of the law, the traditional understanding is probably still a very good starting point. It is helpful to think in terms of three broad categories of OT law: the ceremonial law, dealing with religious practice; the civil law, dealing with societal laws governing Israel as a theocracy in its historical setting; and the moral law, dealing with ethics for life. The OT legal sections merge these categories as all one 'law', but various parts of the NT appear to draw clear distinctions between them. For example, compare Jesus' attitude towards the moral law in Matt. 5 with the treatment of the OT ceremonial law in Heb. 10. The basic rule of thumb for Christian interpreters of the OT is that the moral law, governing ethical behaviour, continues in effect for the Christian, not as a means of salvation, but as a code – based in God's character – by which to live. By contrast, while we can learn from the civil and ceremonial laws, we are not directed by them in the same way.

Some interpreters of the Bible take a different view of the relationship between the law and the Christian. They would argue that the NT also treats the law as a single entity and therefore the separation of the law into three types is artificial. This leads to the conclusion that the law as a whole is valid for the Christian only insofar as obedience to it can flow from faith in Christ, or from the prompting of the Spirit. So some stipulations are set aside, and some are followed in a new way. This approach leads to the conclusion that the moral code indicated by the Ten Commandments continues to direct the behaviour of the Christian believer, with the possible exception of the Sabbath law, which seems to have been radically reinterpreted by Jesus. Whichever approach one takes, the net effect is similar – the moral law continues to have a profound meaning for the life of the Christian.

D. The Old Testament and Christ

Another question worth considering is, 'How should we read the OT *as Christians*?' How does the revelation of God in his Son influence our reading of the OT? When Jesus, in his conflict with the Pharisees, says, 'If you believed Moses, you would believe me, for he wrote about me' (John 5:46), just what does he mean? In what sense does the OT speak about Christ?

There seems to be a threefold sense in which the OT speaks about Christ. First, we come across occasional *prophetic* passages that point to a future individual who will transform the life of Israel and, indeed, the whole world. These passages are infrequent, but when we read them from the perspective of the life of Jesus in the Gospel accounts the correspondence is remarkable. These prophetic passages speak about two types of eschatological figure: (1) a restored Davidic king who will initiate righteous rule over all nations (Isa. 9:6–7, Mic. 5:1–5, Zech. 9:9–10); and (2) a servant figure who will suffer on behalf of Israel (Isa. 52:13 – 53:12; Zech. 12:10 – 13:1). These images provide a complex picture of this mysterious hero, who is king and servant at the same time. In OT terms alone the two images are difficult to synthesize, yet the imagery comes clearly into focus when detail is added in the Gospels.

Secondly, much of the religious and civil life in the OT Israel points towards Jesus in a *typological* sense, i.e. by presenting a typical pattern of how God works. (The OT example is called the 'type', its NT fulfilment the 'antitype'.) We read about practices which were a functioning reality within Israel, yet which also point towards a greater reality in the person of Christ. For example, the temple was an expression of divine presence on earth, the dwelling place of God amongst humanity (Ps. 26:8). Yet there is a sense in which the temple points the Christian reader to a greater reality of divine presence on earth: 'The Word became flesh and made his dwelling among us' (John 1:14). Other significant institutions of the OT also point towards a greater fulfilment in Christ: the system of sacrifices, the roles of prophet, priest, king, judge, sage, etc. However, we can only fully understand the completeness of the work of Christ when we understand the real significance of the original OT phenomena. If we do not grasp the blood-drenched solemnity of the sacrifices for sin in Leviticus on their own terms, then we cannot properly comprehend the significance of the sacrificial work of Christ in the Gospels. The OT institutions point to a greater fulfilment, but understanding the type increases our knowledge of the antitype.

Thirdly, the OT provides essential *theocentric background* to the coming of Christ. This is often referred to as 'salvation history'. The incarnation did not just happen out of the blue, there was a whole long history of God's dealings with his people throughout many generations that leads up to this ultimate revelation of his plan of salvation. Probably the majority of the OT comes into this third category – it is neither prophetic nor typological of Christ in particular, but it teaches us of the covenant God and his dealings with his people in general. In learning about God, we learn about Christ too.

So Christians will read the OT with one eye on the Gospels, but we should never be guilty of fanciful Christology. While Christ is occasionally portrayed in the OT in prophecy and typology, the vast bulk of the OT text teaches us about *God* more generally and about how we should live our lives in his presence.

D. Conclusion

How then should Christians interpret the OT? Just as we would the rest of the Bible – aware of the original cultural and historical setting, seeking the didactic essence of each passage we read, conscious of the literary genre, and looking to place each passage within the broader picture of salvation history. Most of all we should immerse ourselves in 'the Scripture' that teaches, rebukes, corrects and trains – in it we find the very words of life.

Further reading

Good general introductions to the Old Testament include:

John Drane, *Introducing the Old Testament* (Lion, 2nd edn 2000) – excellent, well-illustrated summary of Israel's story and faith.

Tremper Longman III, *Making Sense of the Old Testament: Three Crucial Questions* (Baker, 1999) – concise treatment of OT issues including God's portrayal and Christian usage.

Alec Motyer, *Introducing the Old Testament* (Crossway, 2005) – very readable guide to the various sections and themes of the OT.

Raymond Dillard and Tremper Longman III, *An Introduction to the Old Testament* (Apollos, 1995) – a more detailed standard textbook for evangelical theological study.

Good summaries of OT themes and theology include:

Alec Motyer, *Look to the Rock* (IVP, 1996) – good demonstration of how the OT leads to and is fulfilled in Christ.

Graeme Goldsworthy, *Gospel and Kingdom*, now published in *The Goldsworthy Trilogy* (Paternoster, 2000) – popular short guide, though the theme 'Kingdom of God' fits the NT better than the OT.

Philip Jenson, *The Problem of War in the Old Testament* (Grove, 2002) – best booklet discussion of this difficult subject.

3. Pentateuch

Desmond Alexander

OVERVIEW

The first five books of the Bible (Genesis, Exodus, Leviticus, Numbers and Deuteronomy) have been known collectively as the Pentateuch from at least the third century AD. The designation Pentateuch comes from the Greek term *pentateuchos* meaning 'five-volume work'. While Christians favour the term Pentateuch, Jews have traditionally preferred the title *Torah*. This is a Hebrew term meaning 'instruction', which is commonly – if inappropriately – translated as 'law'.

The five 'volumes' of Genesis to Deuteronomy narrate a remarkable story that begins with the divine creation of the earth and concludes many centuries later with the people of Israel poised on the eastern bank of the River Jordan. From here they anticipate a future across the river in the land of Canaan.

The Pentateuch falls into a number of distinctive chronological stages, which reflect to some degree its structure. Gen. 1 – 11, often designated the 'primeval history', gives a brief but important account of selected episodes in the early stages of human history. Since these events set the scene for all that follows, their significance is immense. Against this background, Gen. 12 – 50 proceeds by focusing on the lives of three men: Abraham, his grandson Jacob, and his great-grandson Joseph. The events associated with this family build around divine promises that are given to Abraham. These promises, which have various components, focus on two main ideas. One concerns the creation of a nation that will come to possess the land of Palestine (or Canaan, as it is called in the biblical text). The other is about the provision of a future king, descended from the patriarchs, who will bring God's blessing to the nations of the earth, reversing the consequences of Adam and Eve's earlier rebellion against God. These two core promises set the agenda for the meta-narrative that runs from Genesis to 2 Kings.

While Genesis concludes by recording how the descendants of Abraham, numbering about seventy, relocate to Egypt, the book of Exodus moves forward several generations to a time when the origin of the Israelites in Egypt is forgotten and Abraham's descendants, now many thousands, are subject to harsh exploitation by the Egyptian pharaoh. Through a series of divine interventions, which conclude with the Egyptian army being drowned, the Israelites are rescued from Egypt and embark upon a journey though the wilderness that brings them to Mount Sinai.

At this stage the pace of the narrative slows down considerably, and detailed attention is given to the process by which the Lord establishes a unique relationship with the Israelites. This is designed to make them into a 'holy nation'. The description of this process begins in Exod. 19 and continues throughout the book of Leviticus and into the early chapters of Numbers. It begins by setting out the covenant obligations that Israel must obey, centred on ten principles commonly known as the Ten Commandments. Following Israel's acceptance of these, the final chapters of Exodus record how the tabernacle is constructed. This unique tent with royal overtones (in its historical and cultural context) will be God's dwelling place among the Israelites. When the tent is assembled, the Lord comes to dwell within it, confirming the special relationship ratified by the covenant. By living in their midst, the Lord transforms the Israelites into a holy nation; his presence sanctifies them.

The book of Leviticus builds on this by detailing various rituals and customs that the Israelites must adopt in order to dwell safely in the presence of a holy God. With almost everything in place, the book of Numbers begins by orientating the people towards the future occupation of the land of Canaan. In due course, they leave Mount Sinai, travelling once again through the wilderness. However, progress into the promised land is halted when the people's trust in God weakens in the face of reports that emphasize the strength of the opposition awaiting them in Canaan. Unwilling to confront the nations of Canaan, the Israelites rebel against God. Consequently, God punishes them by making them spend a further forty years in the wilderness. Only after the death of the adult exodus generation is it possible for the Israelites to reconsider taking possession of the land of Canaan.

While the book of Numbers concludes with several chapters that anticipate the Israelites' future in the promised land, the entire book of Deuteronomy is built around this expectation. With the people camped on the eastern bank of the River Jordan, Moses challenges them regarding their future commitment to God. In two lengthy speeches he invites the people to reaffirm the covenant obligations first made at Mount Sinai. Since the book of Deuteronomy anticipates life in the land, a strong emphasis is placed on the importance of being faithful to the divine Torah that Moses sets out. Obedience to these instructions will bring divine blessing; disobedience will result in God's curses coming on the people.

The book of Deuteronomy concludes by reporting the death and burial of Moses in the land of Moab, outside the promised land. Although the books of Exodus to Deuteronomy are bound together by the birth and death of Moses, the fulfilment of God's promises to the patriarchs in Genesis remains incomplete. The book of Deuteronomy does not mark the end of the story. On the contrary, it merely introduces themes that are developed throughout the books of Joshua to 2 Kings.

While the Pentateuch is often perceived as being a major, self-contained section of the Bible, it is very closely linked to the books that follow. For this reason, the Pentateuch has to be viewed as part of a larger meta-narrative. To consider it simply as an entity in its own right is to fail to appreciate how the books of Genesis to Kings are designed to be understood as a continuous story. The study of the Pentateuch must take into account this connection, for without these books the story recorded in Genesis to Deuteronomy is unfinished.

GENESIS

Genesis is very much a book about beginnings, as its opening words indicate. Starting with the creation of the earth, it traces the progress of a unique family line that begins with Adam and Eve and concludes with Jacob and his twelve sons. Two features structure Genesis around this family line. First, new sections of the book are introduced by a distinctive heading or title, translated 'These are the generations of...' (AV, RSV, ESV) or 'This is the account of...' (TNIV) (2:4; 5:1 with slight variant; 6:9; 10:1; 11:10; 11:27; 25:12; 25:19; 36:1; 36:9; 37:2). These headings function like the zoom lens of a camera, focusing attention on a smaller part of the picture.

Secondly, these titles introduce three distinctive types of material:
1. narrative sections that concentrate upon an individual and his immediate family: Adam (2:4 – 4:26), Noah (6:9 – 9:29), Abraham (11:27 – 25:11), Jacob (25:19 – 35:29) and Joseph (37:2 – 50:26);
2. segmented genealogies that outline a family tree for several generations, giving basic information about characters of secondary importance (10:1–32; 25:12–18; 36:1–8; 36:9–43);
3. linear genealogies that cover ten generations but name only one ancestor in each (5:1–32; 11:10–26).

By carefully combining these different types of material the author of Genesis presents a continuous story that focuses attention on a unique line of descendants, from Adam to Noah, then to Abraham, Isaac, Jacob and Joseph. Crucially, this special family line plays a central role in the outworking of God's purposes for the whole of humanity by anticipating and preparing for the coming of a future king who will mediate God's blessing to all the nations of the earth.

Genesis opens by boldly proclaiming the supreme authority of God in creating the universe and appointing human beings as his vicegerents on earth. Yet one of the key ideas permeating the book is the disruption of the divine–human relationship. Through disobeying God and submitting to the serpent, Adam and Eve throw creation into disorder, reversing the structures instituted by God. Although they were appointed to rule over the animals (1:26, 28), Adam and Eve accede to the serpent's authority when they eat from the tree of the knowledge of good and evil (3:1–6). Their rebellious action immediately alienates them from God, with disastrous consequences for the whole of creation. While Genesis vividly describes the tragic impact of this alienation, especially in chs. 3 to 11, various divine promises hold out hope that one day God's blessing will be mediated to the whole of humanity through a descendant of the family line traced through the book. Readers need to appreciate how the early chapters of Genesis are foundational in describing the origin and nature of our human predicament. Building on this, the whole of Genesis points forward to a divinely promised resolution linked to a future descendant of the unique family line around which Genesis is centred.

The importance of the family line outlined in Genesis is highlighted in more ways than can be enumerated here, and there are interesting twists. The barrenness of the matriarchs, Sarah, Rebekah and Rachel, draws attention to God's role in continuing this special lineage. This motif is especially prominent in the Abraham story where in desperation Sarah mistakenly attempts to provide an heir through her servant Hagar. Later Abraham is tested to the extreme when commanded by

God to sacrifice the long-awaited child of promise, Isaac. This incident, however, brings the Abraham story to a dramatic climax in which God swears by himself that through a future descendant of Abraham all the nations of the earth will experience divine blessing (22:18; cf. 12:3; 18:18). Building on this, the remainder of Genesis describes how God's blessing is uniquely associated with and mediated to others through Isaac, Jacob and Joseph.

In Genesis divine blessing is often associated with the concept of first-born, as seen particularly in the story of Esau and Jacob. While Esau is prepared to sell his birthright for a bowl of stew (25:29–34), Jacob risks everything in order to gain the paternal blessing that promises to the first-born not only authority over nations and peoples but also blessing to those who bless him, echoing God's promise to Abraham (27:29; cf. 12:3). Joseph's misfortune comes due to the jealousy of his older brothers who accept neither their father's promotion of Joseph to the status of first-born nor Joseph's dreams that portray him as a king.

Although Genesis later associates the royal line with Joseph's son Ephraim (48:1–22; another instance of the first-born blessing being given to a younger brother), an alternative kingly lineage from Judah is hinted at in Gen. 38 when Perez breaks out ahead of his 'first-born' twin brother, Zerah. Isaac's blessing of his sons in Gen. 49 confirms this possibility, for future kingship is associated with Judah (49:10), although Joseph receives a comparable blessing. While Joseph's line through Ephraim initially enjoys God's favour, as evidenced by Joshua's leadership of the Israelites, in the time of Samuel the lineage of Ephraim is divinely rejected in favour of David, from the tribe of Judah (see Ps. 78:67–72). Eventually, the divine promises associated with the royal line anticipated in Genesis find their fulfilment in Jesus Christ (cf. e.g. Acts 3:25–26; Gal. 3:16). By pointing forward to the coming of a king who will reconcile humanity to God, Genesis lays the foundation upon which the rest of the Bible builds. Readers need to grasp this agenda in order to understand subsequent developments in the biblical story.

The family line in Genesis not only points forward to the coming of Jesus Christ, it also provides an insight into the nature of the promised king who will emulate fully the positive qualities observed in those who belong to this special lineage. Like Abraham, Jesus will trust and obey God. Like Joseph, he will bring salvation to many (cf. 50:20). As a 'righteous' line of seed that eventually leads to Jesus Christ, the central characters of Genesis also serve as role models for readers who wish to be Christ-like. Throughout the narrative of Genesis indications are given regarding the kind of behaviour that is pleasing to God. While attention is sometimes drawn to their moral weaknesses and their need to overcome sinful tendencies, the members of the main family line display positive qualities that set them apart from others. The contribution of Genesis to a biblical understanding of both God and humanity cannot be underestimated, for it establishes the basis and agenda for God's redemptive purposes in the world.

Genesis poses other questions, which can only be noted here without discussion. Its historical veracity has often been assessed negatively, on the grounds that no known extra-biblical sources confirm the Genesis record of the patriarchs. While this is undeniably so, we are dealing with accounts that relate to around 2000 BC and are largely concerned with the lives of a semi-nomadic family that migrated from northern Mesopotamia to the land of Canaan. Not surprisingly, archaeological investigations and extant texts are highly unlikely to provide explicit evidence about the biblical patriarchs and their families. Such limitations need to be remembered when assessing views for and against the truthfulness of the Genesis record.

Other considerations need to be taken into account when considering the historicity of the early chapters of Genesis. This is especially so as regards ch. 1, given modern theories about how the world was created. We need to appreciate that this chapter sets out to answer the question, 'Why did God do it?' not 'How did God do it?' As many biblical scholars now recognize, the entire chapter is a literary-artistic representation of creation, designed to establish the status, in relation to each other, of the objects and creatures mentioned within it. Since ch. 1 is not attempting to describe the 'how' of creation, the chapter sheds little light on the mechanism by which God created the world. We need to remember that the biblical writers want to communicate particular truths. As readers we need to attune ourselves to what these ancient authors wished to say and not impose our present-day agenda on their writings. We must not expect the biblical text to answer questions that its authors were not addressing.

EXODUS

Continuing the story of Genesis, the book of Exodus divides into three main sections on the basis of geographical location: chs. 1 – 15 are associated with Egypt, chs. 16 – 18 with the wilderness and chs. 19 – 40 with Mount Sinai. While there is a clear continuity between these sections, their contents differ markedly, producing a narrative that moves forward in distinctive stages.

Chs. 1 – 15 record the dramatic deliverance of the Israelites from slavery in Egypt, climaxing in a hymn of praise that extols God's victory over the forces of Pharaoh, the Egyptian god-king. After briefly describing the oppression of the Israelites, the book introduces Moses by recounting his birth and upbringing in the Egyptian court, his stand for the Israelites against their Egyptian slave-masters and his flight to the land of Midian. Then, forty years later, God dramatically commissions Moses to lead the Israelites out of Egypt. Through a series of 'signs and wonders' God reveals his power to the Egyptians, some of whom acknowledge this sooner than others. While Pharaoh stubbornly resists the Lord, he eventually permits the Israelites to go free after all the Egyptian first-born males are struck dead. In marked contrast, the Israelite first-born are protected by sacrificial blood on the door frames of their houses. One further futile attempt by Pharaoh to resist the Lord results in the drowning of his elite troops after the Israelites have safely crossed through the waters of the Red Sea.

Exod. 15:22 – 18:27 covers the seventy days immediately following the exodus from Egypt, when the Israelites travel through the wilderness towards Mount Sinai. Several incidents highlight the ephemeral nature of their trust in God. When confronted with shortages of water and food, they grumble against him. This contrasts sharply with God's care of them and underlines their shallow perception of the one who miraculously delivered them from slavery in Egypt.

Chs. 19 – 40 narrate what happens when the Israelites come to Mount Sinai. After suitable preparations have been made, the Israelites witness a theophany (divine appearance), during which God communicates directly to them the ten principles (Ten Commandments) upon which their future as a nation should be based. To these are added more detailed obligations, mediated through Moses. Then a solemn covenant ratification ceremony seals the special relationship which God establishes with the people (chs. 19 – 24). To finalize this process, Moses receives instructions from God for the construction of a tent or tabernacle that will become his dwelling place in the midst of the Israelite camp. By coming to live among the people, God demonstrates the reality of their unique relationship. Additionally, his presence will have a sanctifying effect upon the people; they will be a 'holy nation' because the holy God lives among them (chs. 24 – 31 and 35 – 40).

All of this, however, is placed in jeopardy by the Israelites (chs. 32 – 34). When Moses is on Mount Sinai receiving instructions for the construction of the tabernacle, the Israelites fashion a golden calf. By doing so, they breach their covenant commitment to be faithful to the Lord alone. Their action is equivalent to a bride committing adultery on her wedding night. But for God's gracious nature and the intercession of Moses, the Israelites' action would have cut short their unique relationship with God. The seriousness of the situation is underlined when Moses breaks the stone tablets containing the covenant obligations. Although a resolution is achieved, the rebellious nature of the Israelites continues to be a significant theme throughout the rest of the Pentateuch. Of the entire adult generation that leaves Egypt, only Joshua and Caleb will enter the promised land.

Running through the book of Exodus is the theme of 'knowing God'. The opening two chapters give the impression of God being somewhat remote from the plight of Abraham's descendants. Then in ch. 3 he reveals himself and his plans for the Israelites privately to Moses. By ch. 15 God has demonstrated through signs and wonders his divine power to both the Egyptians and the Israelites. They now know who the true God is. Through their wilderness experience, the people witness God's ability to provide for them in another hostile environment. Next, at Mount Sinai they see and hear him in an awe-inspiring theophany. Yet God still remains at some distance and the people are prohibited from approaching closer. Finally, Exodus concludes with God coming to inhabit the special tent that is assembled in the centre of the Israelite camp. From the beginning of Exodus to its end, God moves from being distant to being close, from being largely unknown to being intimately known.

While Exodus may be viewed as a story about the liberation of people from cruel oppression, it is essentially a story about changing masters. The Israelites, having been freed from brutal servitude to the god-king Pharaoh, the archetypical tyrant, are invited to submit to the lordship of God. They are to serve him only: the Hebrew word for 'serve' may also be translated 'worship'. The Lord is, however, a very different kind of master, as reflected in his actions and words.

Centred on the theme of knowing God better, Exodus is rich in theological concepts that later play a significant role in defining the gospel. The death of Jesus is closely linked to the Passover sacrifice which both atoned for sin and sanctified those who participated in the meal. Christians are redeemed from the power of evil through a new exodus and enter into a new covenant relationship with God. John's Gospel also contrasts the 'signs' performed in Egypt with those done by Jesus. Whereas the former were mainly punitive, the latter bring blessing: water becomes wine rather than blood; the first-born is raised to life rather than put to death. Further, arising out of this second exodus, the apostles are commissioned to construct a new dwelling place for God: the church becomes his spiritual temple. By appreciating these themes in the book of Exodus, readers may understand better their own Christian experience of God.

In spite of the centrality of the exodus experience in the ancient Israel, as reflected in the various festivals based upon it, modern scholarship is largely sceptical about the historical veracity of these events. This is partly due to presuppositions that discount all accounts of divine activity on earth. It is also partly due to the absence of extra-biblical records that confirm the basic details of the Israelites' departure from Egypt. However, given the limited nature of Egyptian sources for this period and the strong likelihood that Egyptians would not have wished to document their ignominious defeat by the Israelites' god, the silence of the extra-biblical sources is understandable.

LEVITICUS

Leviticus continues the account of the Israelites' sojourn at Mount Sinai in the thirteenth month after their deliverance from Egypt (cf. Exod. 40:17; Num. 1:1). Leviticus presumes from Exodus the construction of the regal tent to enable the divine king to come and reside among his people. This portable residence is placed within a fenced enclosure, designed to maintain a safe distance between the Israelites and their God. All this presupposes that imperfect human beings cannot enter into the presence of a holy God, due to their sinfulness. Against this background, Leviticus consists almost entirely of divine instructions intended to enable the Israelites to dwell safely in close proximity to God.

While these directions facilitate the creation of a new social order in which God and humanity live together in proximity, barriers still exist, preventing the Israelites from having immediate and direct access to the presence of God. The high priest alone may enter into the inner chamber of the tabernacle, the Holy of Holies, and even he is only permitted to do this once in the year, on the Day of Atonement. Although God's presence in the midst of the Israelite camp marks an important new development in reversing the alienation between deity and humanity that begins with Adam and Eve, much more has still to be accomplished before a complete reconciliation is achieved.

The divine instructions that make up about nine-tenths of Leviticus are usually addressed to Moses, with his brother Aaron occasionally included. These directions, however, are normally intended for either the ordinary Israelites (e.g. 1:2; 4:2) or the priests (e.g. 6:9; 21:1).

With the erection of the tabernacle, the priests, under the control of Aaron, take on responsibilities that are entirely new. Never before did the Israelites have a sanctuary in which God lived. Consequently, Leviticus describes the process by which the priests themselves are set apart from other Israelites in order to serve God at the tabernacle.

Fulfilling earlier instructions (Exod. 29), Aaron and his sons are consecrated (chs. 8 – 9). Leviticus then underlines the importance of obeying carefully the Lord's commands by recording how two of Aaron's sons, Nadab and Abihu, are struck dead when they offer 'unauthorized fire before the LORD, contrary to his command' (10:1).

Given the potential danger of living in God's holy presence, the opening chapters provide instructions for sacrifices designed to address human sinfulness in different ways. Five main types are listed, with various names: burnt offerings, grain or gift offerings, fellowship or peace offerings, sin or purification offerings, and guilt or reparation offerings. The instructions for each sacrifice differ, providing clues as to how they function. The burnt offering restores a broken relationship, appeasing the anger of God, i.e. it brings atonement. The fellowship or peace offering possibly celebrates the restoration of peace after having offended God. The grain offering may have been a gift intended to acknowledge God's sovereignty. The sin offering removes the ritual defilement or pollution caused by human sin. The guilt offering makes restitution for a wrongful action by compensating the injured party. These sacrifices reveal that there are different dimensions to human sin, and its consequences need to be dealt with in a variety of ways.

While the sacrifices seek to reverse the results of human wrongdoing, most of the other instructions in Leviticus are geared to encouraging behaviour that minimizes the need for atonement, purification and restitution. To understand these instructions we need to appreciate that Leviticus has a world-view based around the concepts of holiness and its antithesis, uncleanness. While Leviticus emphasizes God's power to make holy or sanctify people and objects, it also highlights the danger posed by the moral and ritual uncleanness associated with human behaviour.

Holiness is associated with wholeness, perfection and life; it derives from God and reflects his perfect nature. In marked contrast, uncleanness is linked to physical and moral imperfection, disorder, illness and death. Holiness and uncleanness are mutually exclusive. Between these two extremes exists a spectrum that moves by degrees from holy to clean to unclean. This may be illustrated spatially in terms of the layout of the Israelite camp. The tabernacle and its courtyard are holy. However, differing degrees of holiness exist within the tabernacle, reducing in intensity as one moves out from the Holy of Holies. The Israelite camp around the tabernacle is clean. The region outside the camp is unclean. Similar degrees of holiness and uncleanness are found among people. In general terms, priests are holy, Israelites are clean and non-Israelites are unclean. However, different factors could affect an individual's condition. For example, those who *touched* an animal carcass became unclean for a day; those who *carried* an animal carcass sustained greater impurity and were required to wash their clothes (11:24–25, 27–28).

Many of the instructions in Leviticus are designed to impress upon the Israelites the need to be holy. Some are largely symbolic in nature. By eating only 'clean' food, the Israelites distinguish themselves from those who are 'unclean'. Consequently, centuries later when the early church is being established God removes the distinction between clean and unclean food in order to signal that the longstanding distinction between Jew and Gentile is now abolished (Acts 10).

Other instructions emphasize the importance of being morally perfect, like God himself. Indeed, for the Israelites to enjoy a meaningful and fruitful relationship with God, they must reflect his holiness in their daily lives. For this reason, the Israelites are commanded, 'Be holy because I, the LORD your God, am holy' (19:2; cf. 11:44–45; 20:26). Leviticus instructs the people on how they may overcome uncleanness and be holy.

To the twenty-first-century Christian reader the book of Leviticus seems remote and irrelevant. God's instructions address a situation very different from that of today. Christians neither offer sacrifices nor eat only ritually clean foods. When we look deeper, however, Leviticus has much to teach us about the holy and perfect nature of God, and how human nature is inclined towards uncleanness. Leviticus also establishes a world-view out of which we come to understand better the significance of Christ's sacrificial death for us, and our calling to be holy as God is holy (cf. Heb. 12:10–14; 1 Pet. 1:15–16). Since this world-view underlies the rest of Scripture, a knowledge of Leviticus is often essential for understanding it.

NUMBERS

Picking up the story of the Israelites' stay at Mount Sinai, the book of Numbers provides a selective record of incidents that cover a period of about forty years. For almost all this time the Israelites are condemned by God to wander in the wilderness rather than enter the promised land. During this extended sojourn in the wilderness all the adult Israelites who experienced the exodus from Egypt die, apart from Joshua and Caleb.

Structurally the book of Numbers falls into three distinctive sections. Chs. 1 – 10 narrate the final preparations which the Israelites undertake prior to leaving Mount Sinai. These activities, spread over two months, are largely focused on helping the people prepare for the onward journey and the task of dispossessing the inhabitants of Canaan. This section concludes with the Israelites leaving Mount Sinai, apparently in a very positive frame of mind (10:35).

The central section, chs. 11 – 25, records various events over the next forty years. The recurring theme of these chapters is the failure of the people to trust and obey God. The main example of this occurs when ten of the twelve spies persuade the Israelites that they cannot possibly overcome the nations of Canaan. Consequently God announces that the Israelites will all die in the wilderness (chs. 13 – 14). On different occasions, arising out of rebellious behaviour, large numbers of Israelites are struck dead so that, by the start of the final section in Numbers, Joshua and Caleb are the only surviving adults of the exodus generation.

Chs. 26 – 36 concentrate on positive developments in the fortieth year that prepare the way for the new generation to enter the promised land. Framed by episodes that focus on the inheritance rights of the daughters of Zelophehad (27:1–11; 36:1–13), this section is clearly orientated towards the future occupation of the land.

The threefold structure of Numbers is reinforced by the fact that the first and third sections begin with a census of all men who are twenty years old or more (chs. 1, 26). Those listed are expected to serve in the Israelite army as it confronts the inhabitants of Canaan. However, of all those recorded in the first census, only Caleb and Joshua remained alive when the second is taken (26:64–65). This second census marks an important new stage in the narrative, confirming that God's punishment has been enacted on the disobedient exodus generation. Although chs. 11 – 25 record various incidents which involve the death of many Israelites, chs. 26 – 36 mention no deaths, not even during a battle against the Midianites (cf. 31:49).

The two censuses record the number of men of military age as 603,550 (2:32) and 601,730 (26:51), which elsewhere is rounded to 600,000 adult men (Exod. 12:37; Num. 11:21). This would give a total population of two to three million. On the one hand, it is mathematically possible that the Israelites increased rapidly during their four centuries in Egypt, and some interpreters take the figures literally. On the other, there are problems with these large numbers: since the number of firstborn males was 22,273 (3:43), the average family unit must have had 35–40 male children; nearly all the figures are exact hundreds, which is highly unlikely (and the figure for Levites is seen as exact, not approximate, 3:39–43); the wilderness stories assume a much smaller group, e.g. all could see the serpent on a pole (21:9); Israel was the smallest of peoples and would meet seven more numerous nations (Deut. 7:1, 7); and archaeology suggests population groups much smaller than these figures. For these reasons, many commentators now argue that mistakes crept into the census figures at an early stage, and that the actual number of Israelites was significantly smaller.

The positive outlook of the opening and closing sections of Numbers contrasts sharply with the very negative presentation of the Israelites in chs. 11 – 24. A variety of stories illustrate well the ungrateful and rebellious nature of the people. In ch. 11, the reason for the people's dissatisfaction with God is their craving for food. Although the Lord has provided them with manna, the Israelites yearn to return to Egypt: 'If only we had meat to eat! We remember the fish we ate in Egypt at no cost – also the cucumbers, melons, leeks, onions and garlic' (11:4–5). Their complaint is full of irony as the people forget the terrible conditions under which they had laboured as slaves in Egypt, and the fact that they are journeying towards a land 'flowing with milk and honey'. Not surprisingly, the Lord interprets their complaint as a personal rejection of him (11:20).

While the central section of Numbers is dominated by incidents that focus on the discontent and rebelliousness of the Israelites and their subsequent punishment, an element of hope is introduced towards the end of this section. This comes through the inclusion of a series of episodes that describe how Balaam, a Mesopotamian seer, is summoned by Balak, the king of Moab, to curse the Israelites. Balaam, however, is forced by God to bless them (22:12) on four separate occasions (23:7–10; 23:18–24; 24:3–9; 24:15–19). In doing so he echoes briefly the divine promises made earlier to the patriarchs in Genesis: 'Who can count the dust of Jacob' (23:10; cf. Gen. 13:16; 15:5); 'The LORD their God is with them' (23:21; cf. Gen. 17:8); 'May those who bless you be blessed and those who curse you be cursed' (24:9; cf. 23:8, 20; Gen. 12:3); 'A star will come out of Jacob; a sceptre will rise out of Israel' (24:17; cf. Gen. 17:6, 16; 49:10). In spite of punishing the exodus generation, God still intends to fulfil through the Israelites his promises to the patriarchs.

The account of the wilderness experience of the Israelites provides a solemn reminder of how prone the human heart is to rebel against God (cf. 1 Cor. 10:1–12). Numbers contains serious warnings about the need to trust God completely and avoid the temptation to grumble against his provision or distrust his ability to keep us secure. Significantly, these are the very temptations that Jesus confronts during his forty days in the wilderness. The repetitive description of the Israelites' behaviour creates a narrative that is designed to encourage the reader to trust God in the face of major obstacles. By reflecting on the experiences and responses of the Israelites, Christians may be helped to avoid failure in their own journey with God.

DEUTERONOMY

With the Israelites standing on the verge of entering the promised land, the book of Deuteronomy consists largely of two speeches delivered by the elderly statesman Moses shortly before his death. The first speech (1:6 – 4:40) reviews the Israelites' relationship with God over the previous forty years, observing what has happened to them since leaving Egypt. Stressing the disobedience of the exodus generation, Moses exhorts the present generation to love and obey the Lord wholeheartedly. His second speech (5:1 – 26:19) contains instructions which are intended to shape the future life of Israel in Canaan. Later this material is recorded on a scroll and designated the 'Book of the Law', better translated 'Book of Instruction' (31:24–26). Because Moses speaks here on his own behalf, passionately exhorting the people to obey God, Deuteronomy often reads like a sermon and differs stylistically from the rest of the Pentateuch.

At the heart of Deuteronomy is a challenge to the next generation of Israelites to embrace the covenant obligations given forty years earlier at Mount Sinai. Because of their failure to fulfil these obligations, the exodus generation died in the wilderness, outside the promised land. As Moses invites a new generation to affirm and embrace their covenant relationship with the Lord, he sets before them an important choice, a choice between 'life and death, blessings and curses' (30:19).

The renewing of the covenant between God and Israel resembles a marriage ceremony. While both parties promise allegiance to each other, the strength of the relationship depends not on the ceremony itself, but on the love and loyalty which each has for the other. For this reason, Moses emphasizes that the Israelites are to adore God with their whole being: 'Love the LORD your God with all your heart and with all your soul and with all your strength' (6:5; cf. 11:13; 13:3; 30:6). Without such devotion the covenant relationship will be meaningless. Moreover, true love will demonstrate itself in perfect obedience. What was true for the ancient Israelites remains true for today's Christian.

In ch. 27 Moses instructs the Israelites to carry out a covenant renewal ceremony after they cross over the River Jordan into the promised land. As part of this, the contents of the 'Book of the Law' are to be inscribed on large plastered stones as a public reminder of the obligations which the people must keep (27:2–8). Six tribes are to pronounce blessings from Mount Gerizim, and the other six tribes are to respond with curses from Mount Ebal (27:12–13). Obedience by the Israelites will ensure blessing in terms of material prosperity and national security; disobedience will have the opposite consequence, resulting in expulsion from the promised land.

Moses emphasizes that the Israelites must be faithful in loving God. In religious terms this means that they are not to practise idolatry; they must worship the Lord alone. Throughout Deuteronomy, Moses reinforces this point through negative warnings against bowing down to, following, serving or worshipping other gods. The Israelites also need to distance themselves from the practices of those who worship idols, otherwise they will be tempted to do likewise. Such is the danger posed by idolatry that the death penalty is imposed on anyone who practises it or entices others to do so. Modern western readers need to transpose the temptation of idolatry into their own context where 'other gods' may take very different shapes. Anything that dethrones God from his rightful position of supreme authority must be shunned.

Although Moses strongly exhorts the people to obey the covenant obligations, Deuteronomy as a whole anticipates that the Israelites will fail to keep them. In his final exhortation Moses clearly envisages a future in which the land will be devastated (29:23) and the people exiled (30:1–4). Not only do God's own words in 31:16–17 confirm this, but he proceeds to instruct Moses to teach the people a special song which will remind future generations of this (32:1–43). Anticipating this negative assessment of Israel's future, the list of blessing given in 28:1–14 is clearly overshadowed by the longer lists of curses that surround it (27:15–26; 28:15–68).

Building on the covenant initiated at Mount Sinai, Deuteronomy underlines the special relationship that exists between the Lord and the Israelites. Out of all the nations they have been chosen to be 'his people, his treasured possession' (7:6; cf. 14:2; Exod. 19:4–6). As such it is God's intention that they should be a light to other nations, reflecting the righteousness which he expects of all people. Consequently, the covenant obligations set out in Deuteronomy emphasize among other things a strong sense of brotherhood, a compassionate concern for the weaker members of society, a generous spirit and an integrity of heart that displays itself in righteous living. God desires that the Israelites should provide a positive example, but even when they fail, their punishment will be a lesson to others.

Deuteronomy underlines how true love for God expresses itself in an unswerving allegiance to him that leads to a lifestyle marked by integrity and righteousness. While the instructions outlined here were specifically intended for the people of Israel, the principles underlying them remain applicable today. Given that the Book of the Law was to instruct the Israelite king (17:14–20), it is interesting to observe how Jesus Christ frequently quoted from Deuteronomy, most notably in the context of being tempted by Satan (cf. Matt. 4:1–11).

During the past fifty or so years, the study of Deuteronomy has been enriched by the observation that its structure and contents closely resemble ancient treaties made between kings of powerful nations and the rulers of weaker, vassal states. While scholars continue to debate the extent and nature of this correspondence, these texts all formalize a special relationship between two parties, one strong and one weak, with the listing of extensive obligations and the pronouncement of blessings and curses. These observations remind us of the importance of understanding biblical texts in their original context.

COMPOSITION

Due to the prominence of Moses in the books of Exodus to Deuteronomy, it is hardly surprising that one of the earliest designations for the Pentateuch was 'the book of Moses' (Mark 12:26) or 'the Law of Moses' (Luke 24:44; cf. John 1:45). Indeed, it was even possible for the Pentateuch to be designated simply by the name 'Moses' (e.g. 2 Cor. 3:15, 'Moses is read'; cf. Luke 16:29; 24:27). While this was an obvious title for the first five books of the Bible, through time it was understood as indicating that Moses was the actual author of these books. Support for this idea also came from within the Pentateuch itself, because various references attribute the writing of blocks of material to Moses (e.g. Exod. 24:4; Deut. 31:9). However, at no point does the Pentateuch attribute to Moses the composition of all five books.

The academic study of the Pentateuch has been dominated for well over a century by a theory known as the documentary hypothesis, which was championed by the German scholar Julius Wellhausen. In his book *Prolegomena to the History of Israel* (English translation published in 1885), Wellhausen presented an entirely new way of understanding the history of Israelite religion. Rejecting the Mosaic authorship of the Pentateuch, Wellhausen borrowed from earlier studies which had pointed to the presence of four different literary styles within the Pentateuch, each associated with a different author. These four supposed authors are now known as the Yahwist, the Elohist, the Deuteronomist and the Priestly Writer.

The first two titles derive their names from the terms used for God in the Hebrew Bible. In Genesis certain passages show a preference for the divine name Yahweh (which usually gets translated into English as 'the LORD', using small capitals). Other passages use the divine name Elohim (which gets translated as 'God'). The uneven distribution of the divine names in Genesis were thought to point to different authors: one preferred the name Yahweh, while another preferred Elohim. The material assigned to the Deuteronomist, as the name suggests, is found mainly in the book of Deuteronomy. The material assigned to the Priestly Writer, much of it in Leviticus, was considered to be of special interest to priests.

While others had identified these four styles of material within the Pentateuch, Wellhausen took this a stage further and assigned to each of them a relative date of composition. He himself was cautious about giving absolute dates for all of the documents, but his position is usually represented as follows:

J   c. 840 BC
E   c. 700 BC
D   c. 623 BC
P   c. 500–450 BC

By so ordering the materials that compose the Pentateuch, Wellhausen challenged the long-standing tradition that Israelite religion was to be traced back to Moses. Rejecting a second millennium BC date for the beginning of Israelite religion, when Moses received the Torah at Mount Sinai, he argued that the true originators of Israelite religion were the prophets of the late ninth and eighth centuries BC. With them ethical monotheism began.

Wellhausen's ideas were quickly and widely assimilated by others. Only the most conservative of Jewish and Christian scholars spoke out against this, and they soon found themselves in a minority. To a large extent they became the victims of the spirit of the age. Perceived as advocates of tradition, their well-founded criticisms of Wellhausen's theory were casually dismissed or ignored. Wellhausen's approach, in marked contrast, represented a triumph for human reason over tradition. This triumph was perhaps all the greater in that it related to the Bible, the very book that for centuries had epitomized the importance of tradition based on divine revelation. Human reason now demonstrated that divine revelation was wrong.

While the documentary hypothesis crystallized by Wellhausen has dominated OT studies for the past century, support for it has diminished significantly, with more and more scholars expressing unease regarding both its methodology and its conclusions. Alternative theories have been advocated, though none has succeeded in gaining widespread acceptance. Consequently, the question of how the Pentateuch was composed remains open.

Two important factors need to be taken into account in considering how and when the Pentateuch came into being. First, the books of Genesis to Deuteronomy consist of a rich amalgam of materials that reflect different literary types. Side by side we encounter, to list but some: narratives of different lengths and complexity, genealogies of different kinds, paternal blessings, hymns, covenant obligations, laws, moral imperatives, instructions for the manufacture of cultic furnishings, and guidelines for the performance of religious activities. The variety of literary types found within the Pentateuch argues against a single author being responsible for everything. Rather, the evidence points to one or more editors taking existing materials and skilfully shaping them together according to an overall plan. As a result the Pentateuch is perhaps best viewed as a literary collage: different types of material have been brought together to produce a story that, while displaying a variety of styles, exhibits an overall coherence of plot and themes.

Second, as it now stands, the Pentateuch is closely tied to the books of Joshua to 2 Kings, forming a continuous story that moves from creation through to the sacking of Jerusalem by the Babylonians in 587 BC. The very last event recorded is the release of King Jehoiachin from prison in Babylon, which probably took place in 562 BC (2 Kgs 25:27–30). Given the interconnectedness of the books of Genesis to 2 Kings, it seems likely that all these books took their present shape shortly after 562 BC. In support of this is the lack of evidence for the existence of the Pentateuch as a five-volume work prior to the period of the exile. This seems to be confirmed indirectly by the discovery of the law book in the time of Josiah (2 Kgs 22). Had the Pentateuch already existed, the contents of the book of the law would have been widely known.

This, however, does not mean that the varied elements that make up the Pentateuch were not in existence much earlier. On the contrary, there is good reason to believe that its contents were known for some considerable time prior to 562 BC.

Speculation regarding the process of composition should not detract attention from the more important issue of understanding the message of the Pentateuch. The significance of these books should not be underestimated, since they provide the theological foundation that undergirds the whole of Scripture. Without the Pentateuch the rest of the Bible would be largely incomprehensible.

Further reading (see **Introduction** for good commentary series)

Gordon Wenham, *Exploring the Old Testament 1. The Pentateuch* (SPCK, 2003) – excellent introduction, with panels highlighting themes and points to ponder.

Desmond Alexander, *From Paradise to the Promised Land: An Introduction to the Pentateuch* (Paternoster, 2nd edn 2002) –

another well-written book, with more detail on all the issues noted above.

Victor Hamilton, *Handbook on the Pentateuch* (Baker, 2nd edn 2005) – good detailed introduction to the books and each section or chapter.

4. Historical Books

Philip Johnston

INTRODUCTION

The Historical Books discussed here are Joshua, Judges, Ruth, 1 and 2 Samuel, 1 and 2 Kings, 1 and 2 Chronicles, Ezra, Nehemiah and Esther. They recount the history of Israel from entry into the promised land under Joshua, through decline under the judges, prosperity in the early monarchy, mixed fortunes in the divided monarchy and eventual exile of both kingdoms, and on to the various returns of some Jews to Judah and their survival in the Persian empire. Between them these books cover about 1,000 years in time, and sweep across some 1,000 miles of the ancient fertile crescent, though most of the story relates to the small territory known variously as Canaan, Palestine or Israel. The story recorded covers much social and political development, but concentrates on God's perseverance with and preservation of his faltering people Israel. (Note that God is often referred to by his Hebrew name Yahweh, usually translated in English as LORD, in small capitals.)

A. Christian and Jewish orders

The order of the Historical Books in English Bibles follows the ancient translation of the Hebrew Scriptures into Greek, commonly called the Septuagint (and abbreviated as LXX). This was made in the third and second centuries BC, though our earliest complete manuscripts come from the fourth and fifth centuries AD. The translation of the Septuagint was done by Jews in the pre-Christian era, but its later preservation and the ordering of books was done by Christians. This order obviously reflects the nature of these books, since together they recount Israel's history. And it contributes to the traditional Christian division of the Old Testament into four sections: Pentateuch, History, Poetry and Prophets.

By contrast, Jewish Bibles have only three sections: Pentateuch, Prophets and Writings. The second is subdivided into the Former Prophets, with four books: Joshua, Judges, Samuel and Kings; and the Latter Prophets, also with four books: Isaiah, Jeremiah, Ezekiel and The Twelve (i.e. the 'minor prophets'). The third section, Writings, includes Ruth, Chronicles, Ezra, Nehemiah and Esther. This division highlights the fact that Joshua, Judges, Samuel and Kings have a distinctly prophetic perspective: they note many prophets who proclaim God's approval or disapproval, and the narrators themselves give similar verdicts. In particular, the man Samuel dominates the first part of 1 and 2 Samuel, while Elijah and Elisha provide a crucial counterpart to the monarchy in 1 and 2 Kings.

The other 'historical' books have different, less prophetic perspectives. Chronicles focuses more on the temple and worship, while Ezra, Nehemiah and Esther recount post-exilic reconstruction and survival. Their placement in the Writings thus has thematic reasons, though may also be due to their later composition and acceptance into the Hebrew canon. In addition, Esther and Ruth were two of the five short books (or 'scrolls'; also Song of Songs, Ecclesiastes and Lamentations), each read at an annual festival. So Jewish and Christian ordering of these books give complementary insights into their nature.

B. Historical setting

When did all this take place? Dating ancient history is a difficult exercise, and becomes increasingly hazardous the further back we go. However, there is one great help. The Mesopotamians were often keen star watchers, and they cross-referenced their historical records to eclipses, comets, etc. Modern astronomy can now give us exact dates for these celestial occurrences, and hence for much of Assyrian and Babylonian history in the first millennium BC. On its own that would be of little use. But fortunately Mesopotamian records occasionally mention battles fought in the Levant (i.e. the eastern Mediterranean lands) and also the names of various kings of Israel and Judah. As a result, we can derive reasonably accurate dates for the Hebrew monarchies back to the time of David. Historians now largely agree on these dates, within about a ten-year margin for most. The following sections use the dates given in the *New Bible Dictionary*.

As we work back to the second millennium BC, however, dating is less easy. 1 Kgs 6:1 states that Solomon started building the temple 480 years after the exodus. The temple construction began in Solomon's fourth year, 967 BC, so this dates the exodus to 1447 and the events of Joshua to 1407 onwards, i.e. the late fifteenth century BC. However, many scholars argue that the archaeological record of destruction in various Canaanite towns places the conquest more in the late thirteenth century. In this case the figure of 480 years is figurative for twelve generations, which in reality would have spanned much less time. For our purposes here, this issue only affects the length of the judges period, where there was some overlap between judges anyway (see below). The following table gives an overview, with the four most important frame-work dates.

Century BC	Events and people
late 15th C	Israelites enter Canaan, taking 1 Kgs 6:1 literally
late 13th C	Israelites enter Canaan, taking 1 Kgs 6:1 figuratively
10th C	David and Solomon
	931, Solomon's death, and division of kingdom into Israel and Judah
9th C	Elijah and Elisha
8th C	722, Assyrians conquer Samaria, and exile many Israelites
6th C	587, Babylonians conquer Jerusalem, and exile many Judeans
	539, Persians conquer Babylon, and allow Jews to return

C. Authorship and date

All these books are anonymous, i.e. they have no named authors, though Ezra and Nehemiah have significant sections apparently written by these two men. Authorship of each book will be dealt with in turn below, but one widespread view merits brief discussion.

Following Martin Noth (1943), many scholars think that Joshua, Judges, Samuel and Kings were put together at the time of the Babylonian exile. Some exiled Jews recorded their history as it had been handed down in various stories and official documents, partly to preserve this history now that Jerusalem and other cities had been destroyed, but mainly to explain why the exile had happened. The stories had different sources but were linked together by a common theology, which explains the diversity of style yet the similarity of interpretation across these books. Deuter-onomy was seen by Noth as a historical and theological introduction, so these books are often called the 'Deuteronomistic History'.

There is some value in this approach. The early stories especially may well have been handed down orally for centuries, preserved in separate parts of the country, and not written down till much later. These books do have similar theological assessments, often using distinctive vocabulary. This theology partly reflects Deuteronomy, regardless of when the later was finalized. And there are many indications throughout the OT of later editing of earlier material.

But several aspects invite caution. First, the books are all significantly different: Joshua is positive and progressive, whereas Judges is negative and cyclical; Samuel has many detailed stories with little overt interpretation, whereas Kings has fewer and briefer stories with explicit theological assessment. This suggests that the stories have different origins, and that later editors showed great respect in preserving their different styles. Secondly, many stories seem to have been recorded early on, as shown by eye-witness-type accounts (e.g. tactics against Jericho and Ai), ancient place names (e.g. Kiriath-Arba for Hebron, Josh. 14:15), or the phrase 'to this day' (e.g. Josh. 15:63, Judg. 1:21, only valid until 2 Sam. 5). Thirdly, the theological interpretation may have been nurtured in prophetic circles right from the start, so that the eventual writer simply standardized the theological assessments of Samuel, Nathan, Elijah, Elisha and many others. In summary, while the books have a common thread, and may truly reflect Deuteronomy, this can be explained as ancient legacy as well as exilic interpretation.

JOSHUA

A. Contents

The book named after him covers the life of Joshua from the death of Moses (1:1) to that of Joshua himself (24:29). It has two quite distinct halves. Chs. 1 – 12 recount the momentous events of entry into the promised land: Joshua's commission and reassurance; crossing the Jordan; the capture of two bridgehead towns, Jericho in the rift valley and Ai in the hills; the grand covenant renewal ceremony at Mount Ebal; the mistaken treaty with the Gibeonites; and finally, in rapid overview, the campaigns in the south and the north, with lists of cities taken and kings captured. This is an all-action story, mostly positive and successful.

The second half, chs. 13 – 24, is quite different. It begins by noting 'very large areas of land to be taken over' (13:1), mostly west and north of Israel's later borders. It then proceeds to detail the allotment of the land to each tribe, noting also the cities of refuge and towns for the Levites. These lists were clearly important, though their inclusion here interrupts the story of conquest. This is resumed in ch. 22, with the return home of the fighting men from the two-and-a-half tribes allotted land east of the Jordan. They set up a commemorative altar which is misinterpreted, and civil war is only averted by their promise of perpetual allegiance to Yahweh and his sanctuary. Finally, there are two rather similar farewell speeches by Joshua, and closing burial notices.

This summary shows that Joshua has three types of material: programmatic theology (chs. 1, 23 – 24), narrative (chs. 2 – 11, 22), and lists (chs. 12 – 21). Thus the book, like many in the OT, seems to be a compilation of different sources brought together.

B. Historical setting

Unfortunately there is no unambiguous extra-biblical evidence for *any* of the characters or events of the early biblical period: the patriarchs, the Israelites in Egypt, the exodus or the conquest. This is not hard to explain. Palestine was off the beaten track, and has left very little writing from the second millennium BC. Also, the Egyptians were notoriously xenophobic, they often had Semitic slaves, and they avoided accounts of defeat. So lack of extra-biblical evidence does not mean that the biblical account is inaccurate. Indeed, many aspects of it fit their historical setting well. But it does mean that the accounts are not supported by external sources.

The main historical issue regarding the Book of Joshua is Israel's entry into Palestine. The book portrays a violent military conquest with the capture of many Canaanite towns, including three which were burned down: Jericho (6:24), Ai (8:28), and Hazor in the north (11:11). Traditionally, this conquest was dated to c. 1400 BC, but no destruction layers in Palestine cities correspond to this early date, on conventional archaeological dating. Alternatively, the conquest has been dated to c. 1200 BC, which gives at least a partial correspondence with archaeological evidence (see Introduction to this chapter). In both cases, however, the cities of Jericho and Ai remain problematic, since the archaeological evidence does not fit a conquest at either date.

These views have been challenged by some evangelical scholars in different ways. For instance, John Bimson suggested an early conquest date by realigning an even earlier destruction layer, conventionally dated at 1550, to the late 1400s. Also Bryant Wood has questioned the standard view on Jericho, arguing that the site's famous excavator Dame Kathleen Kenyon was looking for the wrong evidence in the wrong place. Their views have not generally been accepted by archaeologists. Nevertheless, they indicate some of the uncertainties on the subject and the need for further study.

In recent decades many scholars have suggested that Israel did not enter Canaan violently at all. Rather they emerged from within Palestine, as refugees from lowland Canaanite cities or as nomads who eventually settled down. These groups populated many new villages in the central hills c. 1200 BC, gradually developed a separate identity, and invented for themselves a glorious past. However, this view fails to explain how the biblical tradition arose in the first place. Also, there is some archaeological evidence that the inhabitants of these new villages already had different values, since they did not eat pigs (animals forbidden to the Israelites, Lev. 11:7).

The settlement of Israel in Palestine is probably the most complex issue in OT studies today. Nevertheless, a recent thorough assessment by evangelical scholars concludes: 'we have found nothing in the evidence considered that would invalidate the basic biblical contours'.[1]

One particular incident in Joshua has often intrigued Bible readers: 'the sun stood still and the moon stopped' for 'about a full day' to enable the Israelites to rout the southern kings (10:12–14). Various explanations have been proposed, e.g. suspension of the normal laws of the universe (though claims of scientific corroboration have never been substantiated), or highly unusual light reflection or refraction. More appropriately to the ancient context, John Walton notes that the vocabulary of theses verses reflects that of Mesopotamian celestial omen texts, and has often been misunderstood. To see both the rising sun and the setting moon at the same time on the 'wrong' day was a bad omen, so Joshua prays that his superstitious opponents will see a bad omen and lose heart before they even engage battle.[2]

C. Relevance for Christians

The Book of Joshua has many themes relevant to Christians. Centrally, it shows God fulfilling the promise made to Abraham by bringing his descendants back into the land promised to him. God does this through Joshua, whose name means 'Yahweh saves', a pithy summary of divine activity in human history. This name recurs later (e.g. for the prophet Hosea, and Israel's last king Hoshea), and of course supremely in the person better known by the name's Greek form, Jesus. The covenant God had made with his people at Sinai is reaffirmed immediately after entry, as the people gather at Mount Ebal (8:30–35, cf. Deut. 27 – 28), and again at the end of Joshua's life at Shechem (ch. 24). God's people are now a nation, settled in their land, in covenant relationship with him.

However, the book also poses a major challenge to Christians: the extermination of the Canaanites. This issue more than any other has led many people to reject the OT, and some to reject the whole Bible. So how can we come to terms with this command?

The first thing to notice is the terminology. This is not just any type of war. This is *herem*, variously translated as 'proscription', 'sacred ban', 'devotion to destruction'. *Herem* was a well-known concept in the ancient world: it involved complete destruction of all living beings in devotion to one's god, and sometimes consecration of precious metals to their temple. So it is a religious as well as military term. It is only used of Israel's early wars of conquest and consolidation, in Deuteronomy, Joshua and 1 Samuel. Once the land was firmly secure, warfare became simply defence.

Other passages have complementary emphases. Exodus repeatedly notes that God will 'drive out' other peoples (e.g. Exod. 23:27–30), though whether by death or banishment is unspecified. Deuteronomy allows citizens of surrendering towns to live and non-combatants of conquered towns to be spared (Deut. 20:10–15), though this only applies to distant towns. Perhaps more importantly, the Joshua accounts suggest only occasional application of the *herem*: at Jericho, Ai and some other resisting towns (6:21; 8:26; 11:12). Other texts reveal that many Canaanites were spared, though admittedly this happened because of Israel's military weakness rather than any moral compunction (Judg. 1:27–35). This attenuates the problem historically, but not theologically.

Why did God command it? There are three key elements of the biblical explanation. First, this was divine punishment on people for their sin, not their race: 'the sin of the Amorites' was now complete (Gen. 15:16). Their abhorrent practices included sacrificing their very own children to appease the gods (Deut. 12:31; 18:10). So they were to be punished for basic crimes against humanity, like the nations listed in Amos 1 - 2. Several points show this was punishment for sin, not extermination of race. On the one hand, Canaanites who trusted in Israel's God were spared, like Rahab and her family (2:11). On the other, Israelites who fell into similar sin would meet equally severe punishment, like Achan and his family (7:24–26). And any apostate Israelite town would also be subject to annihilation by *herem* (Deut. 13:12–18). Of course, these texts reflect the group solidarity of ancient times, where all in a family or clan lived or died together.

Secondly, this was prevention for Israel adopting pagan beliefs and practices (e.g. Deut. 7:3–4). God knew how strong their temptation was, and wanted to protect his people. Sadly, the incomplete conquest and the survival of many Canaanites led to exactly what God feared.

Thirdly and most importantly, most of the OT has no developed concept of life after death. So God's punishment of sin had to be seen in this life, if at all. The NT says more about judgment after death, both acquittal and punishment. So in Christian theology divine judgment is equally certain and equally severe, though no longer visible here on earth. How God will ultimately judge those who never had a chance to respond to him is his alone to decide. But the Israelite enactment of immediate judgment reminds us of the Christian doctrine of ultimate judgment.

JUDGES

A. Contents

1:1 – 3:6	Partial conquest and theological assessment
3:7 – 16:31	Oppression and deliverance: twelve judges
17 – 21	Two unattached narratives:
17 – 18	Danite idolatry and kidnap
19 – 21	Rape, murder and inter-tribal warfare

Judges tells the depressing story of Israel's gradual decline between the conquest and the monarchy. It opens positively, with a summary of territory captured (1:1–20). However, it then gives a long catalogue of failure (1:21–36), followed by a historical and religious summary of the ensuing period (2:1 – 3:6). This includes the tragic downward spiral of apostasy – oppression – judge raised up – deliverance – worse apostasy . . . (2:11–19). The opening section thus provides an overview and theological explanation of the whole period.

The second and main section (3:6 – 16:31) recounts the exploits of some twelve 'judges'. Elsewhere this term means judge in the modern sense of one who settles legal disputes, but here it implies more a hero-deliverer who became a ruler. Some clearly exercised leadership already, like the prophetess Deborah (4:4), but many were 'raised up' by God for the occasion. In any case, from what we know of characters like Jephthah and Samson, their justice was probably very rough and ready.

The third section gives two narratives outside the cycle of judges, which illustrate the near anarchy of the times. The first concerns the Danites' migration and the kidnap of a Levite priest. The second recounts horrific rape, murder, inter-tribal warfare and sponsored kidnapping. The refrain 'In those days Israel had no king' (four times), with its addition 'everyone did as they saw fit' (twice), thus suggests that the book was written in the early monarchy, when the order established by David contrasted sharply with this period's lawlessness.

There are two groups of judges, sometimes described as major and minor. The former all have stories about their exploits, the first two fairly briefly and the others at significant length. After the accounts of the first four we read that the land had peace for 40 or 80 years, which look like round figures for one or two generations. Othniel led a successful revolt against 'Cushan-Rishathaim king of Aram-Naharaim' (3:8; since Aram-Naharaim lay beyond the distant Euphrates, this king presumably reigned more locally). Ehud the left-hander assassinated King Eglon of Maob, defeated his forces, and established a long-lasting peace. Deborah the prophetess and her general Barak defeated the powerful King Jabin of Hazor and his general Sisera. Here the prose and poetry accounts in chs. 5 and 6 display some minor differences, though these can easily be explained as complementary rather than contradictory. Gideon leads a rout of the encroaching Midianites with initial humility and courage and then declines the proffered kingship, though later succumbs to pride and idolatry. On his death, one son Abimelech kills the other seventy and proclaims himself king (ch. 9). The disastrous consequences and the implicit suspicion of kingship explain the presence of this non-judge story in this section. Jephthah was illegitimate and ostracized, but later summoned to save the eastern tribes from Ammonite oppression. His military success was marred by his rash vow, fulfilled in the sacrifice of his daughter. Finally Samson, for all his dubious activities, at least kept the Philistines at bay when they were increasingly aggressive.

The 'minor' judges have only a few verses each, in three short sections. Of Shamgar we know nothing except that he 'struck down six hundred Philistines' (3:31), the only military conflict recorded for this group. The other five have brief, formulaic notices of their home town, length of judgeship (in exact rather than round figures) and notice of burial, plus the considerable progeny of three of them (10:1–5; 12:11–15). The different style and content of these brief notices suggests that the final compiler of the book combined two types of material, stories of hero-deliverers and a list of other leaders. The following table summarizes the data.

Reference	Judge (and origin)	Years of oppression and cause	Years of peace	Years of judgeship
3:7–11	Othniel (Calebite)	8, Cushan-Rishathaim	40	–
3:12–20	Ehud (Benjamin)	18, Eglon of Moab	80	–
3:31	Shamgar	Philistines	–	–
4 – 5	Deborah (? Ephraim)	20, Jabin of Hazor (with Sisera)	40	–
6 – 8	Gideon (Manasseh)	7, Midianites and Amalekites	40	–
10:1–2	Tola (Issachar)	–	–	23
10:3–5	Jair (Gilead)	–	–	22
10:6 – 12:7	Jephthah (Gilead)	18, Ammonites	–	6
12:8–10	Ibzan (Bethlehem)	–	–	7
12:11–12	Elon (Zebulun)	–	–	10
12:13–15	Abdon (Ephraim)	–	–	8
13 – 16	Samson (Dan)	40, Philistines	–	20

B. Historical setting

The figures given in Judges for years of oppression, peace and judgeship total 407 (though see above on 40 years as a round figure). If one adds suitable lengths before this for the wilderness period and for Joshua and the elders, and after this for Samuel, Saul and David, the total is clearly more than the 480 years given in 1 Kgs 6:1 for the period from the exodus to building the temple. This means that some of the judgeships must overlap. This in itself is hardly surprising, since it was a period of continued unrest, and there could be simultaneous oppressions or judgeships in the north (Issachar, Zebulun), east (Gilead) and south (Benjamin, Dan). But once overlap is admitted, there is no way of knowing its extent, so the figures in Judges cannot be used to support an early date for the exodus and conquest (see Historical Setting in Introduction to this chapter).

In his dispute with the Ammonites, Jephthah claimed that Israelites had occupied the territory for 300 years (11:26). If true, this would imply a longer period for the judges and hence an early exodus. But Jephthah may well have been exaggerating to bolster his case, or simply ignorant.

Later Israelite history testifies to continued conflict with neighbouring peoples, so the periodic invasion and oppression of the judges period fits the wider context. Unrest in Palestine in c. 1350 BC is related in letters from Canaanite city-states to the nominal overlord Egypt (excavated at El-Amarna, by the Nile). If the Israelites had already entered the land, these letters could reflect their continued attacks. Otherwise they provide general evidence of conflict in the area.

C. Relevance for Christians

A useful initial question concerns the purpose of the book within the OT. Some commentators take their cue from the closing refrain 'Israel had no king', and see it as pointing to the need for a monarch. However, while this is a clear implication from the concluding section, kingship is mostly ignored in the introduction and main section, and once even portrayed negatively (ch. 9). More central to the book is the theme of God's provision for his wayward people, raising up judges to deliver them and enable them to survive. So its overriding message is that of God's grace in response to human failure.

This theme is equally important for Christian interpretation, since it shows God's desire to rescue and restore a wayward people. This can be applied in different ways to both evangelism and the church. Further, the judges can be seen as 'types' of Christ in their role as deliverers, i.e. their activity foreshadows his. However, it is important to note that this relates to their activity, not their morality, which in some case was distinctly dubious.

As to the judges' morality, it is important to remember their times. Obviously there was little knowledge or acceptance of Mosaic law in any form, and the judges were known for military and political leadership rather than religious orthodoxy. Jephthah's foolish vow serves as a sad cautionary tale, even if we note the loyalty of father and daughter to their terribly misguided beliefs (11:30–40). And in the worst case of all, we can see Samson's faith at least in the final act of his life, even if his motives still remain mixed (16:28).

RUTH

A. Contents

The book of Ruth, set in the same period as Judges (Ruth 1:1), provides a delightful and welcome contrast to it. It tells the simple story of an ordinary family struck by tragedy, yet experiencing love and acceptance in unexpected ways. This leads eventually to new hope through marriage and a son, who became King David's grandfather.

Faced with famine, Elimelech and Naomi leave Bethlehem (which ironically means 'House of Bread') for Moab, where their two sons marry but die childless, along with Elimelech. Naomi decides to return home and her daughter-in-law Ruth determines to go too, pledging lifelong loyalty to Naomi and her god. The two women return in poverty, and Ruth the foreigner goes out to glean. She catches the eye of Boaz, who insists she stays in his fields and looks after her. On Naomi's instructions, Ruth then makes a silent approach to Boaz, who responds by redeeming Elimelech's property and marrying Ruth. On the birth of their child, Naomi ((meaning 'pleasant'), who had earlier wanted to be renamed Mara (meaning 'bitter') is again happy, while Boaz and Ruth are lavishly praised by the local women.

B. Historical setting

The book of Ruth provides various historical insights. Foremost is the portrayal of ordinary life continuing at village level, presumably in one of the calmer periods. The anarchy of Judges is complemented by the tranquillity of Ruth. Not that life was easy – famine was a frequent hazard, no doubt exacerbated by political unrest, and it led to Naomi's ten-year voluntary exile. The sojourn to Moab and intermarriage there, even by apparent God-fearers, shows that survival mattered more than any sense of ethnic or religious separateness.

The legal aspects of the book's denouement are intriguing, and involve two features of Israelite law: property redemption and marriage obligation. When someone sold their property, their next-of-kin had both the right and the moral responsibility to buy it back and keep it in the family (Lev. 25:25). Also, when a man died childless, his brother had the moral responsibility to marry his widow and give her a son; the latter would be considered legally as the dead man's son, and would inherit his property and perpetuate his name (Deut. 25:5–6). This practice, attested in many other cultures, is sometimes termed levirate marriage (from the Latin *levir*, 'brother-in-law').

The two concepts are combined here in a way not reflected in Israel's legislation. Elimelech's next-of-kin first agrees to redeem the land, accepting that this includes caring for Naomi (4:1–4). But when he realizes it also involves levirate marriage to Ruth, he declines on the grounds that it will endanger his own estate (4:5–6). He could not afford to buy land which would not become his. At this point Boaz proceeds to redeem the land and marry Ruth. But when Ruth has a son, the father is named as Boaz, not her deceased husband Kilion. While the combination and outworking of these customs did not exactly reflect Pentateuchal provision, the story shows that these customs were known and respected, though also adapted. It gives oblique but strong witness to their antiquity.

C. Relevance for Christians

Ruth is a little jewel. It sparkles like a diamond against black velvet, 'a masterfully crafted response to the politics of despair in Judges'.[3] It provides models of love and loyalty in Ruth, and of compassion and integrity in Boaz, showing how these qualities can redeem tragedy and bring hope. And it wonderfully illustrates the work of the '(next-of-kin) redeemer', or *go'el*. Even in despair, Job still knew that his redeemer would vindicate him (Job 19:25). And Christians know that their Redeemer has done so for them.

1 & 2 SAMUEL

Early tradition followed the Hebrew text in seeing 1 and 2 Samuel as a single book, as attested in the Babylonian Talmud and by church fathers Eusebius and Jerome (fourth century AD). Division into two is commonly attributed to the Septuagint translators, on the basis that the Greek text needed two scrolls whereas one had sufficed for the more compact Hebrew text. The same applies to Kings and Chronicles.

A. Contents

1 Sam. 1 – 7	Samuel as judge
1 – 3	Samuel and Eli
4 – 7	Wars with Philistines, ark captured and returned
1 Sam. 8 – 15	Samuel and Saul
8 – 12	Saul becomes king
13 – 15	Various wars, Saul rejected
1 Sam. 16 – 31	Saul and David
16 – 27	David's rise, Saul's jealousy, David a fugitive
28 – 31	Saul's final battle and death
2 Sam. 1 – 24	David
1 – 4	David's lament, civil war
5 – 10	David as king, Jerusalem as capital, ark installed, covenant, empire
11 – 12	David, Bathsheba and Uriah
13 – 20	Rape of Tamar, Absalom's rebellion, Sheba's rebellion
21 – 24	Appendix

1 & 2 Samuel record Israel's transition from a loose confederacy of tribes partially governed by occasional judges, to a united kingdom with a strong monarchy and a subservient empire. It was a remarkable political transformation in little over a century, involving enormous social, economic and religious change. Some of this is noted directly in the text, but much is simply implied. The development was initiated by popular request for a king, which Samuel interpreted as rejection of the old order, but which God granted. While the first king Saul failed the challenge, the second, David, achieved political success and became the benchmark for future kings, indeed the model for the eventual messiah.

1 Samuel opens with the annual visit of an ordinary Israelite family to the central shrine at Shiloh, giving a rare glimpse into the religious practice of ordinary Israelites. This led to the birth of Samuel, who grew up as an apprentice attendant at Shiloh, and later combined the roles of judge, priest and prophet as 'God's emergency man'.[4] Philistine expansionism marked the careers of Samuel and later Saul, but Samuel initiated spiritual and military recovery, and led Israel during an uneasy peace (ch. 7).

But the situation was unstable, and when Samuel grew old the people demanded a king. For all his qualities, Samuel himself was partly at fault in appointing his sons as judges, even though this was not a hereditary office and they were known to be corrupt. On divine prompting Samuel acceded and Saul was appointed, first anointed privately, then chosen by lot in public, and finally confirmed after exercising impromptu leadership (chs. 8 – 12). Given this succession of events, occurring in different places, and recounted in texts with different emphases, some scholars conclude that the editor merged accounts from different periods, some from the early monarchy when kingship was seen as successful (e.g. 9:1 – 10:16), and others from later centuries when it was unsuccessful and divisive (e.g. chs. 8, 12). However, it must also be noted that there was already longstanding opposition to kingship (cf. Judg. 9), and its anti-egalitarian tendencies were easily visible in neighbouring cultures.

Unfortunately, Saul did not live up to early promise, and quickly lost divine and prophetic endorsement. While his fall appears rapid, it may already be presaged by his ignoring the challenge, hinted at in his anointing, to attack the Philistines (10:5–7). In offering sacrifice and sparing Agag (chs. 13, 15) Saul oversteps his authority and begins a long and painful slide, which leads eventually to his tragic and lonely death (31:4). Meanwhile David gradually rises to be king-in-waiting.

2 Samuel opens with a brief period of civil war, after which David established first a united kingdom then a huge empire. Jerusalem became the political and religious capital, and divine approval was

encapsulated in a dynastic covenant (chs. 1 – 10). However, David's adultery with Bathsheba and murder of her husband Uriah (chs. 11 – 12) are a turning point, and the following chapters relate only family troubles and nearly fatal revolts (chs. 12 – 20). David's despicable actions affected far more than the immediate victims. The final chapters form an appendix of six elements from throughout David's reign, arranged in chiasm: atonement story, warrior list, song; song, warrior list, atonement story (21 – 24).

B. Historical setting

There is ample extra-biblical evidence that the Philistines were a group of Greek-speaking 'Sea-Peoples' who settled in south-west Palestine about 1200 BC. They ruled over five city states as a military aristocracy, and gradually assimilated with the indigenous Canaanites over the following centuries. Their possession of chariots and control of iron gave them military ascendancy over Israel for a long period. Recent excavation has revealed much about them, including the name Goliath (though from the century after the time of David's famous foe).

However, the main problem in finding archaeological corroboration for this period is the difficulty of excavating relevant sites in Jerusalem, for modern political reasons, and the ambiguity of the available evidence. Nevertheless, the existence of some stone building, including an extensive 'step structure', leads many scholars to conclude that Jerusalem underwent significant development at this time. Further, the later 'House of David' inscription found at Dan in the far north clearly shows that a Davidic kingdom stretched that far.

David's empire (2 Sam. 8) was apparently enormous, including all the neighbouring territories and stretching to the distant north, through what is now Lebanon, Syria and north-west Iraq as far as the Euphrates River. So geographically and demographically Israel became only a minority part of this. While some scholars have dismissed this as implausible, Kenneth Kitchen has shown that the eleventh to tenth centuries BC witnessed a power vacuum between the major powers of Egypt, Hittites (central Turkey) and Mesopotamia. This led to several mini-empires, including that of David and Solomon.[5]

C. Relevance for Christians

1 & 2 Samuel abound with lessons. There is the political development from confederacy to monarch to empire, under God's watchful providence, and the implication that different political systems can

work well when leaders are godly and act responsibly. Within this there is the rejection of Saul, whose rebellion hardened, and the approval of David, whose sin was confessed.

There is also the detail of many finely-told stories (the most extensive in the OT), which qualify the big picture with a more nuanced portrayal of characters and events. Close reading of the text (as rediscovered by scholars in narrative criticism) highlights these details, and reminds us of the ambiguity of some actions and the humanness of all the characters, and warns us against simplistic interpretation.

The overall picture and close reading together reveal David in his grandeur and his weakness. Above all, it shows 'a man after [God's] own heart' (1 Sam. 13:14) who regularly sought divine guidance. Despite his terrible sin and its catastrophic consequences, which the text starkly portrays, David's repentance revealed his continued faith in God. No wonder he became the standard against which future kings were assessed, and the model for the one whom a much later hymn writer called 'great David's greater son'.

1 & 2 KINGS

A. Contents

1 Kgs 1 – 11	United Kingdom: Solomon's accession and reign
1 Kgs 12 – 2 Kgs 17	Divided Kingdom:
1 Kgs 12 – 16	Schism and early kings
1 Kgs 17 – 2 Kgs 8:15	Elijah and Elisha
2 Kgs 8:16 – 17:41	Further kings, Israel's exile
2 Kgs 18 – 25	Remaining kingdom: Judah's last kings and exile

The books of Kings cover some four centuries of Israel's history, from the death of David to the death of his kingdom. It opens with David entrusting the kingdom to Solomon, who started well, constructed the temple plus various royal buildings, and led Israel in peace and prosperity (1 Kgs 4:20). But his reign was tarnished by unwelcome economic conditions for the people and his own gradual apostasy (1 Kgs 5:13–14; 11:4–6). Even so, on his death the Israelites would have accepted his son Rehoboam as king. But having known only pampered court life, Rehoboam refused their reasonable request, and the northern ten tribes separated under Jeroboam. They were then known as Israel, in distinction from Judah.

Jeroboam's first task was to create a separate political and religious life, including new temples, priests and festivals. Because of this, he is repeatedly judged to have 'caused Israel to commit sin' (e.g. 1 Kgs 15:26, 34). All Israel's subsequent kings 'did evil in the eyes of the LORD', following Jeroboam's ways. The northern kingdom was inherently unstable, with three new dynasties in its first fifty years, and another three in its last thirty. Only the dynasty of Jehu continued to the fourth generation, and then only briefly. Prophets often pronounce judgment on a dynasty (1 Kgs 14:10; 16:3; 21:21), and some scholars have suggested that they never accepted the monarchy in principle. However, their judgment is always proclaimed on certain kings in particular, not on the northern monarchy in general.

For a large middle section (1 Kgs 17:1 – 2 Kgs 8:15), the focus shifts from kings and politics to prophets and people. Dry records of battles fought and cities built give way to dramatic narratives of miraculous events. Some of these had far-reaching consequences, like the contest on Mount Carmel (1 Kgs 18), but most involved individuals or small groups. Many involved 'the sons of the prophets', who seemed to live on the margins of society, and may have descended from the companies of prophets in Samuel's time (e.g. 1 Sam. 10:5; 19:20). These stories provide intriguing glimpses into ordinary life as well as the role of prophets in ancient Israel.

Israel and Judah together went through cyclical half-century phases of political weakness and strength, with periods of strength in the mid-ninth century (under Omri and Jehoshaphat) and early eighth century (under Jeroboam II and Azariah/Uzziah). This second prosperous period led to Amos's vivid condemnation of ill-gotten and misused wealth. By the third quarter of the eighth century, Assyria was advancing westwards, and in 722 captured Samaria and exiled many Israelites, who never returned. God's assessment was that they refused to listen to 'my servants the prophets' (2 Kgs 17:13).

The Assyrians advanced further and would have conquered Judah too, but for God's intervention to save Jerusalem, in response to the prayers of Hezekiah and Isaiah (2 Kgs 18 – 19). Hezekiah enacted sweeping reforms, including removal of the 'high places'. Sadly his son Manasseh reversed all these, became Judah's worst king, and was seen as a major cause of its later exile. His grandson Josiah again enacted reform, helped by Assyria's rapid decline. But the Babylonians, the new world power, pressured Josiah's weak successors. Eventually Judah too was captured, Jerusalem and its temple were destroyed, and many of its people exiled.

So Kings ends with the tragedy of defeat and exile. God's provision of king, city and temple were all swept away. Other passages like Ps. 137 and Lamentations convey something of the emotional impact of this.

UNITED MONARCHY

Bible	Prophet	King	Dates				
1 Sam.	*Samuel*	Saul	1045–1011				
2 Sam.	*Nathan*	David	1011–971				
1 Kgs 1 – 11		Solomon	971–931				

– – – – – – 931   schism – – – – – –   *10th century*

Bible	Prophet	JUDAH	Dates	ISRAEL	Dates	Prophet	Century
12 – 14		Rehoboam	931–913	• Jeroboam	931–910		
		Abijah	913–911	Nadab	910–909		
15 – 16		Asa**	911–870	• Baasha	909–886		
				Elah	886–885		
17 – 22		Jehoshaphat**		• Omri	885–874		*9th century*
			873–870–848	Ahab	874–853	*Elijah*	
2 Kgs 1 – 8		Jehoram	853–848–841	Ahaziah	853–852		
		Ahaziah	841	Joram	852–841	*Elisha*	
9 – 13		Qn Athaliah	841–835	• Jehu	841–814		
		Joash**	835–796	Jehoahaz	814–798		
14		Amaziah*	796–767	Jehoash	798–782		
				Jeroboam II	793–782–753		
15		Azariah*	791–767–740	Zechariah	753–752	*Amos*	*8th century*
		= Uzziah		Shallum	752		
16 – 17	*Micah*	Jotham*	750–740–732	• Menahem	752–742		
		Ahaz	744–732–716	Pekahiah	742–740	*Hosea*	
18 – 20	*Isaiah*			• Pekah	740–732		Exile to
		Hezekiah**	716–687	• Hoshea	732–722	722 →	**Assyria –**
21		Manasseh	696–687–642				no return
22 – 23		Amon	642–640				*7th century*
		Josiah**	640–609				
24	*Jeremiah*						
		Jehoahaz	609				
		Jehoiakim	609–597				
		Jehoiakin	597	597 ——→			Exile to
25	*(Ezekiel)*	Zedekiah	597–587	587 ——→			**Babylon**
	(Daniel)						Return
				539 ←——			under
Ezra 1 – 6	*Haggai* *Zechariah*	Zerubbabel					**Persia**

(Esther)

5th century

Ezra 7 – 10	*Ezra*	458–...	←
Neh.	*Nehemiah*	445–...	←
	Malachi		

Data simplified from *New Bible Dictionary* 3rd edn 1996, pp. 188–189.

Where three dates are given, the first gives the start of a co-regency.

Key: * = king commended in 1 & 2 Kgs ** = reforming king • = new dynasty in Israel () = books relating to Jews in Babylon and Persia

Kings was probably written during the exile to explain how and why this tragedy had occurred. However, there is a glimmer of hope. The final paragraph shows an improved status for the exiled king Jehoiachin, a portent of the renewal to come.

B. Historical setting

1 & 2 Kings are clearly intended as history and often refer to source documents, notably the chronicles or annals of the kings of Israel or Judah. This implies that the facts could be checked, though these records are now lost (they are *not* the OT book of Chronicles). They also date each king in reference to his contemporary in the other kingdom, showing careful historical method. The figures largely concord, with allowance made for co-regencies – when a son was appointed king while his father was still alive (e.g. 2 Kgs 15:5). This, plus Mesopotamian records of unusual celestial events, allows us to give fixed dates to the whole monarchic period, as in the chart on p. 86.

There are many cross-references between biblical and ancient Near Eastern historical records. OT books frequently mention rulers of both immediate neighbours like Phoenicia (i.e. Tyre and Sidon) and Syria (often called Aram), and the more distant powers of Egypt, Assyria, Babylon and Persia. These rulers are amply attested in extra-biblical sources. Further, these sources also mention many Israelite and Judean kings, as shown in the following table.[6]

Ancient Near Eastern texts	Date BC	Israelite kings mentioned
Tel Dan stele	c. 850	David, Jehoram/Joram, Ahazaiah
Moabite stele	c. 835	(David), Omri
Shalmaneser III, Kurkh Monolith	853	Ahab
Shalmaneser III, Black Obelisk	828	Omri, Jehu
Adad-Nirari III, Calah stele	c. 800	Omri
Adad-Nirari III, Tell Al-Rimah stele	797	Joash
Tiglath-Pileser III, annals	c. 730	Omri, Menahem, Pekah, Hoshea, (Uzziah), Ahaz
Sargon II, annals	c. 720	Omri
Sennacherib's siege, three sources	c. 700	Hezekiah
Essarhadon, Prism B	c. 670	Manasseh
Ashurbanipal, Rassam Cylinder	c. 640	Manasseh
Nebuchadnezzar, ration lists	c. 570	Jehoiachin

A notable absentee from this list is Solomon. But his reign coincided with weakness of the major powers (see above), who were in no position to attack his territory or claim tribute, the usual reasons for mentioning foreign kings. Further, five years after Solomon's death, Pharaoh Shishak carried off all Jerusalem's gold and silver (1 Kgs 14:25–28). Shishak (called Shoshenq in Egyptian records) died the following year, but his son Osorkon soon dedicated vast amounts to Egyptian deities – very probably Solomon's gold.

C. Relevance for Christians

The 'prophetic' book of 1 & 2 Kings gives many big-picture lessons. God blesses obedience and punishes apostasy, though often not immediately. Divine sovereignty and human responsibility are both relevant, e.g. at the schism (1 Kgs 12), even if hard to reconcile logically. High position brings great responsibility.

Above all, Kings shows that God's assessment of value may not be ours. Politically important kings like Omri receive less space than religiously important ones like his son Ahab. Prophets pervade the book, with two receiving more attention than many monarchs. Unnamed women and children from hamlets like Zarephath and Shunem share the story with kings and emperors. And throughout the centuries, God preserves his people.

1 & 2 CHRONICLES

A. Contents and historical setting

1 Chr. 1 – 9	Genealogies and lists
1	Noah & Abraham
2 – 8	The main tribal lines, notably David's family and Levites
9	Post-exilic Jerusalemites
1 Chr. 10 – 29	David: particularly military and religious leadership (difficulties and sins omitted)
2 Chr. 1 – 9	Solomon: particularly temple construction (apostasy omitted)
2 Chr. 10 – 36	Kings of Judah: particularly reformers Hezekiah and Josiah (kings of Israel mostly omitted)

Chronicles retells the history of Israel from Adam to the exile, though only by genealogical list until the death of Saul, and only for the southern kingdom of Judah after the schism. The book has long been misunderstood, e.g. the Greek title 'Omissions' (*Paraleipomenon*) is inappropriate, since much of the history is already given in Samuel and

Kings. Rather, it is a retelling of the story of the monarchy period from a different perspective and for a different purpose.

Chronicles was written well after the exile. 1 Chr. 3:17–24 lists the descendants of Judah's penultimate king Jehoiachin to at least seven generations and possibly twelve, depending on the interpretation of v. 21. This means the book was completed at the earliest c. 400 BC. By this time the exile was long past, various groups had returned to Jerusalem under Zerubbabel, Ezra and Nehemiah (see below), and between them had established a viable if small Jewish community around a rebuilt temple and city. However, they were now firmly within the Persian empire – kingship and political independence were distant memories. So what this community needed was not an explanation of the exile (as in Kings), but encouragement from God's past provision for present circumstances.

This explains the two key features of the book, evident above in the outline. First, it concentrates on David and his line, as those through whom God worked. In consequence, it ignores Saul's reign except for his death, which is seen as judgment on his unfaithfulness (1 Chr. 10:13). It also virtually ignores the schismatic state of northern Israel: they had not been governed by a Davidic king; after conquest by Assyria they had become ethnically and religiously mixed; and in post-exilic times their descendants the Samaritans had actively opposed Jewish re-establishment.

Secondly, Chronicles concentrates on the temple and its worship, as led by priest and Levites. Hence the greater detail in the genealogy of Levi than of other tribes (1 Chr. 6). Hence the focus for Hezekiah and Josiah's reforms on purifying the temple and celebrating the Passover (unlike the focus in Kings). And hence the frequent reference to Levites throughout the book.

This also explains the glaring omissions regarding David's adultery and murder and Solomon's apostasy. The account of these kings concentrates on their preparation for and construction of the temple, with some description of David's early exploits and of Solomon's other activities. The books of Samuel and Kings were clearly known to the author of Chronicles, who copied or paraphrased significant sections, so presumably their contents were known to his community. Like any historian, the Chronicler used his source material selectively to tell a particular story. Just as histories of the British empire or of the Second World War written in, say, 1945 and 2005, would have different contents and interpretation, with complementary insights, so do the OT historical books.

B. Relevance for Christians

Chronicles has a broad vision of God's work and a strong hope for the future. Through his covenant with king and people, God provided security, peace and prosperity, and through obedience in life and worship the small Jewish community can still experience his blessing. The book has relevance for many Christians today, e.g. those with no political influence, or who long for experiences of previous generations, or who desire church renewal. And the model which Chronicles gives of fresh interpretation of the past encourages us to keep rethinking what we can learn from biblical and Christian history.

EZRA AND NEHEMIAH

The Books of Ezra and Nehemiah are closely related, since they present successive episodes of post-exilic history, and the man Ezra appears in both. Indeed, Jewish tradition sees them as a single book (as in the Talmud, Baba Bathra 15a, the earliest known Jewish list of OT books). But there are also differences. For instance, the Book of Ezra has sections in Aramaic (4:8 – 6:18; 7:12–26), including several official letters – obviously early readers were bilingual. And it has two distinct halves, the first of which recounts events long before Ezra's ministry. The Book of Nehemiah is more uniform in its style and more cohesive in its story.

A. Contents and historical setting

These books have four main stages, as shown in the following table.

Stage	Date	Reference	Event	Persian king	Dates
1.	539	Ezra 1:1 – 4:5	**'First return'**, temple started	Cyrus	550–530
				Cambyses	530–522
2.	520–516	Ezra 4:24 – 6:22	**Temple completed**	Darius I	521–486
	?	*Ezra 4:6	Local opposition	Xerxes/Ahasuerus	486–464
3.	458	Ezra 7 – 10	**'Second return' with Ezra**	Artaxerxes I	464–423
	pre-445	*Ezra 4:7–23	More opposition		
4.	445	Neh. 1 – 12	**Nehemiah to Jerusalem**		
	post-433	Neh. 13	Nehemiah's second term		

* Note that this opposition is recorded with earlier opposition, not in chronological order.

The Book of Ezra is in two distinct halves, the first of which records events before Ezra himself was even born. It opens (as Chronicles closes) with Cyrus's decree enabling Jews to return to Jerusalem to rebuild their temple. The initial leader is prince Sheshbazzar (1:8), perhaps Jehoiachin's son (the 'Shenazzar' of 1 Chr. 3:18), but he is soon replaced by Jehoiachin's grandson Zerubbabel and the high priest Jeshua. These latter lead some 50,000 returnees and initiate temple reconstruction. The altar is rebuilt and new foundations laid, to joyous if poignant celebration. But local opposition soon halts activity for nearly two decades. At this point the text inserts two examples of later opposition (4:6–23). The prophets Haggai and Zechariah then encourage resumption of work, and this time local opposition is thwarted by Darius, who rediscovers and reinforces Cyrus's earlier decree. The temple is completed four years later in 516 BC, with a memorable Passover celebration.

The book then jumps some 60 years to 458 BC (7:8). King Artaxerxes sends the learned Ezra to Jerusalem with royal authority and finance, to establish proper judicial procedure. Ezra and his large delegation were descendants of exiles, 'returning' to Jerusalem for the first time. On arrival, Ezra immediately sees the many mixed marriages as a fundamental threat to the nation's very survival. He responds with spontaneous confession and grief, leading to widespread conviction and a resolve to dissolve the marriages. This one glimpse of Ezra's ministry reveals much about his devotion to God's law. Nothing more is said of the repudiated families: some commentators assume this was a callous act, while others argue that a leader like Ezra would have ensured appropriate provision for them.

The book of Nehemiah is the story of one man used by God to protect and re-invigorate Jerusalem, and is drawn largely from his own, first-person memoirs. Like Ezra, Nehemiah was apparently a child of the diaspora, and like Mordecai he rose to high office. With support from King Artaxerxes, Nehemiah travels to Jerusalem in 445/4 BC as its new and energetic governor. He immediately challenges the city's inhabitants and galvanizes them into action. Despite increasing opposition and intimidation, the walls are rebuilt in the amazingly short period of fifty-two days (chs. 1 – 4, 6).

Other reforms proceed apace. Nehemiah vigorously attacks financial abuses, minimizes the governor's costs, reorganizes temple and defence personnel, and repopulates Jerusalem with descendants of the first returnees (chs. 5, 7, 11 – 12). Meanwhile Ezra and others read the law, and the people respond in confession and recommitment (chs. 8 – 10), and the walls are rededicated with joyful festivity, audible miles away (12:27–43).

Nehemiah returns to Artaxerxes after some 11 years, in 433 BC (13:6). He goes back to Jerusalem 'some time later' during Artaxerxes' reign (i.e. before 423 BC), discovers further abuses and sets about reform with typical vigour. These include the recurrent issue of mixed marriages, with the resultant mixed language, culture and religion. Nehemiah's response (13:25) is more physically confrontational than was Ezra's, with some effect amongst priest and Levites (13:30) but no record of wider divorce. The book ends with Nehemiah's characteristic appeal, 'Remember me with favour, my God' (13:31; cf. 5:19; 6:14; 13:14, 22). To the modern reader this may sound arrogant; for Nehemiah it may simply have reflected a sense of personal unworthiness before God and the knowledge that his good work would inevitably be compromised.

B. Relevance for Christians

The post-exilic situation was very different from the pre-exilic. Politically the Jews were now a small part of a large empire, dependent on local governors and the king. Religiously they had moved from syncretism to accepting only Yahweh, but they often became dispirited in their faith and worship. This has many parallels with the Christian era, so the post-exilic books, both prophetic and historical, have much relevance to us. They portray God's overruling in political events, through Cyrus, Darius and Artaxerxes, in conjunction with the faith and action of men like Zerubbabel, Ezra and Nehemiah. They show how unpromising situations can be turned around through faithful action, but also that apathy and inappropriate relationships often recur. And through the highs and lows, God continues to provide for his people.

ESTHER

A. Contents and historical setting

The Book of Esther tells a short story of great consequence. Historically it falls between the two halves of Ezra (see above), though it deals with Jews in the Persian capital Susa rather than in Jerusalem. Xerxes (called Ahasuerus in Hebrew) deposes his queen and chooses Esther instead. Meanwhile his chief official Haman, angered by her uncle Mordecai, plots to kill all Jews throughout the empire. So Esther reveals her identity and pleads for her people. Haman, already humiliated, is then executed in the way he intended for Mordecai, either hanged (NIV) or impaled (TNIV), and replaced by his nemesis. Subsequently the Jews are allowed to defend themselves and attack their enemies. From then on, they celebrate their survival in the new annual festival of Purim.

Esther is an exquisitely told story, whose deft characterization and subtle plot devices continue to delight today. Its annual retelling by Jews at Purim is accompanied by enthusiastic audience participation, cheering the heroes and hissing the villain. Partly because it is so well crafted, some think it is largely fictional.

Surprisingly, Persian records have no mention of the book's events or its main characters: Vashti and Esther, Haman and Mordecai. Many other aspects seem at variance with surviving records of Persian history and practice. There are no records of the empire divided into 127 satrapies, of the immutable 'law of the Medes and the Persians', of laws promulgated in all languages, or of war between Jews and their enemies. And the Greek historian Herodotus calls Xerxes' queen Amestris. As a result, for the last century most scholars have seen Esther as legendary. However, the records for this period are poor, and this alone should invite caution. Further, Vashti and Amestris are both portrayed as strong-willed; and the transcription of Persian names into Hebrew and Greek could be very different, e.g. the king's Persian name Xshayarshan became Akhashverosh in Hebrew and Xerxes in Greek! Noting other evidence, including many historically appropriate elements, Timothy Laniak argues cogently that the story should indeed be taken as historical.[7]

B. Relevance for Christians

From Luther on, many Christians have been troubled by Esther. One problem is that God is unmentioned. But this is a minor difficulty, since a trust in divine providence pervades the book, and is encapsulated in 4:14. More serious are the desire for and the acts of revenge, resulting in the death of some 76,000 (9:12–16). However, we must note three important points: the Jews acted in self-defence, within the law and without taking spoils; the number killed was not large given the number of Jewish communities scattered throughout the empire; and this is seen as justice within an OT perspective.

On a more positive note, the book of Esther reminds us of God's care for his people, his activity 'behind the scenes', his use of faithful people like Esther and Mordecai, and their willingness to stand up for the right, whatever the outcome. So while it is unlike the other historical books in some ways, e.g. its Persian location and its oblique reference to the deity, it is similar in its portrayal of God's response to his people's faith.

Notes

[1] I. Provan, V. P. Long, T. Longman III, *A Biblical History of Israel* (WJKP, 2003), p. 192.

[2] J. H. Walton, 'Joshua 10:12–15 and Mesopotamian Celestial Omen Texts', in A. R. Millard et al, eds., *Faith, Tradition, and History* (Eisenbrauns, 1994), pp. 181–190.

[3] J. G. Harris, C. A. Brown, M. S. Moore, *Joshua, Judges, Ruth*, NIBC (Paternoster, 2000), p. 300.

[4] F. F. Bruce, *Israel and the Nations* (Paternoster, 4th edn 1997), p. 11.

[5] K. A. Kitchen, *On the Reliability of the Old Testament* (Eerdmans, 2003), pp. 98–107.

[6] J. B. Pritchard, *Ancient Near Eastern Texts* (Princeton, 1969), pp. 279–294, 308, 320.

[7] L. C. Allen, T. S. Laniak, *Ezra, Nehemiah, Esther*, NIBC (Paternoster, 2003), pp. 176–182.

Further reading (see **Introduction** for good commentary series)

Philip Satterthwaite, *Exploring the Old Testament 2. The Historical Books* (SPCK, 2007) – excellent introduction, with panels highlighting themes and points to ponder.

Victor Hamilton, *Handbook on the Historical Books* (Baker, 2001) – good detailed introduction to the books and each section or chapter.

Iain Provan and others, *A Biblical History of Israel* (WJK, 2003) – the best detailed study by evangelical scholars of ancient Israel's history, affirming the OT's historical reliability.

5. Poetic Books

Tremper Longman III

JOB

The problem of suffering is one that has plagued ancient and modern people. Why do good things happen to bad people, and bad things to good people? The ancient Hebrews and those who read their sacred literature felt this problem acutely. After all, the very structure of the covenant Israel enjoyed with God would lead one to expect reward for obedience. The book of Deuteronomy is a case in point. Chs. 27 and 28 indicate that those who obey the preceding laws will be rewarded with blessing while those who disobey will be cursed. The historical narrative in Samuel–Kings uses the laws of Deuteronomy, particularly the law of centralization in Deut. 12, to justify the exile. Israel did not worship the LORD only at the place he chose, and so God turned them over to the Babylonians. The prophets, best understood as upholders of the covenant, had anticipated this judgment by warning Israel that they would be punished for their sin. And the book of Proverbs, at least in the bulk of its teaching, emphasizes good outcomes for wise behaviour and negative results for foolishness.

The book of Job grapples with the issue of retribution, and provides a corrective to overconfidence that in this life people necessarily get the reward/punishment that they deserve. However, it would be a mistake to think that retribution was the main concern of the book of Job. A key purpose of the book of Job is to proclaim that Yahweh is the only source of wisdom. This perspective may be observed by following the plot of the book.

A. *Structure and message*

The book opens and closes in prose, while the body (3:1 – 42:6) is in poetry. The prose prologue sets the scene and presents the scenario. Job is a man from Uz, indicating that he is not an Israelite. This fact, and also the description of his wealth, set the story in patriarchal times, though it was almost certainly written later, perhaps much later.

1. The prose prologue (1:1 – 2:13)

Job is 'blameless and upright'. We hear this important fact right at the beginning (1:1). Further, this is confirmed by none other than God himself when he points Job out to 'the Satan' (literally 'the accuser'). However, the latter uses God's evaluation as an occasion to question Job's integrity. He agrees that Job is blameless, but he throws doubt on his motivation. Job is blameless because of the rewards that come from such behaviour. Challenged in this way, God then grants permission to allow the Accuser to bring suffering into Job's life and then observe whether or not he maintains his integrity.

Job's suffering is severe and, in response to his pain, three friends come to commiserate with him. They sit in silence for seven days (2:13), and Job is the first one to break this silence with a bitter lament (ch. 3) that begins the poetic portion of the book. This lament provokes responses from the three friends: Eliphaz, Bildad and Zophar. The debate between them and Job provides the bulk of the book (4 – 31) and it has a very set pattern.

2. The debate (3:1 – 31:40)

The friends speak in turn, each being answered by Job before the next voices his concerns. There are three cycles of the debate, though the last is somewhat truncated, perhaps indicating that the friends are running out of steam. The section is extensive and there are three speakers, but their message is fairly repetitive. They represent a hard-and-fast view of the relationship between sin and suffering. As they observe Job's suffering, they reason that sin results in suffering, so suffering is the result of sin. As a result, the solution to Job's conundrum is quite clear: he must repent.

Job, however, has a conflicting perspective on the situation. He knows he does not deserve to suffer. While everyone sins (9:2), he has not sinned so much that he deserves such horrific suffering. He questions God's justice (9:21–24). At the end of his speeches, he says he wants God to charge him properly, so he can then meet him and justify himself (31:35–37). As we will soon see, Job gets his wish for an encounter with God, but it doesn't go the way he expects.

In a word, Job's view is really not substantially different from that of the three friends. All of them believe that consequences follow from one's deeds. The difference is that Job thinks God is unfair towards him, while the friends insist that God is fair and that Job is being punished for his sins. Eventually, the three friends run out of arguments without convincing Job.

3. Elihu's monologue (32:1 – 37:24)

Into the silence steps a man named Elihu. He is young and full of bluster, upset that the three friends, whom he had respected as wise elders, have not adequately shown Job that he is wrong. He reasons that it must not be age, but the spirit that renders a person able to discern the proper state of a situation (32:6–9). However, when all is said and done, Elihu too expresses a simple retribution theology (34:11, 25–27, 37). This explains why no one responds to Elihu and, even at the end, God does not address him.

While the debate has centered on the reasons for Job's suffering, this is not the heart of the debate. The question behind the issue of suffering is: who is wise? Both Job and the friends set themselves up as sources of wisdom and ridicule the wisdom of the other side (11:12; 12:1–3, 12; 13:12; 15:1–13). The question of who is wise is central to the book.

4. Yahweh's speeches and Job's repentance (38:1 – 42:6)

The answer to this question comes in the climax to the book with Yahweh's speeches (38:1 – 42:6). As mentioned earlier, Job desired an interview with God so he could set him straight and accuse him of unfairness. God now appears to Job, but the latter does not get the opportunity to challenge him. On the contrary, God appears to Job in the form of a whirlwind and challenges him by giving him a surprise test. God asks Job a series of questions that only the Creator could possibly answer. The questions demonstrate God's full knowledge and control of the natural order that he created and this contrasts with Job's ignorance. When so confronted, Job recognizes God's superior power and wisdom and responds with repentance. He submits himself to the almighty God of the universe.

5. The prose epilogue (42:7–17)

In the epilogue, the story comes to a happy conclusion. Job is reconciled with God and his fortune is restored. God blesses him and allows him to live a long life. Thus this book wrestles with the issue of proper retribution and concludes that God is wise.

B. Date and authorship

The book of Job is notoriously difficult to date. No author or date is specified in the book itself. The early setting of the story (see above) has led some to suggest that it is early, perhaps even the first book of the Bible to have been written. This conclusion is unlikely. Others have put forward the idea that Job is one of the last books to be included in the OT. This viewpoint too is unprovable. The language of the book is unique, but its specific characteristics have been pressed into service to demonstrate both an early and a late date. The best conclusion is to remain agnostic about its date of composition and fortunately the answer to this question does not bear on its interpretation.

C. Historicity

A similar debate surrounds the historicity of the book. It is true that the figure of Job is mentioned outside of this book (Ezek. 14:14, 20), alongside Daniel and Noah. Further, the opening of the book bears resemblance to the opening of Judg. 17 and 1 Sam. 1, two passages with fairly certain intention to communicate historical events.

Thus there appears to be a historical intention in the book. We are probably to understand Job to be a real person who lived in the past and who suffered, though this cannot be proven by reference to extra-biblical material like archaeological data. However, although the book of Job intends to be historical at least in a general sense, there are other indications that suggest that the book does not consider historical precision a high priority. For instance, the dialogues are in poetic form. Clearly people did not speak to each other in poetry, especially when they were in deep pain. Poetry elevates the book from a specific historical event to a story with universal application. The book of Job is not simply a historical chronicle; it is wisdom that should be applied to all who hear it.

D. Continuing significance

The book of Job continues its relevance today as witnessed by the fact that it is one of the best-known books of the OT. It grapples with the issue of suffering, and people suffer today as they always have. People of faith come to the book of Job and learn that not all suffering can be explained as penalty for evil behaviour. The book teaches us that we should not be quick to judge the morality of those who suffer. If we do, we might end up in the position of the three friends whom God clearly reprimands at the end of the book (42:7–9).

Christians read this book from the perspective of the cross. The NT brings us to a deeper understanding of God's dealing with the suffering in our life. In Jesus, God enters the world and endures the most horrible suffering on our behalf. Jesus Christ is the only truly innocent sufferer, the only one completely without sin. He submits himself to suffering voluntarily (unlike Job), for the benefit of others. No wonder the early church read the book of Job during Passion week.

It is not as if Christ has put an end to the suffering of his people. 2 Cor. 1:3–11 describes the church as those who receive comfort in the midst of suffering. But the hope of the NT is that Jesus suffered on our behalf and so we anticipate a glorious future (Rom. 8:18–27).

PSALMS

The book of Psalms is a collection of 150 separate poetic texts. There are indications that a few of the psalms that are now separate were originally a single composition (e.g. the refrain in Pss. 42 and 43), but, if so, we do not know the reasons why they were split.

A. Titles

Many of the psalms have brief introductions, traditionally called 'titles', that are part of the Hebrew text. These were probably added later than the composition of the psalms, but before the canonical collection was closed. It is debated whether they should be considered canonical or not. If one takes the titles as authoritative or as reliable early tradition, they inform concerning composition and function of the psalms. For instance, the titles make it obvious that psalms were sung, since they often use the labels 'song' (*shir*) and 'psalm' (*mizmor*). However, phrases that are generally taken to be tunes are unclear (e.g. 'Do Not Destroy' for Ps. 58). There are also references to instruments, and the parenthetical expression *selah* is best understood as some kind of musical direction, even though its exact meaning is unclear. Thus the psalms are songs as well as prayers.

Many titles associate certain individuals with particular psalms. The largest number of such psalms, seventy-three in total, are associated with David (known in Amos 6:5 as a great musician; see also 1 Sam. 16). The earliest attribution is Moses (Ps. 90), and then there are others such as Solomon (Ps. 72), Asaph (a temple musician at the time of David, Ps. 73), and more. Some songs clearly come from the latest period of OT history (Pss. 126; 137). So if the titles are taken to indicate authorship, which seems their intention, then the psalms were written over the long period of time from Moses to the post-exilic era. Even if the titles indicate a looser association with the named individuals, as some interpreters suggest, the psalms still come from many different writers, times and situations.

The titles also give evidence for the purpose behind certain psalms. There are a handful of historical titles that cite the occasion for composition. Ps. 51 is well known for its connection to David after Nathan the prophet confronted him following his sin with Bathsheba (2 Sam. 11). Indeed, when one reads the psalm two things are immediately apparent. First, the contents, a petition to God to forgive the psalmist's sins, is very appropriate to that historical occasion. Second, the psalmist does not refer to the specifics of the story as we know them in 1 Samuel. The request is for forgiveness from sin generally, not adultery specifically. Thus if, as is likely, the composition of the psalm was inspired by a particular experience, the psalmist intentionally avoided specific reference to that experience in order that later worshippers could use the psalm when they found themselves in a similar though not identical situation. 1 Chr. 16 pictures David handing a psalm to Asaph, the Levite in charge of music, thus providing a narrative to bolster the claim that psalmists were mindful of later users in their compositions.

Most scholars today would agree that the book of Psalms functioned as the hymn book of ancient Israel. Its primary setting was corporate, though individual use of psalms is portrayed in the OT (1 Sam. 2:1–10; Jon. 2). The label 'hymn book' is also appropriate because the church's hymns often came into existence in a similar way. 'Amazing Grace', for instance, may have been written by the author John Newton because he was moved by his own conversion, but he wrote it so that others who sang the song would marvel at their own conversions, not his.

B. Structure

One obvious difference between modern hymn books and the Psalms is their structure. While most hymnals have a topical or liturgical structure, that of the Psalms is unclear. There have been many attempts over the years to discern an underlying structure of the psalter, but these have failed to convince a majority of readers. Since a clear structure has not been observed in the past millennia, one should be suspicious of any new insight that claims to have discovered it.

While there is no apparent overall structure in terms of how one psalm moves to the next, there are still some useful observations about which there is general agreement. The first has to do with the presence of 'mini-collections' in the book. One example will suffice, the Songs of Ascent. Pss. 120 – 134 are so named in their title, probably because they were used by pilgrims as they were 'going up' to Jerusalem to celebrate one of the annual festivals. Mini-collections like the Songs of Ascent were then incorporated in the Psalter as a group.

The second observation is that there are intentional placements of psalms at the beginning and at the end of the book. Early rabbis called Ps. 1 the gatekeeper of the psalms, making an analogy between the holy physical space of the temple, where the gatekeeper kept the wicked out, and the holy textual space of the psalms, where Ps. 1 encourages the righteous and condemns the wicked. Ps. 1 also places the Torah front-and-centre, thus making a connection between Penta-teuch and Psalms. After entering the literary sanctuary, readers then encounter the other psalm that forms the introduction, Ps. 2, which brings them into contact with the LORD and his anointed one. In the monarchical period, the 'anointed one' was the Davidic king, and the psalm was probably composed as a coronation or pre-battle song. But after the monarchy's demise, when the psalter was compiled, thoughts would have turned to a future messianic deliverer. There is also a clustering of praise songs at the end. Pss. 146 – 150 resound with hallelujahs, especially the last of that group. These psalms form a final doxology to end the book.

Finally, picking up on the observation made above in regard to Ps. 1 and the Torah (Pentateuch), the final canonical form of the book of Psalms is divided into five books:

Book 1: 1 – 41
Book 2: 42 – 72
Book 3: 73 – 89
Book 4: 90 – 106
Book 5: 107 – 150

Each book ends with a doxology. The idea behind this division is again to make an intentional connection between Torah and Psalms and thus support the latter's claim to authority. Though these are prayers to God, they are also God's Word.

Though one can make some general observations, the final form of the Psalter gives the general impression of a rather random order of psalms. This may be observed in terms of the different types of psalms that the book contains, to which we now turn.

C. Genre

In terms of genre, we first observe that the psalms are poems. Of course, the book is not unique in this regard. Most of the wisdom books, large sections of the prophetic books, and even some parts of the Torah (e.g. Exod. 15) and the historical books (e.g. Judg. 5) are poetic. Hebrew poetry is characterized by brevity of expression, parallelism within lines, and an intense use of imagery. In addition, poets utilized a host of other poetic conventions on a more occasional basis, e.g. acrostics, alliteration, and other types of word play and sound play. In a word, poetry is compact language, and must be read slowly and reflectively to be read well.

The Psalms are a certain type of poetry, namely lyric. Lyric poetry conveys the emotional expression of the composer. Indeed, the different categories of psalms discerned by scholars are mainly recognized by the emotional state of the poet. For illustrative purposes, we name four main categories as follows:

Hymn: These are songs of unalloyed joy (24; 98). They are songs sung when everything is going well and one wants to celebrate God. They have been called descriptive songs of praise and psalms of orientation.

Lament: These are songs of disorientation. The psalmist expresses discouragement, anger, disappointment, grief with oneself, the 'enemy', or even God himself. There are laments of the individual (77) and corporate laments (83). Interestingly, while there are exceptions (88), most laments turn at the end to some statement of praise or confidence (69).

Thanksgiving: These psalms are very similar to hymns. They often begin that way (30), but in the body of the psalm there is some recognition of previous trouble and an earlier lament to which God has responded. These psalms are psalms of new orientation.

Confidence: Ps. 23 is an excellent example of a psalm of confidence, that expresses trust in God in the midst of a struggle.

D. Theological message and continuing significance

Though the psalms are the prayers of Israel to God, they also have a theological function that is recognizable through the many images of

God that the psalmists invoke. In the psalms God is a king (47), a warrior (24), a shepherd (23), a mother (131), and so on. These metaphors throw light on the nature of God and his relationship to his people.

The book of Psalms continues to be significant in the light of the NT people of God. First, attention should be paid to the fact that the book is frequently cited in the NT, indeed second only to the book of Isaiah. This should not be surprising, since Jesus himself said that the Psalms anticipated his suffering and glorification (Luke 24:25–27, 44). Admittedly, 'Psalms' here stands for the whole third part of the Hebrew canon, but of course that includes this book. We see that Jesus' own emotional state is occasionally expressed through psalm citation (Matt. 27:45–46).

Further, Christians continue in the line of later worshippers who use the psalms to help them express their own thoughts and feelings in prayer to God when they have similar though not necessarily identical experiences. Calvin described the psalms as a 'mirror of the soul'. As worshippers read a psalm, they find themselves being read. They find words to help them express their own feelings, and the psalm, whether hymn or lament, brings them face to face with God.

PROVERBS

Proverbs is a book of wisdom similar in many ways to the wisdom literature of the broader ancient Near East, especially Egypt. The predominant style of the book is that a father instructs his son in the pursuit of wisdom and avoidance of folly.

A. The nature of wisdom

At first glance the wisdom of Proverbs seems largely and simply practical advice. The preamble of the book (1:1–7) gives the purpose of Proverbs: to give the simple-minded prudence and the wise increased wisdom, including how to avoid problems, deal with difficult people, and maximize the good things of this life (wealth, health, happiness). In other words, wisdom is a skill of living, navigating life's hardships. In many ways, wisdom is similar to the modern idea of emotional intelligence, knowing how to say and do the right thing at the right time in order to enjoy life.

This description of the wisdom of Proverbs is true as far as it goes, but it does not go far enough. Wisdom is not just a practical skill; it is more profoundly a theological idea, since it involves relationship with God.

The last verse of the preamble, often called the book's motto, makes this clear from the start:

The fear of the LORD is the beginning of knowledge,
but fools despise wisdom and instruction. (1:7)

Thus knowledge (a synonym of wisdom, see the statement at 9:10) is not just skill, but involves a particular type of relationship with God, one characterized by godly fear, the recognition that God is the centre of the universe, not human beings.

The idea that wisdom is a theological category is also presented in the interesting figure named Woman Wisdom. While Woman Wisdom is first encountered in 1:20–33, she is extensively described in ch. 8. There we see that she accompanied God during creation (8:22–31). The implicit message here is that if one wants to know how the world works, one must have a relationship with this woman.

But what or whom does Woman Wisdom represent? The clearest evidence to answer this is found in 9:3, where the reader learns that her house is on the highest point of the city. It is common knowledge that only the deity has a house on the high place in an ancient Near Eastern city, and thus the reader should recognize that this woman is a personification of Yahweh's wisdom and ultimately stands for Yahweh himself.

With this background the reader can recognize the main purpose of the book. As mentioned, the literary form of the book is primarily a father who is encouraging his son to pursue wisdom. The book itself may be divided into two parts: the discourses of chs. 1 – 9 and the proverbs (brief observations, prohibitions, admonitions) in chs. 10 – 31. The proverb section is mostly practical advice, but must be read in light of chs. 1 – 9 in the following way.

Readers of the book of Proverbs are supposed to identify themselves with the son. The son/reader is walking on the path, a metaphor often found in the first nine chapters of the book. In ch. 9, the path takes the son past the high hill where Woman Wisdom dwells. She invites him in for a meal (9:1–6). But another voice also beckons (9:13–18). This is Woman Folly, whose house is also located on the highest point of the city. This indicates that she too stands for a deity, in this case a false god. The reader must choose with which woman (which god) to enter into an intimate relationship. Thus, at the heart of the book of Proverbs there is a fundamental religious choice. Will the son be wise and therefore godly and righteous, or foolish and therefore ungodly and wicked?

The teaching of the book spans a broad spectrum of behaviours and actions as it differentiates wise speech and actions from foolish. Some of the main topics addressed are: speech, friends and neighbours, business ethics, honesty, planning ahead, family relationships, behaviour before kings, even table manners and moderation in the use of alcohol.

B. Date and authorship

The superscription of the book associates it with King Solomon (970–930 BC), renowned for his wisdom (1 Kgs 3 – 4). While there is no good reason to dissociate Proverbs from Solomon, the internal evidence of the book indicates that others were involved in its final form. For instance, 22:17 and 24:23 mention a group simply called 'the wise'; 30:1 and 31:1 name two otherwise unknown kings named Agur and Lemuel respectively; 10:1 and 25:1 mention Solomon again, but the latter verse also ascribes a role to the 'men of king Hezekiah of Judah'. Another complicating factor is the fact that a comparison with other ancient Near Eastern texts, some coming from before Solomon (e.g. the Egyptian *Instruction of Amenemope*) shows a strong likelihood that some proverbs were adopted and adapted from non-Israelite sources. It appears that the composition of Proverbs, like that of the Psalms, took place over a long period of time, before the book came to a close and no more proverbs were added.

C. Continuing significance

The book of Proverbs retains its relevance in the Christian canon and for the Christian church. Theologically, it should be noted that Jesus Christ is revealed as the very pinnacle of God's wisdom (1 Cor. 1:30; Col. 2:3). But even more, Jesus uses language that identifies himself with Woman Wisdom (Matt. 11:18–19) and the NT writers also describe him in language closely associated with her (John 1; Col. 1:15–17). Thus when Christians read Prov. 9 they should take it as a choice between Jesus and some kind of false god.

And further, the advice that the proverbs offer is still relevant for navigating life. Principles are expressed in this book that help in marriage, society and self-understanding. However, readers need to remember two important things about the genre of 'proverb'. In the first place, a proverb states a truth which is time-conditioned: the proverb must be stated in the right circumstance to be true. In other words, the wise must read the circumstances before knowing whether to 'answer fools according to their folly' or not (compare 26:4 and 5). The time-conditioned nature of proverbs is true no matter what the language. In English, sometimes 'too many cooks spoil the broth' is appropriate, but at other times, 'many hands make light work'. In the second place, proverbs are not in the job of giving promises. If one 'start[s] children off in the way they should go' as 22:6 suggests, it is more likely, but it does not guarantee that 'when they are old they will not turn from it'. It will come true, everything else being equal, but not in all contexts.

When read properly, Proverbs is a source of great richness, presenting its readers with an image of God as a female sage. It also provides helpful advice about how to get along in the world.

ECCLESIASTES

The book of Ecclesiastes is best known for the repeated refrain that proclaims 'everything is meaningless' (Hebrew *hebel*; see 1:2; 12:8 and throughout), and for this reason the book's appropriateness for the canon has often been questioned. However, a thorough reading of the book demonstrates that 'meaninglessness' is not its final conclusion.

A good way to interpret Ecclesiastes is to note its two voices, that of 'the teacher' (Qohelet in Hebrew), who speaks in the first person ('I') in 1:12 – 12:7, and a second unnamed wisdom teacher who speaks about Qohelet in the third person ('he') in 1:1–11 and 12:8–14. The second speaker is teaching his son (12:12) by exposing him to Qohelet's thinking and then evaluating it.

A. The message of 'the teacher'

To understand the book of Ecclesiastes, we must first understand the logic of Qohelet's thought. In a sentence, the nub of his point is 'Life is hard and then comes death'. Death renders everything meaningless. In this regard he surveys various areas where one expects to find meaning. In turn, he examines work (3:9–13; 4:4–6), pleasure (2:1–11), relationships (4:9–12), status (4:13–16), wealth (5:8–10), even wisdom (2:12–16), and though there might be a relative advantage, say, to wisdom over folly, death is the great leveller. Two other issues plague Qohelet and lead him to the conclusion that life is meaningless. First, as a wise man he knows that it is vitally important to know the right time to say the right thing or perform the correct action. However, though God has created everything appropriate for its time, he has not let human beings in on the secret (3:1–15). Second, wisdom thinking would lead one to believe that good things happen to good people and bad things happen to bad people. However, Qohelet's observations on life lead him to conclude that life is essentially unfair (7:15–22; 8:10–15).

Qohelet does have some advice for people in the light of the fundamental meaninglessness of life: seize whatever enjoyment comes along. This attitude is often summarized by the Latin phrase *carpe diem*, 'seize the day'. These passages (2:24–26; 3:12–14; 3:22; 5:18–20; 8:15; 9:7–10) indicate that the benefit of such momentary joy is to keep from thinking about the hard realities of life.

B. *The message of the book*

But, as mentioned, Qohelet is not the final voice heard in the book. That role belongs to the second speaker, sometimes called the frame narrator since his words frame the long quotation from Qohelet. The prologue (1:1–11) simply introduces and sets the mood for Qohelet's dark thoughts, but the epilogue interacts with the substance of Qohelet's thought. In the first place, he tells his son that what Qohelet says is indeed true. After all, while Qohelet's perspective encompasses 'everything', it is circumscribed by the phrase 'under the sun', that is, apart from a heavenly perspective. Due to a number of allusions to the language of Gen. 2 – 3, we can say that Qohelet rightly describes the world as a function of the fall. But the frame narrator wants to point beyond an 'under the sun' perspective, and he does so in 12:13–14, where he instructs his son to 'fear God', 'keep his commandments', and expect the coming judgment.

Of course, readers ancient and modern are to take this admonition to heart and adopt this attitude in order to avoid Qohelet's pessimistic thought. In a word, the book of Ecclesiastes is an idol-buster. If one tries to make anything other than God the source of meaning in life, it will ultimately fail. Thus, fear God.

C. *Date and authorship*

The authorship and date of this intriguing book are matters of debate. Some believe that there is only one voice in the book, that of Qohelet who is identified with Solomon. Most scholars today would disagree, believing that the connection with Solomon is a matter of literary argument. Thus, even the name Qohelet, which literally means 'one who assembles (a group)', is a way to associate this figure with Solomon (since he summons and addresses 'the assembly', Hebrew *qahal*, in 1 Kgs 8) rather than a means of identifying the two. It is best to think of Ecclesiastes as an anonymous book. There is some evidence that the book was written late in the history of the OT.

D. Continuing significance

Christians who read the book of Ecclesiastes can also benefit from the book's function as an idol-buster, reminding them that no true meaning comes apart from God in a world suffering the effects of the fall. Rom. 8:18–27 has a fascinating association with Ecclesiastes when in v. 20 it describes how God subjected creation to 'frustration'. The Greek here is the same word as that used to translate the Hebrew *hebel* ('meaningless') in the Greek OT (the Septuagint). But here Paul tells us that God did so 'in hope' of a future redemption. That redemption, we learn in the NT, is accomplished by Jesus Christ, who subjected himself to the fallen world (Phil. 2:6–11) in order to free us from the curse (Gal. 3:13). Indeed, he does so by subjecting himself to death and defeating it on the cross (1 Cor. 15). Thus Jesus had victory over death, the issue which particularly robbed this life of significance for Qohelet. A canonical reading of Ecclesiastes encourages us that, once we make God the source of ultimate meaning in our lives, we can find enjoyment and significance in other areas such as work, money, pleasure and wisdom.

SONG OF SONGS

The Song of Songs presents the reader with passionate dialogue between an unnamed man and an unnamed woman, filled with intensely sensuous imagery. Occasionally, a chorus of women chime in to encourage, help, or learn from the couple, and once we hear from the woman's brothers (8:8–9).

The erotic nature of the language of the Song concerned early interpreters, who felt that sexuality and spirituality were at polar opposites. For them, the Song could not truly be saying what it seemed to be saying on the surface, but rather must have a deeper spiritual sense. Thus was born the allegorical interpretation of the book. The idea that matters of the spirit and matters of the body were dissonant resulted from the influence of Platonic thought on early biblical interpreters.

A. Genre

Both Jewish and Christian interpreters adopted an allegorical approach to the Song. Typical early Jewish interpretation is presented in the Targum (eventually completed AD 700–900). Here, when the woman (standing for Israel) urgently asks the man (representing Yahweh) to bring her into his bedroom (1:2–4), this allegorically describes the exodus from Egypt. Or when the woman demurs at her dark skin (1:5–6), the blackness signifies the sin and shame of the worship of the golden calf in the wilderness (Exod. 32). Christians simply adapted this interpretive strategy to their distinctive theology. In a Christian allegorical reading, the man represented Jesus Christ and the woman either the church or the individual Christian. As with Jewish interpretation, the details of the text were also thought to be allegorically significant. Cyril of Alexandria, for instance, stated that the sachet of myrrh lodged between the woman's breasts (1:13) stood for Jesus Christ who spanned the Old and the New Testaments. This interpretive tradition was passed down from generation to generation until the period of the Enlightenment.

It was especially in the nineteenth century that opinion about the genre of the Song began to change. Due to the diminishing influence of neo-Platonic ideas on theology, biblical scholars no longer felt that a book celebrating sexuality was inappropriate for the canon. The arbitrary character of allegorical interpretation was also recognized. Further, it was during the nineteenth century that the literature of the ancient Near East was rediscovered and among those treasures were love poems, especially those in Egyptian, similar in theme and imagery to the Song.

Thus, for the past century and a half interpreters have recognized that the Song was not primarily about the love between God and his people, but a celebration (and warning) of passionate love between a man and a woman.

Even so, debate remains. Does the Song tell a story (the dramatic approach) or is it a collection of love poems (the anthological approach)? The Song can be made to tell many stories, and that is problematic. There is no overarching narrative voice to guide the reader through a plot. Thus it is best to think of the Song as a love psalter, a number of different love poems, loosely united by consistency of character, occasional refrains (compare 2:6 with 8:3, and 2:7 with 3:5 and 8:4), and echoes particularly between chs. 1 and 8. It is truly a song composed of many songs, producing the most sublime song of all.

B. The message

The message of the Song is thus a celebration of love. The poem in 4:1 – 5:1 is an excellent example. This is a type of poem known as a *wasf*, an Arabic word for 'description'. In this *wasf*, the man describes the physical beauty of the woman from the head down to her 'garden', a euphemism for her most private bodily part. At the climax of the poem, she opens her previously locked garden to allow him to enter it, as the chorus chimes in their approval. Not only is the woman's body often likened to a garden, the man and the woman frequently make love in a garden-like locale, thus recalling the Garden of Eden (Gen. 2) where the man and the woman were naked and felt no shame. Thus the Song has the message of the restoration of the marriage relationship after its disruption at the Fall (in Gen. 3 Adam and Eve feel compelled to cover their nakedness).

Even so, some of its poems acknowledge there are still problems in the garden of love. In the narrative of 5:2 – 6:3, the man approaches the house where the woman lives and knocks on the door, a double-entendre suggesting sexual desire. Instead of opening the door the woman demurs, but the man persists in his attempt to enter. At this point, the woman's passion heats up and she moves to the door to open up to her lover. However, when she does, he is gone. Rather than simply giving up she goes in pursuit of him, moving through the watchmen (represent-ative of social custom), and enlists the aid of the daughters of Jerusalem to whom she gives a passionate description (a *wasf*). Finally, they achieve union in the garden of love.

Thus, the Song is a celebration of human love. In the context of the canon where only marital love is permitted such intimacies, we are certainly right to imagine that the unnamed couple are a married couple, at least in many of the poems. Just as the Psalms give those who praise and lament words that will help them pray, so the Song gives married lovers encouragement to develop their own language of love and permis-sion to seek physical intimacy with each other.

C. Theological significance

But there is more to the song than simply love and sex. It is also a theologically rich book when read in the context of the canon. After all, throughout the Old and New Testaments, marriage is a metaphor of the divine–human relationship. This is often expressed negatively when Israel breaks its intimate and exclusive love relationship with God, but it also has a positive expression, especially in the NT. Eph. 5:22–33 likens the relationship of Christians to Jesus to that of husband and wife.

D. Date and authorship

Not much is known for certain about the composition, authorship and date of this book. The superscription mentions Solomon, but it is debated whether this means he is the author (of all or of part), or a character, or whether it is written in the tradition of wisdom of which he is the figurehead. If it is an anthology, there is the possibility that its separate poems were composed at different times by different people on analogy with books like Psalms and Proverbs. Fortunately, the authorship of the book bears no significance for its interpretation.

LAMENTATIONS

In 587 BC the armies of Nebuchadnezzar of Babylon captured the city of Jerusalem, destroyed its temple, and exiled a large number of its inhabitants, especially its leading citizens. The devastating effect on the community was enormous and is nowhere more emotionally expressed than in the book of Lamentations. This honest book struggles with this destruction, realizing that, though Nebuchadnezzar was its human agent, the ultimate author was none other than God himself.

A. Genre, structure and style

The book as a whole is a corporate lament, generally similar to laments in the book of Psalms (e.g. Pss. 44; 60; 74; 79; 80; poems that bemoan defeat in battle). It is true that some parts of the book speak in the first person singular (3:1–21), but it is best to understand the first-person speaker here as personified Jerusalem, or in some way to stand for the community as a whole.

The book neatly divides into five parts, following the division into five chapters. The first four chapters are individual, complete acrostics, though they differ in their detail. Chs. 1 and 2, each twenty-two verses long (the number of letters in the Hebrew alphabet), are three-line acrostics, that is, the first letter of the three-line stanza begins with a successive letter of the Hebrew alphabet. Ch. 3, composed of sixty-six verses, also contains three-line stanzas, but in this case all three of the lines begin with the relevant letter (similar to the stanzas of Ps. 119). Ch. 4 has two-line stanzas, more in keeping with the style of chs. 1 and 2. Even ch. 5, which is not an acrostic, nonetheless alludes to the acrostic by having twenty-two verses.

The predominant emotional note of the book is sadness and shocked despair. However, there is a note of hope found, surprisingly, in the middle (3:19–27). After this, though, there is a return to sadness, and the book ends with an appeal to God to 'restore' his people, while expressing concern that God may have 'utterly rejected' them and be angry at them 'beyond measure' (see 5:19–22).

B. Date and authorship

Lamentations is an anonymous book, but tradition has assigned its authorship to Jeremiah. While not impossible, such a position is unlikely and in any case does not affect the interpretation of the book. The vividness of the description of the destruction of Jerusalem and the rawness of the emotional expression have led many scholars to identify the time of writing as relatively soon after the destruction of the city in 587 BC. However, some scholars dissent, claiming that the book's ancient Near Eastern background argues for a later date. The argument is as follows. First, no one seriously doubts the close generic relationship between the book of Lamentations and a number of Sumerian city-laments, e.g. the 'Lamentation over the Destruction of Sumer and Ur' and the 'Lamentation over the Destruction of Ur'. These compositions also express deep sadness and bewilderment over the divine realm's involvement in the destruction of their cities. Interestingly, some of these ancient Near Eastern texts date not to the time of destruction but to the time of rebuilding the destroyed temples. Thus some scholars date the biblical book of Lamentations closer to the time of the rebuilding of the Jerusalem temple in 520–515 BC.

In either case, the content struggles with the fact that God had abandoned his city and his people. He not only allowed the enemy to defeat them, but he had become an enemy himself (2:1–5) and had attacked and destroyed them. The theological purpose of the book is to acknowledge God's judgment against Jerusalem and to move him to intercede for and restore his people.

C. Theological message and continuing relevance

The leading theological theme of the book is certainly the divine warrior. While much of the OT pictures God as fighting on behalf of his people (the Red Sea, Exod. 14:14; Jericho, Josh. 6:16; etc.), he also attacked his own people when they disobeyed him (Ai, Josh. 7). Lamentations pictures God as divine warrior in the second sense. This attack should not have surprised the faithful in Israel. After all, in the covenant, God not only promised that he would protect faithful Israel, he also announced that he would attack and defeat them if they disobeyed the covenant (Deut. 28:15, 49–50).

But the final word is not negative. As already pointed out, there is also an expression of hope in the book (3:22–33). Here the poet voices his assurance that God does not abandon those who turn to him for help. Although Israel has sinned in the past (1:8, 14, 18; 2:14; 4:13), they appeal to him for help, expecting that he will forgive and restore.

Reading Lamentations from a NT perspective, we know that God did end the exile and returned a remnant to the land (Ezra 1 – 6). We also know that the exilic and post-exilic prophets looked forward to a future intervention of the divine warrior to free them from their oppressors (Dan. 7; Zech. 14; Mal. 4). The NT identifies Jesus as the divine warrior who defeats the forces of evil on the cross (Col. 2:13–15) and as the one who will come again in the future for the final battle against all human and spiritual enemies of God (Rev. 19:11–21).

Further reading (see **Introduction** for good commentary series)

Ernest Lucas, *Exploring the Old Testament 3. The Psalms and Wisdom Literature* (SPCK, 2003) – excellent introduction, with panels highlighting themes and points to ponder.

Daniel Estes, *Handbook on the Wisdom Books and Psalms* (Baker, 2005) – good detailed introduction to the books and each section or chapter.

Tremper Longman, *How to Read the Psalms* (IVP, 1988) – helpful and inviting exploration of the many facets of the Psalms.

Barry Webb, *Five Festal Garments* (Apollos, 2000) – Christian reflections on Ecclesiastes and the Song of Songs (as well as Ruth, Lamentations and Esther).

6. Prophets

Ernest Lucas

PROPHETS IN ANCIENT ISRAEL AND ELSEWHERE

The first mention of prophecy within Israel is the story in Num. 11:16–17, 24–30. When seventy elders were appointed to help Moses, they received some of the spirit which empowered Moses and prophesied, but they did so only on this occasion (v. 25). Moses is referred to as a prophet in Deut. 18:15, where God promises to raise up a prophet like him from among the Israelites. This has been taken to refer to both a continuing line of prophets and a final unique prophet.

Prophecy was not unique to Israel, as references to Canaanite prophets of the god Baal and goddess Asherah show (1 Kgs 18:19). The Egyptian story of Wen-amon (twelfth century BC) tells of someone in a frenzied state giving an oracle in the name of the god Amon during a sacrifice in a temple in the Phoenician city of Byblos. The eighth-century BC inscription of Zakir, king of Hamath, says he received an answer to prayer through prophetic oracles. Prophecy was not common in Mesopotamia, but excavations at Mari, a city on the Euphrates, have found seventeenth-century BC texts with oracles that were written down and sent to the king. These came from both men and women. Some were attached to the worship of the goddess Ishtar, and apparently exhibited frenzied behaviour. Others had no official office. Prophets are mentioned in seventh-century BC texts from

Assyria. Some of these prophesy in a frenzied state while others have visions or dreams.

A. *The early prophets*

By the time of the early Israelite monarchy prophecy seems a well-established phenomenon. The story of Saul's meeting with Samuel in 1 Sam. 9:1 – 10:13 provides a picture of it:

- It was often a group phenomenon (10:5, 10).
- Prophets were sometimes found at 'high places', the local centres of worship (9:13; 10:5, 10).
- It involved frenzied or ecstatic behaviour (10:6, 10; see also 1 Sam. 19:23–24).
- It could be stimulated by music (10:5; see also 2 Kgs 3:15).
- Prophets might give oracles of guidance for payment (9:7–8), and were often consulted (see 2 Kgs 4:23).

In this period many of the prophets lived communally. Elisha appears as the leader of such a community (2 Kgs 4:38; 6:1). The organization of the group seems to have been fairly loose. Prophets could marry, have their own homes (2 Kgs 4:1–2; 5:9) and travel around (2 Kgs 4:8).

Most of the prophets mentioned in the books of Samuel and Kings seem to be on the fringe of society and independent of its power structures. Yet some get deeply involved in politics. Two things seem to have motivated them in this. One is zeal for the defence of the worship of Yahweh, the God of Israel. This led them to oppose kings who tolerated or encouraged the worship of Baal (Elijah in 1 Kgs 18) or other foreign gods (prophets who opposed Manasseh, 2 Kgs 21:10–15). They were also nationalistic in the sense that they were concerned that Israel should be respected among the nations because Yahweh's reputation was related to theirs (1 Kgs 20:13–15). Prophets sometimes instigated revolutions, for example Ahijah of Shiloh (1 Kgs 11:26–40) and Elisha (2 Kgs 9:1–10).

There were some prophets at the centres of power. David had two court prophets, Nathan and Gad (2 Sam. 7:1–3; 24:11–12). They were not mere yes-men: Nathan fearlessly rebuked David's sins of adultery and murder (2 Sam. 12:1–15); and Micaiah courageously opposed Ahab, unlike the four hundred prophets who said what Ahab wanted to hear (1 Kgs 22:7–28).

The ethical concern evident in the books of the prophets is fore-shadowed in the earlier prophets. Two prominent examples are Nathan's rebuke of David and Elijah's rebuke of Ahab for his murder of Naboth (1 Kgs 21:20–23).

B. The later prophets

The prophetic books come from prophets active from the eighth century BC onwards. Why not until then? Several answers have been offered. Maybe the spread of writing was important. There is archaeological evidence of writing in Israel from the tenth century onwards, but it seems to become more widespread in the eighth century. Then, as we shall see, there is the fact that many of the 'writing prophets' about whom we have information came from those nearer the centres of power – unlike most of the early prophets. This begs the question why prophets should arise from that sector of society at that period and not earlier. Finally, the fact that the prophecies of doom uttered by Amos and Hosea were vindicated within a few decades, by the destruction of Samaria, must have been important. This was a shattering event for Yahweh's covenant people, and one can understand why the oracles of the prophets who foretold it would be collected, preserved and studied, to understand both why it happened and what could be learned from it.

There is very little evidence of how the books were put together. In Isa. 8:16–18 the prophet called on his disciples to preserve his warnings against appealing to Assyria, which King Ahaz had rejected, until after the disaster he had foretold. A century later Jeremiah dictated some oracles to his scribe Baruch so that he could read them in the Temple. After King Jehoiakim burned the scroll, Jeremiah dictated it again, adding other oracles (Jer. 36). These incidents may give some clue as to how and why prophetic oracles began to be written down.

The activities of the 'writing prophets' cluster around four periods: the fall of Samaria (Jonah, Amos, Hosea, Micah, Isaiah 1 – 39), the fall of Jerusalem (Zephaniah, Habakkuk, Nahum, Jeremiah, Ezekiel), the return from exile (Isaiah 40 – 66, Haggai, Zechariah) and the ministry of Ezra and Nehemiah (Obadiah, Joel, Malachi).

INTERPRETING THE PROPHETS FOR TODAY

The clustering of the 'writing prophets' in particular periods provides an important pointer to their function and to how we are to understand their message for us today. Many Christians think of the prophets primarily in terms of foretelling the future. They read them looking for predictions about the coming of Jesus, the new covenant age and the end of the world. However, less than 5% of OT prophecy describes the new covenant age, less than 2% is 'messianic' (even broadly speaking), and less than 1% concerns the end of the world. Most OT prophecy can be described as 'forth-telling', declaring to the hearers God's perspective on them and their situation, usually in terms of exposing their sinful state. So most 'foretelling' elements warn of imminent judgment, though some tell of salvation beyond judgment. This judgment and salvation involved events that lay in the prophets' near or medium-term future, but which happened long ago from our perspective. So what does most of the material in the prophetic books have to say to us? Before answering that we need to think further about the role of the prophets.

A. *The role of the prophet*

The first thing to say is that the prophets were God's ambassadors. They did not speak on their own authority but were spokesmen for the God of Israel. This is made clear by their use of the phrase 'This is what the LORD says' (1 Kgs 14:7; 2 Kgs 22:15; Jer. 31:2, 7, 15, 23). When a king sent a message to another king in the ancient Near East the messenger would read or recite the message, beginning with a 'messenger formula' such as 'This is what king X says'.

Israel had made a covenant with God at Sinai. For this reason the major part of the prophets' role was that of 'covenant enforcers'. Their forth-telling is based on Israel's covenant traditions. Their exposure of sin is rooted in the covenant law. The echo of the Ten Commandments in Hos. 4:2 is a particularly clear example, but there are many other allusions to the covenant law. Their threats of judgment are not arbitrary. The specific calamities threatened in Amos 4 are based on the curses pronounced on covenant breakers, and the promise of restoration in Amos 9:13–15 has its roots in the blessings of the covenant (Lev. 26; Deut. 28). God had also made a covenant with David (2 Sam. 7) and this is the basis of the 'messianic prophecies' of hope and restoration, such as those in Isa. 9 and 11. The better acquainted you are with Israel's covenant traditions (especially Exod. 20; Lev. 26; Deut. 4, 28), the better you will be able to understand much of what the prophets said.

As covenant enforcers, the prophets became interpreters of God's activity in the history of Israel. Before the exile in Babylon their main task was to confront their hearers with the fact that they were living in disobedience to the covenant law and to warn them that, unless they repented and changed their ways, God would visit the covenant curses upon them. After the exile, when at least some had learned the lesson it taught, the prophets brought a message of hope and restoration. The prophets interpreted key events in the history of Israel and Judah within this context: the fall of Samaria and the destruction of the kingdom of

Israel; the fall of Jerusalem and the end of the kingdom of Judah; Cyrus' capture of Babylon and his edict allowing the return of the Jews to Jerusalem; the rebuilding of the temple by Joshua and Zerubbabel; and the rebuilding of the walls of Jerusalem by Nehemiah. This means that the more you know about the historical situation within which a prophet was active (see chs. 2 and 4), the better you will be able to understand his message.

B. Prophetic speech

The prophets were primarily preachers, and the prophetic books consist mostly of the written record of originally spoken words. Most of the prophets' preaching took the form of fairly short poetic 'oracles' rather than lengthy prose sermons. The use of poetry is understandable in a culture where only a minority were literate. Poetry is highly 'patterned' speech. It uses patterns of rhythm (metre) and sound (rhyme, alliteration). Hebrew poetry also contains patterns of thought (parallelism). All this makes poetry easier to remember than prose. Poetry also makes far greater use of figurative language than does prose. This gives it its emotive power, but also gives it a 'mind-teasing' quality since the meaning of figurative imagery is not always obvious. It is important not to treat the figurative language as if it were straightforward prose. For example, the language of cosmic upheavals in Isa. 13:10, 13 might lead one to take this as talk of the end of the world. However, what follows shows that the language is figurative since it is referring to the end of the Neo-Babylonian Empire (vv. 17–19). The figurative language is used to make the point that this historical event is an epoch-changing act of God's judgment.

When reading the collections of poetic oracles in the prophetic books it is important to try to recognize the individual oracles. They may be linked together in a variety of ways, for example by theme (Jer. 23:9–24 is a collection on the theme of false prophets), or by catchwords (Isa. 1:2–3 is linked to vv. 4–6 by the catchword 'children', and vv. 7–9 to the following oracle by the catchwords 'Sodom' and 'Gomorrah'). These kinds of links often do not result in the logical flow of thought that would be expected in prose teaching. Therefore looking for that kind of flow will result in misunderstanding.

The messenger formula is a helpful indicator of the beginning of an oracle. Recognizing individual oracles is helped by an awareness of some of the common types of oracle:

- 'Woe' oracles (threats of judgment) are easy to spot because of the word 'woe' or 'ah' at the beginning (Isa. 5:8–23).

- 'Lawsuit' oracles are recognizable by the elements they contain: summoning the jury; the complaint; the defendant's response; the sentence (Mic. 6:1–8).
- The 'promise of salvation' oracle has the phrase 'do not be afraid' (Isa. 43:1–4, 5–7).
- 4 Oracles using other literary forms, such as love song (Isa. 5:1–7), number proverb (Amos 1, 2), allegory (Ezek. 17).

C. Interpreting the prophets

So, in the light of what we've said, how are we to interpret the message of the prophets for today? There is no simple method that guarantees a right interpretation, but there are a number of steps that provide a helpful way of dealing with prophetic texts. Of course the whole process should be done in prayerful reliance on the God who spoke through the prophets.

1. Begin by trying to separate out the individual oracles in a passage. Then summarize what you understand to be the main message of each oracle. Knowing something about the type of oracle you are reading will be a help.
2. If the oracle is part of a cluster, note how it is linked to those before and after it. Does the fact that it is in the cluster throw any particular light on its meaning, or emphasize some aspect of it?
3. What is the significance of the oracle in the historical context in which it was given? Some oracles can be related to a specific time or event in the prophet's life, others only to the general context.
4. Finally, consider how the message that the oracle had in its original historical context might apply to us in our context. Often this is not as difficult as it may seem. What were sins under the old covenant (personal immorality, social injustice, idolatry, hypocritical worship) are still sins under the new, though they may take different forms. Some of the more material blessings of the old covenant were related directly to Israel being a political community living in a specific land, and do not apply to the new covenant, where the emphasis is more on spiritual blessings in Christ (Eph. 1:3). Sometimes the message will point to some truth about the nature of God, or principle upon which God acts in the world, which we can then relate to our lives today.

The fact is that down the centuries Christians have found that the words of the OT prophets continue to be the living and active word of God (Isa. 55:10–11).

ISAIAH

A. Historical setting

Isaiah was active from about 740 BC until at least 700, a period of growing Assyrian power. He lived through some major crises. In 735/4 Israel and Syria invaded Judah. Against Isaiah's advice King Ahaz of Judah appealed to Assyria for help, becoming a vassal and introducing aspects of Assyrian worship into the temple (2 Kgs 16; Isa. 7 – 8, this is the setting for the Immanuel prophecy of 7:14). The kingdom of Israel was destroyed by the Assyrians in 722/1 (2 Kgs 17), becoming three provinces of its empire (cf. 9:1; Galilee, 'the Way of the Sea', 'beyond the Jordan'). When Ashdod, Edom and Moab rebelled against Assyria in 713–711, appealing to Egypt for help, Isaiah opposed Judean involvement (14:28–32; 18 – 19). He also opposed a similar revolt in 705 (30 – 31) which resulted in Sennacherib's devastating invasion. Because of the Assyrian's pride and blasphemy Isaiah prophesied the miraculous deliverance of Jerusalem (36 – 37; 2 Kgs 18 – 19).

Isa. 40 – 55 assumes a different historical setting, being addressed to the Judeans in exile in Babylon (587–539). These chapters promise that the time of deliverance is near (40:1–2). God has chosen Cyrus as the agent who will set them free to return to rebuild Jerusalem (44:24 – 45:7). Isa. 56 – 66 seems concerned with events after the return, when faithfulness to God has begun to decline.

B. The book of Isaiah

The three parts of Isaiah have other differences besides historical setting. The oracles in chs. 1 – 39 have a terse style that is different from the hymnic poetry of chs. 40 – 66. While some themes do run through the whole book (e.g. God's holiness and sovereignty), there are differences of emphasis: the remnant and the Davidic messianic hope in chs. 1 – 39; God as Creator and Redeemer in chs. 40 – 55; the new heaven and earth in chs. 56 – 66. This raises questions about the origins of the book.

Traditionally Isaiah of the eighth century has been taken as author of the whole book. There are two indications of occasions when some of his oracles were written down (8:16; 30:8). Some scholars still support this view. Others think that the differences in style, content and historical setting suggest different authors. They argue that, since the prophets generally spoke to their own generation and about the fairly near future, the book of Isaiah probably contains the words of two, three or more different prophets from different periods. Some take Isa. 8:16 as evidence of a group of disciples around Isaiah. These could have formed a 'school' that preserved his words for generations and produced later prophets who added to them. Of course, Isaiah's prophesying could have been different from the more common pattern. The debate continues (see commentaries for more details).

In recent years, even those who assume several different authors increasingly treat the book as a single volume encompassing different emphases rather than as three separate volumes. Whoever was responsible for the final form of the book has given it a measure of unity and coherence in its themes and theology.

C. Structure

1 – 12	Judah judged and redeemed
13 – 27	God's sovereignty over the nations
28 – 35	Oracles of judgment and hope (a righteous king)
36 – 39	Jerusalem saved, but the Babylonian exile prophesied
40 – 55	Return from exile promised
56 – 66	Oracles of judgment and hope (a new heaven and earth)

D. The message of Isaiah

The sovereignty, holiness and grace of God are portrayed in Isaiah's call vision (Isa. 6). They are themes that run through the whole book.

God's sovereignty is displayed in history. He uses Assyria to punish his people for their sins (10:5–19; 14:24–27) and Cyrus to deliver them from exile (44:24 – 45:7). In chs. 40 – 55 another aspect of God's sovereignty is brought out: he is the Creator of heaven and earth (40:12–26). This gives the exiles hope because Israel's Creator (through the exodus) is *the* Creator (51:9–16). A new exodus is promised (52:11–12). The proper human response to God's sovereignty is faith (7:9; 28:16; 30:15). Since God is the Creator it is appropriate that salvation is presented in terms of a new heaven and a new earth (65:17–25).

In 1 – 12 and 56 – 66 there is emphasis on the moral aspect of God's holiness, his justice and righteousness (5:16; 59:15b–17), as Isaiah exposes Judah's sins and calls for repentance (1:16–20; 56:1–2). Chs. 40 – 55 emphasize God's holiness as his 'uniqueness', with phrases like 'the first and the last', 'apart from me there is no God', 'I am he' (44:6, 8; 46:4). All other gods are worthless idols (44:6–20).

God's grace is expressed in chs. 1 – 39 in terms of the purified 'remnant' that will survive judgment (10:20–23). In chs. 40 – 56 God is spoken of as Israel's Redeemer (41:14) who will bring about the new exodus (43:1–7; 62:10–12).

Isa. 9:2–7 and 11:1–9 are classic 'messianic' passages which speak of the coming ideal ruler from the line of David. In both, righteousness and justice are marks of this ruler, a theme taken up in 32:1–8. This messianic vision falls into the background in chs. 40 – 55, where the promise to David is applied to the people as a whole (55:3) and the central human agent of God's salvation is 'the servant of the LORD'. The servant is portrayed in four 'songs' (42:1–4; 49:1–6; 50:4–9; 52:13 – 53:12). Although David can be called God's servant (Ps. 89:3), the servant in Isaiah seems more like a prophet. He is called by God to proclaim salvation, not just to Israel but to the nations. His ministry involves suffering and death, though there is a hint that death may not be the end for him. His death is spoken of as an atoning sacrifice for all. The servant is identified with Israel (49:3) and may represent the righteous remnant. Isa. 61:1–3 is often linked with the servant songs.

In the NT Jesus is seen as the Davidic Messiah, and Matt. 1:23 refers to Isa. 7:14. This gives the 'sign' a double application, first to the child born in Ahaz's day and then to Jesus. Jesus is also identified with the Suffering Servant (Matt. 12:18–21; Acts 8:32–33). He himself described his ministry in terms of 61:1–2 (Luke 4:18–19).

Isaiah's rich portrayal of the nature of God is one that should inspire the same responses today as he looked for: faith in God in the midst of the problems of life; a life in which true worship is linked with the practice of justice and righteousness; and a concern to share the message of salvation with all nations. The picture of a new heaven and new earth shows that God's saving purpose includes all his creation, not just humans, so we should be concerned about the non-human creation too.

JEREMIAH

A. Historical setting

Jeremiah was a priest from Anathoth, a town three miles north-east of Jerusalem (1:1). He may have been a descendant of Abiathar, one of David's chief priests, who was banished to Anathoth by Solomon (1 Kgs 2:26–27). Jeremiah's ministry began in the thirteenth year of Josiah (626 BC) and continued beyond the destruction of Judah and Jerusalem in 587 BC. This period included several important events: Josiah's reform (begun in 621); Josiah's death in battle with Pharaoh Neco (609); the Babylonian defeat of the Egyptians at Carchemish, which brought Judah under their control (605); the Babylonian capture of Jerusalem and the first deportation of Judeans (597); the fall of Jerusalem and the exile of many Judeans to Babylon (587); the murder of the Babylonian-appointed governor, Gedaliah, and the flight of some Judeans to Egypt, taking Jeremiah with them (39 – 44; 52; cf. 2 Kgs 22 – 25).

B. Structure

The book contains three different kinds of material, all mixed together: poetic oracles, prose sermons and prose narratives. The poetry probably comes more or less directly from Jeremiah. Most of the prose narrative tells stories about him and so was probably written by somebody else. Some of the prose sermons repeat what is said in the poetic oracles, suggesting that they are reports of Jeremiah's preaching written by someone else. In style and vocabulary the prose resembles Deuteronomy and Kings:

1 – 10	Pronouncements of judgment and calls to repent
11 – 20	The broken covenant and the prophet's laments
21 – 25	The failure of Judah's kings and prophets
26 – 29	Controversies with false prophets
30 – 33	The 'book of consolation', hope beyond judgment
34 – 36	King and people reject Jeremiah's words
37 – 45	Events before and after the fall of Jerusalem
46 – 51	Oracles against foreign nations
52	Another account of the fall of Jerusalem (cf. 2 Kgs 25)

Jeremiah's oracles include poems in which he protests to God about the pain and grief he is suffering, about how God is treating him, and he sometimes prays for punishment of his enemies (11:18–23; 12:1–6; 15:10–14, 15–21; 17:14–18; 18:18–23; 20:7–12, 14–18). They are called his 'confessions' but might better be called 'laments' since they resemble the psalms of lament.

C. Jeremiah's message

Two Hebrew words characterize Jeremiah's preaching: *sheqer* (lie, deception, delusion) and *shub* (turn, turn away, return, repent). A major theme is that Judah has lost her true identity as God's covenant people because deceit permeates her life, destroying the social fabric (9:1–6). Only genuine repentance can avert disaster (3:12–14).

Jeremiah attacks three particular forms of *sheqer*.

(1) *Idolatry*. Since entering Canaan Israel's history was one of apostasy after the Baals (2:7–8). Jeremiah uses Hosea's imagery of the unfaithful wife (3:1–5, 20) and the delinquent child (3:19, 21–22). He declares that idolatry is a delusion and calls the idols 'non-gods' (3:22–23; 16:19–20), contrasting their powerlessness to help with the power of the LORD who is the living God (10:1–16). God's power is seen in his control of other nations (46:1 – 51:64). This makes Israel's apostasy an incredible and unnatural thing (2:9–13).

(2) *A false sense of security*. This is highlighted in the 'temple sermon' (7:1–15; 26:1–24). The people believed that because the temple was the LORD's sanctuary he would never let it, the city and the nation be completely destroyed. They may have based this on the covenant traditions and the memory of the deliverance of the city from Sennacherib in 701 BC (Isa. 37; 2 Kgs 19). Jeremiah declared this attitude a delusion because they were constantly breaking the covenant law (7:4–10). Once before God had allowed his sanctuary, then at Shiloh, to be destroyed because of Israel's sinfulness (7:12–15). Worship that is not linked with obedience to God is worthless (7:21–26).

(3) *False prophecy*. Jeremiah prophesied imminent disaster unless there was repentance. He was opposed by prophets who declared that all would be well. Some of his strongest words are addressed to them (14:13–16; 23:9–40). That they could prophesy 'peace' (enjoyment of the covenant blessing) when the nation was breaking the covenant showed that they were not sent by God.

Jeremiah offers three liturgies of repentance (3:22–23; 14:7–9, 19–22), but seems pessimistic about the possibility of his hearers repenting (13:23). He does, however, have a message of hope. He promises that the exiles in Babylon will return after seventy years (24:1–10; 29:10–14; the figure may mean 'a lifetime'). Because of this hope he bought land at Anathoth despite it being useless to him (32:6–44). Though 22:28–30 might imply the end of the Davidic covenant, it refers just to Jehoiachin's descendants since elsewhere Jeremiah promises a restored Davidic monarchy (30:9) and an ideal Davidic king (23:5–6; 33:14–16).

Jeremiah's most striking word of hope is the promise of a new covenant (31:27–34; 32:37–40). The old covenant led to disaster because of the stubbornness and corruption of the human heart (7:23–24; 17:9). The new covenant promises a God-given change of heart so that each individual will know God and his law, and want to do it. Jeremiah puts an emphasis on the individual not found in the earlier prophets. He stresses the importance of the individual's heart being right before God, and calls repentance the 'circumcising' of the heart (4:1–4) – in Hebrew thought the heart is the centre of thought and the will, rather than emotion. The nation will find its God again when they seek him with all their heart (29:13–14). There are parallels between Jeremiah's preaching of repentance and Deut. 4:25–30; 30:1–6. Deut. 30:6 foreshadows the new covenant promise when it says that God will circumcise the nation's heart.

Jeremiah's exposure of *sheqer* as a corrupting force is as relevant as ever, though the particular forms it takes today in the church and in secular society may be different. For Christians the hope of the new covenant is fulfilled in Jesus (Luke 22:19–20; Heb. 8 – 9), who also fulfils the promise of a Davidic descendant (Luke 1:68–74).

LAMENTATIONS

See ch. 5 pages 111–113

EZEKIEL

A. *Historical setting*

Ezekiel was a priest who was among those deported from Judah when the Babylonians took Jerusalem in 597 BC. In 592 he had a vision which was his call to be a prophet to the exiles in Babylon (1:1–3). He was active for at least twenty-two years (29:17). The 'thirtieth year' (1:1) probably refers to his age. This was when priests were meant to enter fully into their duties (Num. 4:3). The Kebar was probably a major irrigation canal. The destruction of Jerusalem in 587 was a watershed in Ezekiel's ministry (24:2; 33:21). Before it he prophesied judgment, challenging the exiles' complacent view that it would not happen. Afterwards he brought messages of hope, deliverance and restoration. Ezekiel sometimes acted out his message and used allegories and parables.

B. *Structure*

1 – 3	Ezekiel's commissioning
4 – 7	Messages of judgment
8 – 11	A vision of Jerusalem's sin and judgment
12 – 24	The sins of Israel, Judah and Jerusalem
25 – 32	Oracles against the nations
33 – 39	Oracles of salvation
40 – 48	Vision of a renewed city, temple and land

The unity of thought in Ezekiel leads most scholars to conclude that a significant core of the book derives from the prophet, with some additions and expansions by his followers (though there is little agreement on these).

C. The message of Ezekiel

Much of Ezekiel's preaching can be related to three aspects of God's nature that are evident in his call vision: holiness, glory and sovereignty.

For Ezekiel, God's holiness is primarily his awesome 'otherness'. This colours his attack on Israel's sinfulness, which concentrates on cultic sins such as apostasy and idolatry. The worship of other gods is the central theme of chs. 8 – 11. These sins impugn the otherness of the only true God. Ezekiel presents sin as a deep-seated resistance to God. This is expressed in three horrifying recitals of Israel's history (16, 20, 23). At the heart of Israel's sin is unfaithfulness to the Sinai Covenant (5:6–12), and the punishments threatened echo the covenant curses (Lev. 26).

Hope for the future rests on the nature of God, especially his concern for his glory, his 'reputation' among the nations. In Ezekiel, God's glory is closely linked with his 'name', because his name is related to his nature as understood by people. In the past he withheld judgment to prevent his name being profaned among the nations (20:9, 14, 22). The depth of Judah's sin means that he must now risk this reputation by sending her into exile. Ezekiel is sure that God will act to restore the nation in order to vindicate his reputation (36:22–23, 32). The vision of the valley of dry bones (37:1–14) shows that this will be a miracle of divine grace and power, as does the promise in 36:22–32, which has three elements: cleansing (forgiveness), a new heart (attitude towards God), and the gift of God's Spirit (the power to obey God). This means a new covenant, as implied by the words 'you will be my people, and I will be your God' (36:28). Also the blessings promised (36:29–30) echo the blessings of the Mosaic covenant (Lev. 26). Ezekiel has little to say about the 'messianic hope', but does expect the monarchy to be restored (21:26–27; 34:24; 37:24–25).

The sovereignty of God over Israel's history is clear from the three surveys of Israel's history. Although he allows their rebellion, he is always there, free to act or refrain from acting. The oracles against the nations show his sovereignty over all nations. He wants all the nations to know that he is God and to accept him as such (20:41; 36:23).

The ultimate blessing for God's people is that he should dwell in their midst. Their sin had driven him out (11:22–23), but he would return to a repentant and purified people (37:26–28). The symbolic vision in 40 – 48 gives a picture of this.

Ezekiel's emphasis on God's awesome 'otherness' needs to be heeded today when holiness is often limited to moral purity. Grasping the larger concept enriches worship. Bringing glory to God as the prime motivation for how we live is endorsed by Paul (1 Cor. 10:31). Ezekiel's view of the deep-seatedness of human sin is also shared by Paul (Rom. 7). The 'new heart' promise lies behind 2 Cor. 3:1–6. The valley of dry bones vision, with its message of God overcoming human sinfulness and failure by his grace and power, has been a constant source of hope to God's people. Jesus' claim to be the Good Shepherd is clearly rooted in Ezek. 34, where the Sovereign LORD condemns Israel's shepherds (kings) and says he will shepherd his people.

DANIEL

A. Historical setting

Dan. 1 – 6 contains stories which cover the period from 606/5 BC (1:1) to after Cyrus' capture of Babylon in 539 (6:28), recounting the experiences of some Jewish exiles in Babylon. Darius the Mede (5:30–31) is not known in historical records, but this may be another name for Cyrus the Persian, since 6:28 can be translated 'the reign of Darius, *that is*, the reign of Cyrus'. The visions of chs. 6 – 12 focus on the persecution of the Jews by Antiochus IV in 169–165 BC. He banned Jewish religious observances. In 167 he desecrated the Jerusalem temple by erecting a statue of the god Zeus Olympius and sacrificing pigs there (11:31). The Maccabean Revolt led to the rededication of the temple in 164. Some scholars date the whole book to the sixth century. Others, while often accepting this date for the stories, date the visions and final form of the book just prior to Antiochus' persecution (see commentaries for detailed discussions).

B. Structure

Chs. 2 – 7 are in Aramaic rather than Hebrew and form a distinct section, beginning and ending with dream-visions of four world empires. Chs. 3 and 6 are about faithful Jews, while chs. 4 and 5 concern proud kings.

1	Introduction
2 – 7	Faithfulness under pagan rulers
8 – 11	Faithfulness under persecution
12	Resurrection and judgment

The stories resemble ancient stories known as 'court-tales' (the Joseph and Esther stories are other biblical examples). The visions resemble those in apocalypses, like Revelation, and contain symbolic imagery.

C. The message of Daniel

The overarching theme of Daniel is God's sovereignty over history (4:17). The surveys of history (2; 7; 11 – 12) end with the establishment of God's eternal kingdom. God is faithful to those who trust him under persecution (3; 6) and martyrdom (11:33–35). Dan. 12:1–4, the first clear promise of resurrection and judgment in the OT, gives hope to the martyrs.

The message of Daniel has often encouraged Christians facing the pressures of a pagan environment. Jesus' use of 'the Son of Man' is rooted in 7:13. Here, after judgment of the beast-like empires, a human figure represents the kingdom of God which fulfils God's original purpose for humanity (Gen. 1:26–28). Jesus inaugurated that kingdom.

HOSEA

A. Historical setting

Hosea's ministry, beginning soon after Amos', lasted at least thirty years (755–25 BC), and covered the turbulent final decades of the kingdom of Israel, where he prophesied. There is no reference in the book to the fall of Samaria in 722/1 BC. His marriage shaped his message. Most scholars think chs. 1 and 3 describe his marriage. Hos. 1:2 may indicate that he married Gomer knowing she was sexually promiscuous, or may describe her in retrospect. The third child's symbolic name (1:8–9) suggests that Hosea was not his father. Ch. 3 implies that Gomer became a prostitute, possibly in a Baal temple. Baalism was a fertility religion which involved ritual prostitution. Hosea bought her freedom and sought to restore their relationship.

B. Structure

1 – 3	Hosea's marriage, Israel's unfaithfulness
4 – 7	Sins of the people, priests and leaders
8 – 11	Apostate worship
12 – 14	Past failure, future repentance and restoration

C. The message of Hosea

Ch. 2 makes Hosea's experience a picture of the broken covenant relationship between God and Israel, summarizing the prophet's message. He concentrates on Israel's unfaithfulness to God. People were worshipping the Canaanite rain-god Baal, alongside, or instead of, the LORD. Yet the LORD is the true God of nature and fertility (2:8). Political intrigue involves seeking security from other nations, and is also unfaithfulness to God (7:8–13). Hosea urges Israel to repent and acknowledge God, showing faithfulness (4:1–3), steadfast love (6:6, TNIV 'mercy'), righteousness (10:12) and justice (12:6).

Hosea presents two profound and enduring pictures of God's love for sinners. One is the deserted husband who continues to love his wife and pays the financial and emotional cost of redeeming her and restoring the relationship (Hos. 1 – 3). The other is the parent who loves and refuses to give up on a delinquent child (11:1–11).

JOEL

A. Historical setting

Since the prophecy assumes temple worship, Joel was not prophesying during the exile. There are verbal parallels with several other prophetic books (see commentaries for details), which may indicate that Joel lived after the exile. The nation faces a crisis from a locust plague – but was this literally of locusts, or metaphoric of a military invasion?

B. Structure

1:1 – 2:17	Locust plague, the Day of the LORD and calls to repent
2:18 – 3:21	Promises of salvation
2:18–27	Plague-damage restored
2:28–32	Outpouring of the Spirit
3:1–14	Judgment of the nations
3:15–21	Judah restored

C. The message of Joel

The locust imagery asserts that God is Lord of nature as well as history, and can act in either realm for judgment and blessing. The calls to repent, implying hope of averting judgment, rest on God's character (Joel 2:13, a classic definition; see Exod. 34:6). Joel's special contribution regarding the Day of the LORD is the promise of the outpouring of the Spirit, which was fulfilled at Pentecost (Acts 2:16–21).

AMOS

A. Historical setting

Tekoa, Amos' home, was ten miles south of Jerusalem. As a sheep-breeder ('shepherd' in 1:1 means this) he probably owned land. His seasonal sideline tending sycamore fig-trees (7:14) involved travel to areas where they grew. Although he came from Judah, Amos prophesied in the northern kingdom of Israel. The visions (7:1–9) may record his call experience. Amos distanced himself from the 'professional' prophets serving at sanctuaries like Bethel (7:14).

The earthquake (1:1) happened around 760 BC. (It was still remembered centuries later; Zech. 14:5.) By then Israel and Judah had enjoyed a period of peace and prosperity due to the weakness of Egypt and Assyria.

B. Structure

1:1 – 2:16	Oracles against the nations – including Israel and Judah
3:1 – 5:17	Judgment oracles
5:18 – 6:14	Woe oracles
7:1 – 9:10	Vision reports
9:11–15	Promise of restoration

C. The message of Amos

Israel has fallen short of God's standards (7:7–8); judgment has been withheld (7:1–6), but must now fall (7:8–9; 8:1–3). These standards are the covenant demands (3:1–2). Amos alludes to covenant laws (2:4–16) and curses (4:6–12). He condemns rampant materialism, social inequality, perversion of justice, sexual immorality, and hypocritical worship. The 'Day of the LORD', when God punishes evil, will mean disaster for Israel (5:18–20). There are exhortations to repent (5:4, 6, 14–15) but the promise of restoration addresses Judah, perhaps after Israel's fall, making Amos' message relevant to Judah too.

God is sovereign over all nations, the judge of evil and upholder of good worldwide (9:7–8). His demand for social justice and righteousness applies today, as does his rejection of lavish, enthusiastic worship which ignores these demands (5:21–24).

OBADIAH

A. Historical setting

Obadiah prophesied against Edom, Judah's south-eastern neighbour. There was a history of conflict between them. Obadiah probably prophesied after 587 BC, when the Edomites joined in the Babylonian destruction of Judah (Ps. 137:7).

B. Structure

vv. 1–4	Judgment declared on Edom's pride
vv. 5–14	Edom will be destroyed for plundering Judah
vv. 15–21	The Day of the LORD: judgment for all nations and deliverance for Israel

There are many parallels between vv. 1–5 and Jer. 49:7–16. Verse 17 has links with Joel 2:32.

C. The message of Obadiah

Obadiah gave encouragement to post-exilic Judah. Edom and Judah were brothers (v. 10) since Edomites were descended from Esau the brother of Jacob, Judah's ancestor. Thus Edom's behaviour was an act of betrayal, and Obadiah strongly condemns it. Edom would be punished by the Sovereign LORD, who acts justly (v. 15). This encourages us to trust God's justice when we are badly betrayed by someone close to us.

JONAH

A. Historical setting

The book is mostly a story about a prophet, and contains only one brief oracle (3:4b). Jonah prophesied in the reign of Jeroboam II of Israel (about 760 BC; 2 Kgs 14:25), when Assyria was relatively weak. Scholars debate whether Jonah should be read as an historical narrative or as a parable. Among other features, there is hyperbole ('great' occurs fourteen times) and satire (in the portrayal of Jonah), which point to the story being told primarily as a parable conveying a message. Of course, parables may be based on actual events.

B. Structure

1   Jonah's first call: flight
2   Jonah's prayer, thanksgiving and deliverance
3   Jonah's second call: obedience
4   Jonah's prayer and argument with God

C. The message of Jonah

The enduring message of Jonah is found in its affirmations about God. He is the Creator of all (1:9) and so worthy of worship by all people, including pagan sailors and Ninevites, not just Israelites. He is compassionate and loving, ready to forgive all who repent (4:2, echoing Exod. 34:6). His loving concern even extends to the non-human creation (4:11).

MICAH

A. Historical setting

Micah came from Moresheth, a town twenty-five miles south-west of Jerusalem. The reigns during which he prophesied (1:1) spanned over fifty years, including Israel's final troubled years before its destruction in 722 BC, and Sennacherib's invasion of Judah in 701. An auto-biographical note (3:8) expresses his sense of calling and inspiration. The word 'justice' in it refers to the rights and duties flowing from the Sinai covenant. Micah was zealous for the covenant. A century later his preaching was remembered as a cause of Hezekiah's reform (Jer. 26:18–19).

B. Structure

1 – 2   Samaria and Jerusalem judged – but deliverance promised
3 – 5   Jerusalem condemned – but redeemed
6 – 7   Israel proven guilty – but pardoned

Most scholars see the prophet's own words in chs. 1 – 3. Debate continues about possible additions by his followers in chs. 4 – 7, particularly 4:6–13 and 7:8–20, which may reflect the exile in Babylon. Mic. 4:1–4 is very like Isa. 2:2–4; both may quote a temple hymn.

C. The message of Micah

Mic. 6:1–8 (a 'covenant lawsuit' oracle) sums up much of the book's message. The LORD defends himself against his people's complaints, stressing his graciousness towards them and condemning dependence on religious observances without obedience to the moral demands of the covenant.

The book's message of hope concerns a 'remnant' that will survive judgment (2:12–13; 4:6–8; 5:7–9). Mic. 5:2–6 (a classic messianic text, cf. Matt. 2:4–6) promises a 'new David'. Ultimately hope rests in God's compassion and forgiveness (7:18–19).

God's 'requirement' (6:8) remains today: live by his standards ('act justly'), treat people as he does ('love mercy'), and live appropriately ('walk humbly'), aware of his presence ('with your God').

NAHUM

A. Historical setting

Nahum prophesied against Nineveh, the capital of Assyria, and so dates from before the destruction of Nineveh in 612 BC. Reference (3:8) to the fall of Thebes dates the prophecy after that event in 663 BC. The site of Nahum's home town, Elkosh, is uncertain.

B. Structure

1:1–8	God's character and power
1:9 – 2:2	God will deliver his people from oppression
2:3–13	Nineveh's destruction depicted
3:1–19	Judgment pronounced on Nineveh

C. The message of Nahum

Nahum asserts God's sovereignty over the world; though 'slow to anger' (1:3) he will eventually punish oppressors. God is 'a refuge in times of trouble' to those who trust him (1:7). This belief, not a nationalistic desire for revenge, underlies the book. Assyria is condemned for cruelty towards all nations, not just Judah.

Nahum means 'comfort' and his prophecy brings hope to God's people whenever they face oppression by seemingly invincible powers or ideologies. These will eventually fall, like Nineveh.

HABAKKUK

A. Historical setting

Hab. 1:6 suggests a date in the late seventh century, when the Babylonians were rising to power. Hab. 1:2–4 probably refers to the state of Judah in Jehoiakim's reign, when Josiah's reforms were being reversed.

B. Structure

1:1–11	Habakkuk's lament and God's response
1:12 – 2:5	Habakkuk's protest and God's response
2:6–20	Five woes against Babylon
3:1–19	Psalm of confidence in God

C. The message of Habakkuk

Habakkuk complains that God is inactive when the sinful state of society cries out for action. When God replies that he intends using the Babylonians to punish Judah, the prophet protests at his use of a wicked nation to punish a relatively righteous people. God's answer is a call to trust in him and an assurance that the Babylonians will be punished for their wickedness. Habakkuk responds with a psalm expressing confidence in God.

God's people are often perplexed by current events. Habakkuk shows how to deal with this. He commits his problem to God. When the answer is primarily a challenge to renewed faith in God's justice, he responds with an expression of trust in God to preserve him through troubled times.

ZEPHANIAH

A. Historical setting

Zephaniah is given an unusually long genealogy, possibly because the Hezekiah mentioned was the Judean king of that name. He prophesied during Josiah's reign, before the destruction of Nineveh (612 BC) and probably before Josiah's reform (621), since he condemns practices that were common before it.

B. Structure

1:1–6	Warning of judgment
1:7 – 3:8	The Day of the LORD – judgment
1:7 – 2:3	A day of wrath
2:4–15	Oracles against the nations
3:1–8	Condemnation of Jerusalem
3:9–20	The Day of the LORD – salvation

C. The message of Zephaniah

Zephaniah asserts the two-sidedness of the Day of the LORD, as both judgment and salvation. Idolatrous worship and social injustice provoke God's judgment, expressed in terms echoing the covenant curses (1:13, 15, 17–18). Beyond judgment lies salvation and blessing for 'the remnant', those who humbly trust in God and seek righteousness (2:3; 3:12–13). Both judgment and salvation are presented as universal since the LORD is the universal king.

Zephaniah asserts the kingship of the God of justice in the midst of a corrupt and oppressive society. It is therefore a call to faith and endurance to the 'remnant' in any society who 'seek first [God's] kingdom and his righteousness' (Matt. 6:33).

HAGGAI

A. Historical setting

Haggai and Zechariah 1 – 8 share a common framework of dating. Haggai's ministry coincided with Zechariah's (Ezra 5:1; 6:14). He prophesied in Jerusalem in 520 BC, early in the reign of Darius I of Persia. Eighteen years earlier Jews returned from Babylon intending to rebuild the temple. Opposition halted the work (Ezra 4:1–5). Since then they had continually postponed restarting it, concentrating on meeting their material needs.

B. Structure

The four sections are each introduced by a date.

1:1–15	An exhortation to rebuild the temple
2:1–9	An encouraging word
2:10–19	A promise of blessing
2:20–23	A messianic promise (cf. Jer. 22:24)

C. The message of Haggai

The temple was God's ordained 'means of grace' for the Judeans, a source of blessing. Its ruined state evidenced their spiritual state and caused their plight (1:10–11 echo the covenant curses). Like a dead body, it contaminated all they did (2:10–14). Any tendency to feel daunted by the task of rebuilding was met by promises of empowering, resources and blessing. Under the new covenant we have different means of grace, which we neglect to our detriment. When God gives us specific tasks to do, he will provide what we need to complete them.

Haggai gave an assurance that the covenant with David still stood and the messianic kingdom would come. Christians see this promise fulfilled in Jesus.

ZECHARIAH

A. Historical setting

Zechariah 1 – 8 shares Haggai's historical setting. Zechariah began prophesying a month before Haggai finished (1:1), and his last dated prophecy came two years later (7:1; dated 7 December 518 BC). He may be mentioned in Neh. 12:16 as a priest. The historical setting of chs. 9 – 14 is unclear.

B. Structure

Chs. 1 – 8 and 9 – 14 differ in content, style and vocabulary. Since 9:1; 12:1 and Mal. 1:1 are each headed 'prophecy' (or 'oracle', NIV), chs. 9 – 11 and 12 – 14 may be independent collections of prophetic sayings, perhaps by Zechariah's disciples. They develop the message of chs. 1 – 8.

1:1–6	Israel's past sins and God's judgment
1:7 – 6:8	Visions of encouragement
6:9–15	Joshua crowned as a symbol of the coming king
7 – 8	The covenant renewed and a call to renewed obedience
9 – 11	Salvation and judgment. The coming King
12 – 14	Final judgment and salvation. The LORD worshipped as universal King

C. The message of Zechariah

Zechariah's visions brought encouragement to those rebuilding the temple. Their main thrust is that the exile is over, Israel's past sins are cleansed and God is beginning to fulfil the promises of salvation given by the earlier prophets. Here was encouragement to persevere and complete the rebuilding.

Promises of salvation for Israel predominate in chs. 9 – 11, centred on a coming king (9:9–13). This will mean judgment on Israel's enemies (9:1–8), but also on the faithless in Israel (10:2–3; 11:4–17).

Chs. 12 – 14 tell of the final victory of God on behalf of his people. This will involve their repentance and cleansing (12:11 – 13:9). Ch. 14's symbolic imagery depicts God's final victory over evil, which establishes God's rule, with people of all nations worshipping the LORD Almighty.

Under the new covenant God is ready to forgive our past sins if we truly repent (1 John 1:9) and give us a new start in serving him. Matthew sees Jesus in the figures of the coming king (9:9–10; cf. Matt. 21:4–5) and rejected shepherd (11:12–13; 13:7; cf. Matt. 26:15, 31; 27:9). He inaugurated God's kingdom on earth. Zechariah's vision of God's final victory encourages us to persevere in the work of the kingdom.

MALACHI

A. Historical setting

'Malachi', which means 'my messenger' (the same Hebrew term occurs in 3:1), is not a name elsewhere in the OT, so here it may introduce an anonymous prophecy. It is often dated to the early fifth century BC because it mentions religious abuses which Ezra and Nehemiah dealt with later that century.

B. Structure

Malachi is a collection of 'disputes' between God and the covenant community.

1:1–5	God's love for Israel
1:6 – 2:9	God's dispute with the priests
2:10–16	Dispute about marriage and divorce
2:17 – 3:5	God's justice and judgment
3:6–12	Dispute over tithes
3:13 – 4:3	God's final judgment
4:4–6	Moses and Elijah

C. The message of Malachi

The assertion of the LORD's love for Israel assumes the covenant

(Deut. 7:7–11). The basic sin of priests and people is covenant-breaking (2:8, 10). The covenant was meant to be a living relationship like that of a child with its father (2:10), but the people had become lukewarm towards God and apathetic in worship (1:13; 3:8). The broken relationship with God led to broken relationships in society (2:14). God's love is not to be presumed upon. As the God of justice (2:17), he punishes sinners (3:13 – 4:3).

Malachi gives a fitting end to the OT, looking back to Moses, mediator of the old covenant (4:4), and forward to a future 'messenger of the covenant' (3:1), who will make God's people righteous. He will be preceded by 'the prophet Elijah' (4:5), with whom John the Baptist is later identified (Matt. 11:14; Mark 9:12–13).

Malachi's challenge not to become lukewarm towards God remains today. The risen Lord Jesus warned the church in Ephesus of judgment for abandoning its first love (Rev. 2:1–7), and called the church in Laodicea to repent of its lukewarmness (Rev. 3:14–18).

Further reading (see **Introduction** for good commentary series)

Gordon McConville, *Exploring the Old Testament 4. The Prophets* (SPCK, 2002) – excellent introduction, with panels highlighting themes and points to ponder.

Robert Chisholm, *Handbook on the Prophets* (Baker, 2002) – good detailed introduction to the books and each section or chapter.

Brent Sandy, *Plowshares and Pruning Hooks: Rethinking the Language of Biblical Prophecy and Apocalyptic* (IVP, 2002) – engaging study of prophecy's language and imagery.

John Sawyer, *Prophecy and the Biblical Prophets* (OUP, 1993) – good general scholarly survey.

7. Between the Testaments

Carl Mosser

A. *Times of great change*

Many people attempt to read the Bible like a modern book, straight through from beginning to end. Christians are sometimes encouraged to begin with the NT and then read the OT. However, the perceptive reader immediately notices that Jewish life and faith in the NT is very different from that in the OT. The obvious reason is the gap of about 400 years between the end of the OT and the beginning of the NT. A great deal happened during this time to shape Jewish society.

At the close of the OT story the Jewish homeland is a province of the Persian empire, and Aramaic is the language of diplomacy and commerce. Jews have recently begun returning from exile to rebuild Jerusalem and its temple. But when the NT story begins Persia has long ceased to be a major power. Rome is the dominant empire but Greek, not Latin, is the language of diplomacy and commerce. The Jewish homeland is a kingdom ruled by Herod the Great, an ethnic Idumean (see E and F below) placed on the throne by Rome. Jewish piety is expressed in synagogues as well as the temple. There are religious and political groups like the Pharisees, Sadducees and Samaritans, but their origins and beliefs are not explained. Knowledge of the developments that took place during the intertestamental period will greatly assist our understanding of the NT.

This chapter will give a survey of the four centuries between the testaments. For the social and literary developments of the final century or so, see New Testament Background in ch. 8.

B. From independent kingdoms to Persian province

Following Solomon's death the twelve tribes of Israel were split between two kingdoms: Israel in the north and Judah in the south. The Assyrians conquered Israel in 722 BC, exiled some inhabitants and brought in other displaced peoples to dilute their ethnic and religious identity (and reduce the likelihood of rebellion). These groups settled together and became known as the Samaritans. Though they later accepted the Jewish law, they were excluded from the Jewish people because of their mixed background.

A century later the Babylonians conquered the Assyrians, and in 605 BC Judah became their resentful vassal. Judah eventually rebelled, and in 587 BC Babylon responded by destroying Jerusalem and the temple. Many of its inhabitants were exiled to Babylonia.

The Babylonian empire was short-lived, and fell to an alliance of Persians and Medes in 539 BC. The Persian empire sought the loyalty of its inhabitants by reversing many Babylonian policies and permitting exiles to return to their homelands. They were also allowed to take the statues of their gods and other sacred items that had been removed from their national temples. A minority of the Jewish population took advantage of this policy and returned to Judah, now a Persian province called Yehud.

The biblical books of Ezra and Nehemiah recount many of the difficulties faced by several groups of returning Jewish exiles down to the late 400s. Relatively little is known about events in Judah after this time, but archaeological evidence suggests that the province eventually prospered under Persian rule. We also know that Judeans served in the Persian army. For example, documents and the remains of a Jewish temple have been discovered at Elephantine in southern Egypt. These indicate that a Jewish military garrison was stationed there to protect the south-west border of the Persian empire.

Many significant events took place under Persian rule that would have a lasting affect on Judaism. The Jerusalem temple was rebuilt, though less grand than its predecessor. It remained the central focus of Jewish piety until it was destroyed in AD 70. The priesthood came to control many secular as well as religious affairs within the province. The high priest came to rule Jerusalem as a temple city with some degree of autonomy. He was viewed as the chief representative and leader of the Jewish people around the world. Jewish identity came to be determined by descent through the mother. The study and interpretation of the law of Moses took on greater significance than it had in the pre-exilic period.

C. Alexander the Great and the spread of Hellenism

Another formative stage in the development of Judaism was ushered in by Alexander the Great's conquest of the Persian empire in 333–330 BC. Alexander sought to unify his vast domain by spreading Hellenistic (i.e. Greek) language and cultural institutions throughout his newly acquired territories. He did this primarily by founding hundreds of new cities, settling them with colonists from Greece and veterans from his army. These Hellenistic cities included an acropolis (central fortress), a market, temples dedicated to Greek deities, a theatre and a gymnasium. The gymnasium was particularly important as the primary centre for education and training in sports and combat. The goal was to train body, mind and soul in preparation for citizenship in a Greek city. Pious Jews objected to the gymnasium because athletic activities were conducted in the nude. They also objected because gymnasia were associated with homosexual activity, especially pederasty.

The Greek inhabitants of these new cities became a cultural elite. The indigenous peoples reacted in ways similar to the way people in modern non-Western countries respond to the encroachment of Western ideals and fashions. Some embraced Greek culture and language. They did so because they were either enamoured by its chic 'modernism' or because doing so provided means of social and economic advance. Others considered Hellenism a threat to their traditional way of life and resisted it as much as possible. But as these Greek cities became permanent fixtures in a region, the surrounding peoples were all affected by Hellenism to some degree, the Jews no less than others.

D. Judea under the Ptolemies and Seleucids

When Alexander died in 323 BC his massive kingdom was divided among his generals. After several wars between the generals, the non-European territories near the Mediterranean were divided between Ptolemy and Seleucus. The Ptolemaic empire was centred in Egypt. The Seleucid empire initially spread from eastern Syria to Afghanistan, but soon came to be centred in Syria and Asia Minor. Considerable numbers of Jews made their homes in both empires.

The Jewish homeland was included in territory initially assigned to Seleucus, but Ptolemy seized it in 301 BC and incorporated it into his holdings. This served as the pretext for a number of Seleucid invasions of the Ptolemaic empire. Like the Persians and Alexander, the Ptolemies granted Judea limited freedom in the administration of internal affairs, though little is known about Jewish attitudes toward them. Hellenism continued to exert influence on Jewish society generally, with many wealthy Judeans freely adopting the Greek language and aspects of Greek culture.

In 200 BC the Seleucids were finally successful in taking control of this territory. They were initially generous towards their Judean subjects because the inhabitants of Jerusalem sided with them at a crucial moment in their conflict with the Ptolemies. The Seleucid king Antiochus III even gave financial support to the temple. Little changed under his successor, Seleucus IV. However, the situation changed dramatically when Seleucus was murdered and his brother Antiochus IV 'Epiphanes' became king in 175 BC.

Though Onias III was the high priest, his brother Jason bribed the cash-strapped new king to obtain the high priesthood, and actively promoted Hellenism. As part of his agreement with Antiochus, he secured the right to establish a gymnasium in Jerusalem. This effectively re-founded Jerusalem as a Greek city. Young men from the nobility were enrolled in the gymnasium, and priests participated in its athletic competitions. Because they were conducted in the nude, participation violated Jewish law and defiled priestly purity. Greek customs were introduced on a wide scale, but they were not imposed. Individuals who chose to do so could still maintain traditional Jewish practices, and the temple remained dedicated to Yahweh. But this too would change.

After three years Jason was replaced by Menelaus, who was not even a member of the priestly family descended from Zadok (cf. 1 Kgs 2:35; Ezek. 40:46). But the only qualification Antiochus was concerned about was whether Menelaus could deliver a larger sum of money than Jason. This proved more difficult than Menelaus anticipated, and he resorted to stealing gold vessels from the temple. Meanwhile Jason waited for an opportunity to regain the office. Following a rumour that Antiochus had died, he gathered a small force and attacked Jerusalem, but was forced to withdraw. Antiochus, however, was very much alive. Hearing that Jerusalem was in rebellion, he attacked the city and massacred many inhabitants. Afterwards he entered the most holy place of the temple, guided by Menelaus himself, and pillaged its wealth.

For reasons that are not entirely clear, Antiochus then instituted a policy of forced Hellenization. Completing the transformation of Jerusalem into a Greek city, the temple was dedicated to Olympian Zeus, and a pig and other 'unclean' animals were sacrificed on the altar. The Judean people were forbidden to keep the Sabbath or festivals, or circumcise their sons, under pain of death. Once a month they were required to celebrate the king's birthday with a festival dedicated to the god Dionysus. The king's representatives went to Jewish villages and required the locals to prove their abandonment of Judaism by sacrificing a pig and eating a portion of its flesh. Many people obeyed while others resisted to the point of martyrdom. In one famous episode a mother refused to compromise even as she was forced to watch her seven sons being tortured and killed one by one (2 Maccabees 7).

E. The Maccabean revolt and Hasmonean period

Open rebellion began when the king's representatives went to the village of Modein. A priest named Mattathias refused to make the required sacrifice. When a fellow Judean stepped forward to offer it, Mattathias killed him and the king's officer. He called upon all who were zealous for the Jewish law to follow him and his sons to the hills, where they began a guerrilla war against the Seleucids. In addition to harassing Seleucid troops, they went through Jewish villages tearing down pagan altars, forcing boys to be circumcised and killing collaborators. Mattathias soon died, but his son Judah Maccabee ('the Hammer') took command of the growing army and won a string of stunning victories. In 164 BC he captured Jerusalem and rededicated the temple, an event still celebrated today in the Jewish festival of Hanukkah. Judah was succeeded by his brothers Jonathan and Simon, who managed to secure concessions from the Seleucids and finally independence.

The family of Mattathias were known as the Hasmoneans after the name of one of their ancestors. At first they ruled as high priests; later they added the title of king. John Hyrcanus (134–104 BC) expanded the nation's borders to their greatest extent since the time of Solomon. Taking advantage of weakness in the Seleucid empire, he conquered territory east of the Jordan, including several Greek cities. To the north he conquered Samaria and destroyed the rival temple on Mount Gerizim. To the south he conquered the Idumeans, descendants of ancient Edom, forcing them to submit to circumcision and convert to Judaism. The Seleucid empire continued to weaken as Rome began intervening in the eastern Mediterranean. This allowed subsequent Hasmonean rulers to expanded Judea's borders further.

In 76 BC King Alexander Janneus died, leaving the kingdom to his wife Alexandra. She was able to rule as queen but had to appoint one of her sons as high priest. She chose her eldest son Hyrcanus II because he was not politically ambitious. By contrast, his younger brother Aristobulus II was ambitious, and proclaimed himself high priest and king when his mother took ill. Alexandra did not recover, and civil war broke out between Hyrcanus and Aristobulus after her death.

Hyrcanus was initially defeated and forced to give up his power and titles. A wealthy Idumean named Antipater advised Hyrcanus to seek the support of Aretas, ruler of the south-eastern Arab kingdom of Nabatea. Antipater brokered a deal in which Aretas promised to help Hyrcanus regain the throne in exchange for territory lost to Judea in earlier wars. Hyrcanus and his Nabatean allies were able to besiege Aristobulus in Jerusalem. At the same time the Roman general Pompey arrived in the eastern Mediterranean with a commission to pacify various territories and organize provinces. Hyrcanus and Aristobulus both appealed to Pompey to intervene on their behalf. At first the Romans preferred Aristobulus, but Pompey distrusted him. Pompey committed his troops in support of Hyrcanus. Three months later in the autumn of 63 BC Aristobulus was defeated and Pompey entered Jerusalem. Pompey insisted on entering the holy place of the temple, an action that sowed seeds of distrust against the Romans among the populace. A few years later Julius Caesar returned political power to Hyrcanus, appointing him ethnarch (a title lower than king) in addition to high priest. He would be the last member of the Hasmonean dynasty to rule.

The Hellenization crisis led to several developments within Judaism during the Hasmonean period. The chief result of the attempt to forcibly Hellenize the Judean people was a backlash that solidified Jewish identity. The crisis under Antiochus IV was widely seen as divine judgment for tolerating idolatry and for neglecting the commandments of the law of Moses, and the Maccabean victory was attributed to uncompromising zealousness for the law. Afterwards monotheism was finally secured among the Jewish people once and for all. Obedience to the law in basic matters of Jewish identity such as circumcision, Sabbath-keeping and food laws became the norm.

Commandments pertaining to purity, priesthood, sacrifice and festivals were also looked at with renewed seriousness. The proper implementation of the purity laws became a particular concern among some groups because the Mosaic law indicated that the well-being of the nation was directly contingent upon purity (Deut. 23:14). Ambiguities in the biblical commandments led to debates about their proper interpretation. Combined with various political factors, these debates led to the development of distinct parties within Judaism such as the Pharisees, Sadducees and Essenes. These groups enter the historical record during the reign of John Hyrcanus and remain very influential until the destruction of the temple in AD 70.

F. Herod the Great

When Julius Caesar granted Hyrcanus II the title of ethnarch, he also recognized Antipater the Idumean as administrator of Judea. Caesar seemed to like Hyrcanus and was persuaded by him to grant Jews within the Roman empire significant rights and privileges that would later prove beneficial to the spread of the Christian movement. These included the right to meet in synagogues, gather for public meals, keep the Sabbath and pay the yearly temple tax. But Antipater was the real power behind the throne. In 47 BC he moved to secure additional power for his family by having his son Phasael appointed governor of Jerusalem and another son Herod appointed governor of Galilee. This set the stage for the end of the Hasmonean dynasty.

When the young Herod was appointed governor, Galilee was an unruly territory terrorized by a brigand named Ezekias. Herod quickly proved himself an effective (albeit harsh) leader by pacifying the region. This earned him the respect of the Galilean Jews and Romans. He served as governor of Galilee until members of Hyrcanus' court felt he was becoming too powerful. He was brought to trial before the Jewish ruling council, the Sanhedrin, but the Roman governor of Syria intervened on his behalf. Herod was then appointed as governor of the Roman territory of Coele-Syria for a term, again proving himself an effective leader.

For the next few years Herod was embroiled in the intrigues of Roman politics and various controversies in Judea. An adept politician, he outmanoeuvred his enemies and increased his power. Things nearly came to an end for him when in 40 BC Judea was invaded from the east by Rome's arch-rival, the Parthian empire. They sought to depose Hyrcanus and place his brother's son Antigonus on the throne. Hyrcanus and Herod's brother Phasael were captured by the Parthians through a ruse and Antigonus was installed as king. Herod managed to escape and eventually made his way to Rome. Sensing the need for a strong and effective ruler in Judea, the Roman Senate appointed Herod king of the Jews. With Roman support he returned to Galilee and captured it. From there he moved on Judea. In 37 BC he captured Jerusalem and beheaded Antigonus. Shortly before this Herod married Mariamne, a Hasmonean princess, to strengthen his claim to the throne.

Herod ruled as king of the Jews from 37–4 BC. In the first few years of his reign he consolidated his power by eliminating various rivals and critics. Once power was consolidated, Herod revitalized the kingdom's economy. He used his wealth to build fortresses, palaces, theatres and various civic buildings throughout his territory. He had a small coastal town rebuilt into a prominent port city and renamed it Caesarea

Maritima in honor of Caesar Augustus. Pagan temples were built under his patronage in Gentile areas both within and without his kingdom. His most notable building project, however, was a massive renovation and expansion of the temple in Jerusalem.

The final stage of Herod's reign was plagued by domestic problems. Many of these were generated by the fact that he had ten wives, each of whom wanted her son to inherit the throne. His wives and children plotted against one another and attempted to discredit their rivals. Herod's favour tended to shift between his sons, leading him to rewrite his will six times. Always known as a harsh ruler, Herod's actions became more erratic in the final years of his life. He was growing ill and was increasingly paranoid about possible plots against him. During these years Herod had numerous alleged conspirators put to death, including several of his wives and sons. It is against this background that Matthew records Herod's order to kill all the children in Bethlehem aged two and under in an attempt to eliminate a possible rival (Matt. 2:16).

When Herod died in 4 BC the Roman Senate divided his kingdom between three of his sons. Archelaus was appointed ethnarch over Samaria, Judea and Idumea. Herod Antipas was appointed tetrarch of Galilee and Perea. Philip was made tetrarch of various outlaying territories. Archelaus was promised that he would be elevated to king if he proved an effective ruler. He instead proved to be an inept and oppressive ruler hated by his subjects. This explains why Joseph and Mary were afraid to return to Judea after the death of Herod (Matt. 2:22). In a rare show of unity, in AD 6 a delegation of Jews and Samaritans complained to Caesar Augustus about Archelaus' tyranny and he was deposed. Antipas and Philip retained their territories, but those of Archelaus were placed under direct Roman rule. As a concession to the Judean people, Antipas was given the right to appoint the high priests and officiate at the annual festivals. This basic political arrangement was maintained throughout most of the NT era.

G. The rise of Jewish messianism

Judaism developed in many ways during the intertestamental period. One of the most important concerned the expectation that God would send one or more messiahs to redeem Israel.

Upon their return from exile, Jews hoped that the Davidic monarchy would soon be restored. But their homeland remained under the control of foreign powers until the Maccabean revolt. The Hasmoneans managed to free Judea from Greek rule and rededicate the temple, but did not return the high priesthood to the descendants of Onias III, the last legitimate Zadokite high priest. Nor did they re-establish the Davidic monarchy. Instead they took for themselves the titles of high priest and (later) king, which some Jews saw as usurpation and blatant violation of God's law. The same was felt about Herod's ascendancy to Israel's throne. Greek and Roman oppression contributed further to messianic hopes for a time when God would set things right by sending a righteous Davidic king and/or a priest anointed to redeem Israel from foreign oppression and internal corruption.

The roots of messianism lie in the OT, though it nowhere refers to 'the messiah' as an individual who is anointed by God to redeem Israel in the last days. The word *messiah* comes from a Hebrew term meaning 'anointed'. In the OT, priests, prophets and kings were anointed with oil as part of their installation to office (e.g. priests: Exod. 28:41; prophets: 1 Kgs 19:16; 1 Chr. 16:22; kings: 1 Sam. 10:1; 16:13). Kings were especially known as 'the LORD's anointed', though most were criticized by the prophets for their failure to rule in a godly manner. Some of the prophets express hope for a new Davidic king who would reign righteously and justly (see, e.g. Isa. 11:1–5; 32:1–2; Ezek. 34:23–24; Hos. 3:5; Amos 9:11; Mic. 5). In some texts an anointed priest is hoped for alongside this ideal king (Jer. 33:15–18; Zech. 4:14).

Three OT texts were widely interpreted in a messianic sense and played a particularly important role in the rise of messianic ideas. Gen. 49:10–11 says that the royal sceptre and ruler's staff will not depart from the tribe of Judah. This text implicitly indicted both the Hasmonean and Herodian kings as pretenders to Israel's throne. It was also understood to be a divine promise which God would fulfil by establishing one of David's descendants as king. The second important text was Num. 24:17: 'A star will come out of Jacob; a sceptre will rise out of Israel.' Many Jewish texts written near the first century interpret this prediction to refer to a messianic figure of the last days, e.g. Aramaic paraphrases which expand the line to say: 'a king shall arise out of Jacob and be anointed the messiah of Israel.' The third text was Isa. 11:1–9, where the prophet foretells of a day in which a 'shoot will come up from the stump of Jesse', an allusion to a restored Davidic monarchy. The passage describes this 'shoot' or 'branch' as a just and righteous ruler filled with the Spirit of the LORD, and goes on to associate his rule with the establishment of harmony in nature (e.g. 'the wolf will live with the lamb', v. 6) and universal knowledge of the Lord (v. 9). These and other texts came to be understood as predicting a messiah who would deliver Israel and usher in a new age of peace and righteousness.

Jewish literature written around the turn of the eras attests a variety of messianic expectations. Some of the Dead Sea Scrolls portray a priestly messiah from the house of Aaron, sometimes alongside a kingly messiah from the house of David. Most texts, however, mention only a kingly messiah. A variety of roles are attributed to the messiah(s). Inspired by the imagery of Ps. 2, he is usually depicted as a warrior who plays a decisive role in an end-time war in which unrighteous Israelites and foreign oppressors are destroyed. The messiah is always a remarkable figure, but he is not a supernatural being and he is never expected to perform miracles.

The rise of messianism in the intertestamental period prepared the way for Jesus to be proclaimed the messiah. In harmony with common expectations, the NT describes Jesus as a descendant of David anointed by God's Spirit. He is referred to with recognized messianic titles such as 'son of David', 'Branch', 'Son of Man', the 'Chosen One' and 'the Christ' (Greek for 'messiah'). Features approximating Qumran's priestly messianism are also attributed to Jesus throughout the epistle to the Hebrews. But in other ways the messianism of the NT is unique. Instead of immediately waging war against God's enemies, Jesus performs miracles, preaches and engages in religious controversy. He is killed, raised from the dead and ascends to God's right hand, from which he will return. The NT also insists that Israel's messiah did not come just to deliver righteous Israelites. He came to redeem sinners and reconcile to God people from every race, tribe and tongue. In light of pervasive Jewish attitudes towards Gentiles at the time (see New Testament Background in ch. 8), this became one of the most distinctive and controversial features of Christian messianism.

Further reading

Anthony Tomasino, *Judaism Before Jesus* (IVP, 2003) – informative retelling of the story of Israel between the testaments.

James Vanderkam, *An Introduction to Early Judaism* (Eerdmans, 2001) – useful overview of intertestamental history and literature and of early Judaism.

8. Introducing the New Testament

Ian Paul, Carl Mosser, Mark Strauss and
Brian Rosner

NEW TESTAMENT STORY

A. *The story of Jesus*

The New Testament is the story of the coming of the promised kingdom of God in the person and work of Jesus of Nazareth. This highlights some important aspects of what the NT is and what it does:

It is primarily a story. The longest sections consist of stories: Jesus' life and teaching and the church's missionary expansion. And the more doctrinal letters are part of this story, addressing issues raised in the fledgling churches.

It is about the fulfilment of promise. The early pages of the Gospels are full of expectation, and at numerous points there is a sense of hope fulfilled, disappointed or reapplied. This finds no better expression than in John the Baptist's question (through his disciples) to Jesus: 'Are you the one who was to come, or should we expect someone else?' (Matt. 11:3).

Sections in this chapter were written as follows – Ian Paul: New Testament Story; Carl Mosser: New Testament Background; Mark Strauss: New Testament Theology; Brian Rosner: New Testament Interpretation.

It is about the kingdom of God. The expectation found in the NT concerns the coming of the just and perfect rule of God, recognized as king first by his people and then in the wider world. But this kingdom does not come in the abstract. It breaks into a world full of competing kingdoms and would-be rulers, political and personal, and inevitably comes into conflict with all of them in different ways.

It is about the person of Jesus. As typical for a rabbi in his day, Jesus gathers around him a group of followers to be with him and to learn from him. However, it is striking that time and again, it is not so much how people respond to his teaching that matters to Jesus, but rather how they respond to him. Even in the later parts of the NT, the theme of response to the person of Jesus is paramount. In the book of Revelation, the challenge for late first-century Christians is to be faithful witnesses just as Jesus was a faithful witness.

It is about the work of Jesus. The NT appeals throughout for a response to Jesus on the basis of his death and resurrection. Thus Paul could be misunderstood as teaching about the two gods 'Jesus' and 'Anastasis', the Greek word for resurrection (Acts 17:18). Paul always pointed people to what Jesus could mean to them because of what he had done for them.

It is about the particular and the cosmic. The story of what God has done in Jesus is rooted in a particular time and place. And yet the events which happened then and there constantly spill over into here and now – indeed, into every here and now there has been, since the NT claims that this person and these events have cosmic significance: 'God has made this Jesus, whom you crucified, both Lord and Messiah' (Acts 2:36).

The gap between the Old Testament and the New is sometimes called the 'silent years' – but they were far from inactive. Expectation of God's intervention in the history of his people focused around a number of issues important to different groups. God's people would have the land of Israel restored to them, free from oppressive rulers. The temple would be restored, and pure worship would be re-established, free from compromise or corruption. There would be a renewal of covenant relationship with God, and this would be marked by the presence of God with his people through the gift of the Spirit of God. As a result, the law would be kept, and the people would have no king over them but God. These diverse ideas, all rooted in OT promise, were held together in the twin ideas of 'this age', in which God's face is hidden and his people suffer oppression, and the 'age to come' brought about by God's anointed one ('messiah' in Hebrew), in which God's presence is clear and his people liberated.

B. Quiet beginnings

The story of the NT starts quietly enough, though even here there are hints of what is to come. In a troublesome corner of the great Roman empire, towards the end of the reign there of Herod the Great (probably before 4 BC), a young woman is visited by a messenger from God who brings a startling message: she will conceive miraculously and the child who is born will be the one to fulfil all these hopes. The account of Jesus' birth is given mostly from the men's perspective in Matt. 1 and 2 and mostly from the women's perspective in Luke 1 and 2. Zechariah's song (Luke 1:68–79) spells out how this Jesus will be the hope of Israel. But the threat of another king sets the paranoid and insecure Herod on a murderous frenzy as he orders the killing of boys aged two and under in the Bethlehem area (Matt. 2:16). And yet the wider significance of the coming king is already there, as the wise 'Magi' from nations to the east come and pay homage in response to the cosmic sign of the star. All this 'fulfils' the prophets (Matt. 1:22; 2:17, 23; 4:14); with vivid detail it paints in the hope sketched in outline in the former Scriptures.

C. Dramatic developments

The story moves on, jumping perhaps twenty-five or thirty years to the dramatic arrival on the public scene of John the Baptist. Here all four Gospels join the story, each bringing its own distinctive emphasis. John's cousin Jesus joins the thronging crowds in this 'repentance' movement that has drawn large crowds ('the whole Judean countryside and all the people of Jerusalem', Mark 1:5, and 'the whole region of the Jordan', Matt. 3:5). Already there is recognition that Jesus is someone special, as John hesitates to baptize him. But special though Jesus is, his ministry cannot begin without the anointing of the Holy Spirit (signified by the descent of a dove from an open heaven), the word of affirmation as the beloved Son, and the discipline of temptations in the desert.

The drama of John's ministry is matched by the drama of the beginning of Jesus' own ministry. He strides across Galilee, proclaiming in word and deed the coming of the long-awaited kingdom of God, calling people to follow him as they turn from old ways of thinking and acting, to think again (the meaning of the term translated 'repentance') and trust in God.

D. The eye-witness view

Mark depicts Jesus' ministry in particularly dramatic fashion. A typical day sees Jesus driving out demons, healing the untouchable, clashing with the religious authorities, forgiving sins and calling those on the fringes to belong to his new community. All this is accompanied by radical new teaching that redefines traditional understandings of Sabbath, family, law and spiritual reality. This teaching comes from Jesus' own authority, and is authenticated by the spiritual power of his actions (Mark 1:27). And the result is crowds pressing in from every direction, straining to hear his words, longing to feel his healing touch.

Matthew too has this double emphasis on Jesus' action and his teaching, organizing his account into five blocks of teaching interspersed with stories of Jesus' healing. Here we have a new Moses bring a new law from the mountainside (Matt. 5:1), though this time with blessings as much as commands. And yet this new teaching is not so much new set against the old, but rather a new understanding of what has always been true (Matt. 5:17).

For Luke, this combination of teaching and healing spring from Jesus' understanding of his mission – to proclaim the year of the Lord's favour prophesied in Isaiah (Luke 4:18–19), a time which would bring wholeness of understanding as well as wholeness of life. Luke sees in Jesus' ministry a distinctive concern for those without power – women in a world belonging to men, the poor in a world controlled by the wealthy, the diseased in a world acclaiming the unblemished.

John's perspective is rather different. Less concerned with chronology, he appears to be writing for those already familiar with the other Gospels, perhaps especially the Gospel of Mark. The truth about Jesus is seen in seven of his miracles, depicted as seven 'signs' – not proofs, but glimpses into the reality of who he is – starting with the changing of water into wine at Cana (John 2:1–11) and ending with the raising of Lazarus (John 11:1–44). But the truth is also seen in Jesus' claims, in this case his seven declarations that 'I am', related to the seven signs and connecting his identity with the God of Israel. He is the bread of life (6:35), the light of the world (8:12), the door for the sheep (10:7) and the good shepherd (10:11), the resurrection and the life (11:25), the way, truth and life (14:6), and the true vine (15:1). John does not record the language of the kingdom of God on Jesus' lips as do the other Gospels. Instead he records Jesus' kingdom ministry as opening the way to 'eternal life', literally, 'life of the age [to come]' of Jewish expectation.

E. The turning point

As Jesus' ministry grows in its impact, it becomes a shared ministry; Jesus commissions and sends first the twelve (Matt. 10:5–14; Mark 6:7–13; Luke 9:1–5) and then seventy-two (Luke 10:1–12) to spread the good news of the kingdom, teaching, healing and driving out demons as he has done. But a crucial moment comes when Jesus hears of the execution of John the Baptist by Herod the Great's son, Herod Antipas (Matt. 14; Mark 6). This shows clearly the personal cost of the clash between the kingdom of God and the kingdoms of men. The turning point comes at the most northerly point of this Galilean phase of his ministry. In response to Jesus' question, Peter declares Jesus' true identity as messiah (Matt. 16:16; Mark 8:29; Luke 9:20), and yet the disciples still have much to learn about what true messiahship entails. From then on, Jesus 'resolutely set out for Jerusalem' (Luke 9:51) to meet his destiny and to take the conflict with the authorities to the heart of the nation's worship, the temple. From now on, his work and teaching are done 'on the way' to the cross. Glory and agony are set alongside one another as the path that Jesus must follow – and along with him, any who want to be his followers. Even at this turning point, the overflow of Jesus' ministry to the lost sheep of the house of Israel is a blessing to those beyond God's historic people (Matt. 15:21–28; Mark 7:24–30), giving a foretaste of what is to come.

F. The finale...

Like other 'lives' of important people in the ancient world, the Gospels focus most of their attention on the time which showed above everything else the importance of and the truth about their subject. If the subject was a great general, then the focus would be on an important battle; for a politician, perhaps an important speech. For Jesus, the telling moments were the days leading up to his crucifixion and resurrection, and in particular that final week.

Jesus enters Jerusalem on a donkey, as a king coming to his people in peace, just as it has been foretold. But he finds few who welcome his reign; his cleansing of the temple and his challenge to the religious authorities upset too many vested interests. While many of the people are still entranced by his teaching, the pressure amongst their leaders mounts, until they find in Judas a way to seize Jesus and bring him to trial. Knowing what is at hand, Jesus shares a last Passover meal with his disciples. Here he makes clear the purpose of his coming; the deliverance of God comes only at a great price. He is to be a new Passover lamb, following the pattern of the OT, but this time setting God's people – and not just them, but 'many' others too (Mark 10:45; 14:24) – free from the root of all bondage, from sin that enslaves all humanity. And at this moment of greatest sacrifice, even the disciples cannot face the cost of faithfulness, and one by one they betray him in his hour of greatest need.

But as in his temptations, as through all the demands and testing of his ministry, Jesus stays true to the end, even asking for forgiveness for those torturing him (Luke 23:34). John depicts this moment of greatest humiliation and apparent defeat as in fact the moment of greatest glory (John 12:23, 28) which ends with a cry of triumph: 'It is finished!' (John 19:30). Everything has been accomplished; Jesus' mission is complete. The promised water of life flows from his broken body for the sake of a thirsty world (John 19:34). And in this moment of victory-in-defeat, the truth of it, missed by the religious leaders, is understood by foreigners. The truth of Jesus' kingship is written in all the major languages (John 19:19–20) and a Roman centurion recognizes Jesus' identity in death (Mark 15:39).

G. ... or perhaps only the beginning

But this is not, of course, the end of the story. Even the tomb of a rich man, with a stone rolled across the entrance, could not contain this king. On the first day of the week, symbolizing the beginning of the new age, the stone is rolled away and the tomb is empty. Seeing the grave clothes still laid out, as if the body had passed through them (John 20:6–7), the disciples begin to grasp the truth of what has happened. As before his death, so after his resurrection, Jesus turns the conventions of his day upside down and appears first to women, even though their testimony has no status in Jewish law. One by one, he restores his disciples, forgiving their failure and nurturing their understanding. He is the one who fulfils all the Scriptures (Luke 24:27) – not so much in satisfying isolated predictions, but in following the pattern of God's dealings with his people. God turns into redemption the moments of supreme rejection by his people, leading ultimately to restoration for those who would receive it.

H. A new chapter

Mark's Gospel leaves us with an incomplete ending, and perhaps in that an invitation to write ourselves into the story. Luke takes up the challenge, and starts by showing how Jesus continued to do all the things he had begun in his earthly ministry (Acts 1:1). Having dealt with sin and broken the power of the ruler of this age in his death and resurrection, Jesus now ascends to be with his heavenly Father so that he might release the gift of the Spirit on his followers. Just as Jesus brought the kingdom of God into people's lives by the power of the Spirit (Matt. 12:28), so the same Spirit would empower Jesus' disciples for similar kingdom ministry.

The feast of Passover, which celebrated the exodus from Egypt, was followed fifty days later by the feast of Pentecost, which celebrated the giving of the law on Mount Sinai, showing God's people how they were now to live, free from the tyranny of slavery. As Jesus' death on the cross was a new Passover, so a new Pentecost came in the gift of the Spirit (Acts 2), the new way God would shape his people for a life of freedom and witness. Peter explains how this is the climax of God's dealings with his people (Acts 2:14–39), many people come to recognize Jesus as God's anointed one and put their faith in him (Acts 2:41), and the kingdom advances forcefully (see Matt. 11:12).

But as for Jesus, so for his followers: kingdom ministry leads to persecution. The apostles perform 'signs and wonders' amongst the people, who are at once fearful and amazed (Acts 5:12), but they are then arrested and flogged (Acts 5:40). Practical pressures lead to the appointment of seven men to manage the care of the growing group of followers of 'the Way', but one of them, Stephen, is eventually stoned to death for blasphemy (Acts 6 – 7). This leads to wider persecution and many believers are scattered to other cities. But hardship leads to fruitfulness, and the scattered believers share the message about Jesus wherever they go (Acts 8:4).

I. A new mission

The desire of the dispersed believers to share the message about Jesus leads them, almost inadvertently, to talk to non-Jews who also believe (Acts 11:19–21). At the same time, Peter is given a vision from God explaining that no-one should be considered unfit to hear the message. As a result, Peter tells a God-fearing Gentile centurion called Cornelius and his household the story of what Jesus has done. He knows that the message applies to them when he sees the Holy Spirit come upon all the listeners (Acts 10:44)!

One of the leading persecutors of Jesus' followers, a Pharisee named Saul, encounters the risen Jesus on the road to Damascus when heading there to arrest believers. He immediately starts sharing the good news, first to his fellow Jews, but then also to Gentiles. Eventually he becomes one of the leaders of the church in Antioch, and is sent by them on three successive missionary journeys, establishing communities of believers throughout the area now known as Turkey and on into Greece.

Because of the numbers of Gentiles coming to faith, there is a dispute about how far Gentile believers have to follow Jewish patterns of life to be followers of Jesus, and this is largely resolved at a council in Jerusalem (Acts 15). Other issues arise in the fledgling churches, and in response to some of these issues Paul writes letters to the different communities. Some of his letters are circulating more widely and are collected, eventually being added to accounts of the life and words of Jesus as part of the apostolic teaching.

Paul's letters address questions such as:

- How can Gentile believers be sure that they do not need to become Jews to be followers of Jesus?
- Will Jesus return soon, and what will happen to those who have already died?
- What is life like when led by the Spirit?
- What is the appropriate discipline for those who are not living out a life of holiness?
- How should we conduct ourselves when we meet together?
- What has Jesus' death achieved for us?
- What pattern of living follows on from understanding what God has done for us in Jesus?

Other leaders, including Peter and John, also wrote letters addressing further questions:

- How can we live with integrity whilst suffering for our faith?
- What does it mean to follow Jesus' example?
- What are the marks of a believing community?
- How can we understand what Jesus has done from the perspective of Jewish hope?

J. A new future

The story finishes with a vision, in the book of Revelation, in which the widening circle of mission eventually reaches every corner of the earth. It is a vision of the risen Jesus, walking amongst and protecting his persecuted people, in this case in the west of modern Turkey. Despite dissent from within and pressure from without, despite natural disasters and imperial oppression, Jesus the faithful witness will keep faith with his redeemed people from every nation, and invites them to keep faith in response. Their particular situation, like all the generations to follow, is caught up in the grand vision of the renewal of the whole created order, where God will meet his people face to face when Jesus comes again. In that moment all God's promises will reach their fulfilment, the kingdom will be made manifest, the work of Jesus will have achieved its full effect, and Jesus himself will be at the centre of it all.

NEW TESTAMENT BACKGROUND

A. A time prepared

Significant changes took place throughout the Mediterranean world during the time between the testaments that prepared the world for the advent of Christianity (see ch. 7 for historical survey). For example, the empires of Alexander and his heirs established Greek as the common language of commerce, diplomacy and scholarship. This allowed people from numerous ethnic groups in and around the Roman empire to communicate with one another on an unprecedented scale. The Roman system of roads and shipping lanes allowed people to travel throughout most of the empire with relative safety. It also served as the infrastructure for a communications network that allowed geographically distant persons and communities to stay in contact with one another. The new institution of the synagogue arose as an important institution in Jewish communities both in Palestine and in the diaspora (Jews living outside Palestine). Each of these developments allowed the Christian message to spread quickly from Palestine to the far reaches of the empire and beyond. They also set the stage for the Jesus movement to develop into the first truly multi-ethnic religious movement.

By NT times some Gentiles (non-Jews) were becoming discontented with the implausibility of polytheism and the separation of religious and moral practices. While Gentiles worshipped at temples dedicated to various deities, they typically looked elsewhere for moral instruction, such as to philosophers. The Hellenization crisis in the second century BC (see ch. 7) increased Jewish antipathy toward Gentiles, yet also made Judaism attractive to discontented Gentiles because of its commitment to monotheism and the Mosaic law. In Judaism religious devotion and ethics were entailed by one another. Food laws and Sabbath-keeping made the Jewish way of life distinctive and gave it the appearance of wholesomeness.

Sometimes Jews outside Palestine were treated harshly for being foreigners (as were other ethnic groups). But Gentiles could be found in many cities who were attracted to the 'Jewish philosophy'. A few would convert, an act requiring circumcision. Others, known as 'God-fearers', attended synagogue and followed Jewish moral standards but did not convert due to the repulsion many Gentiles felt toward circumcision. Early Christian preachers found a receptive audience among the God-fearers. It was through them that the Christian message was able to spread into the Gentile world.

B. Early Christians and Judaism

The NT should be read as the literary product of a *Jewish* religious movement, including those few books probably written by Gentiles (e.g. Luke and Acts). This will seem counter-intuitive to modern readers accustomed to thinking of early Christianity as a new religion that quickly separated from Judaism. But it should be remembered that *Jewish* and *Christian* were not mutually exclusive categories in the first century. Moreover, Jesus and his earliest followers all lived and died as Jews. The earliest Gentile members of the Jesus movement were God-fearers who had already associated with the Jewish community. In fact, the earliest Christians were more integrated into Second Temple Jewish society than some other Jewish groups. Knowledge of this fact was forgotten because of the way in which Rabbinic Judaism and Christianity developed in polemical distinction from one another after the temple's destruction in AD 70. But it can be readily illustrated by comparing the participation of different groups in the sacrificial worship of the temple.

The Jerusalem temple served as the most visible and concrete marker of Jewish identity until its destruction. Signs warned non-Jews not to enter its sacred precincts on pain of death. Samaritans worshipped the God of Israel and accepted the Mosaic law but they were still prohibited from offering sacrifice in the temple because they were not considered Jews. At the same time, a few Jewish groups did not worship at the temple but nonetheless remained Jewish, for example the Qumran community responsible for the Dead Sea Scrolls who thought the temple had become defiled.

In contrast, the Jerusalem church often met in the temple courts (Acts 2:46; 3:1; 5:25). The apostle Paul was arrested while at the temple to offer a sacrifice in fulfilment of a vow (Acts 21:17–26). According to early tradition, James the brother of Jesus frequently prayed at the temple for long periods of time until he was killed in AD 62. The fact that Christians were *permitted* to worship in the temple shows that they were recognized as Jews. The fact that they *wanted* to worship at the temple shows that they thought of their faith as a form of Judaism.

In fact, the early Christians considered their faith to be the true Judaism. As far as they were concerned, the rejection of Jesus called into question the authenticity of the Judaism practised by non-Christian Jews (cf. Rev. 2:9; 3:9). According to Paul, true Jews are followers of Christ who experience the circumcision of their hearts (Rom. 2:28–29). The earliest Christians perceived no contradiction between the confession 'Christ died for our sins according to the Scriptures' (1 Cor. 15:3) and participation in the sacrificial system, at least as long as the temple stood (cf. Heb. 9:8–10). On the contrary, they were zealous to obey God's law (cf. Acts 21:20). After all, it was only natural for sinners who repented in response to the gospel to worship God in the ways ordained in his law. This is also why some initially insisted that Gentile believers had to be circumcised, keep the Sabbath and follow the food laws (cf. Acts 15:1–29).

C. Other Jewish groups

First-century Judaism was diverse. Rabbinic Judaism did not begin to emerge as normative to most Jews until the second century, a generation or two after the temple was destroyed. Prior to that several competing groups could be identified. The most prominent of these were the Pharisees, Sadducees and Essenes. These groups disagreed with one another about various political and religious issues (politics and religion were inseparable). Some of their disagreements were theological and similar to issues debated by Christians today, e.g. predestination and free will. Their most serious disagreements, though, were about issues related to ritual purity, sacrificial procedures, the dates of Jewish festivals and the rules regulating the priesthood and operation of the temple. At the centre of their disputes was the proper interpretation of the various laws found in Exodus, Leviticus, Numbers and Deuteronomy. While all Jews accepted this Mosaic law as normative, they disagreed about how to apply it because there are inconsistencies in the formulation of various commandments and ambiguity about what to do when more than one law governs a situation. For example, when a festival falls on a Sabbath, do you offer the Sabbath offering, the festival offering, or both?

The *Essenes* were the smallest of the three major groups and required members to go through a three-year initiation process. They lived communally and one branch was also celibate. They were known for praying before sunrise, taking a daily purification bath and wearing distinctive white clothes. They ate common meals in silence, regarding them as sacred. They rejected free will and believed that God had predetermined everything. The sources disagree as to whether they believed in the resurrection of the righteous dead or a disembodied afterlife as in Greek thought. Many scholars think that an offshoot of the Essenes were responsible for the famous Dead Sea scrolls discovered at Qumran. This is not certain, but there were at least some significant commonalities.

The *Sadducees* were associated with the temple and the priesthood and were prominent in the Sanhedrin, the Jewish ruling council. They disagreed with the Pharisees on many legal issues related to ritual purity, temple ceremonies and Sabbath regulations. At times, though, the political and social climate obliged them to follow Pharisaic practices. They were known for rejecting any form of predestination in favour of a robust notion of human free will. They were also known for dismissing the elaborate hierarchy of angels espoused by others and the notion of resurrection (cf. Acts 23:8). Furthermore, they appear to have disregarded the notion of an afterlife altogether. In some ways the Sadducees might strike the modern reader as 'liberal', but in fact they were conservative in that they would not accept beliefs and practices that could not be clearly established from the Torah (i.e. the Pentateuch). The later two canonical divisions of the Hebrew Bible, the Prophets and the Writings, support some of the positions rejected by the Sadducees (e.g. Dan. 12:2 on resurrection). This suggests that they did not consider these writings to be as authoritative as the Law. Deeming them innovations, they also rejected practices which the Pharisees regarded as sanctioned by authoritative oral traditions.

The *Pharisees* are the most important of the Jewish groups for understanding the NT. They play a prominent role in the Gospels and Acts, and the Apostle Paul was a Pharisee. Theologically, the Pharisees were known for their belief in the resurrection of the dead, an elaborate hierarchy of angels, the compatibility of free will and predestination, and an authoritative legal tradition. They were laymen, not priests, and had a reputation as expert interpreters of the Mosaic law. Of special concern were issues related to ritual purity, tithing and the Sabbath. Today the Pharisees are popularly associated with legalism, but the nature of Pharisaic 'legalism' is often misunderstood.

Like other Jewish groups, the Pharisees believed that they should keep the law as part of the covenant between Israel and God. They prided themselves for being experts in the law who zealously kept it. But, their zeal to keep the law was not always what it appeared to be. The Pharisees employed clever legal reasoning and drew fine distinctions to determine precisely when the various commandments had been fulfilled or broken. Positive commandments require Israelites to do certain things. The Pharisees wanted to know the minimum that had to be done in order for them to have fulfilled the commandment. Other commandments are prohibitions. The Pharisees wanted to know precisely at what point the commandment was violated, i.e. how much they could do before breaking a commandment. In this regard their motive was probably like that of young people who want to know exactly how far they can go with their boyfriend or girlfriend before doing something immoral. Determining the precise parameters of the commandments in this way allowed the Pharisees to maintain a reputation for strictly observing the law while devising self-serving ways to constrict some commandments and liberalize others.

In the Dead Sea scrolls the Pharisees are accused of being 'seekers after smooth interpretations'. This seems to be a way of saying that the legal expertise of the Pharisees was used to find loopholes and make distinctions that would make following the law easier. Jesus similarly criticized the Pharisees for using extra-biblical legal traditions and distinctions to avoid fulfilling commandments that might prove costly or difficult (see Mark 7:9–13). The heart of Pharisaic legalism was not an attempt to impose legal requirements and good works in order to merit salvation. Rather, it was the tendency to devise self-serving interpretations of the law. These interpretations could also be used to attack the reputation of opponents. This is seen in the Gospels, for example, when Jesus is repeatedly accused of violating the Sabbath (e.g. Mark 2:23–28; 3:1–6; Luke 13:10–17; John 5:9–18; 9:1–34). But not all Pharisees approached the interpretation of the law in this manner. Some genuinely desired to serve and love God. While the Pharisees are often depicted as Jesus' chief opponents, a Pharisee named Nicodemus is portrayed as a disciple (John 3:1–21) as was his friend Joseph of Arimathea (John 19:38–39), probably also a Pharisee.

It is tempting to think that the Jewish groups functioned like competing religions or modern denominations. They did not. In the first century Judaism was not primarily a religion of bounded beliefs and practices. Rather, it was an ethnicity whose identity was expressed through various foundational beliefs and practices common to the entire ethnic group. These included belief in and worship of the God of Israel, the inspiration and authority of the Mosaic law, circumcision as a mark of God's covenant with his people, the observance of the Sabbath and food laws, and the centrality of the promised land and its temple. Just how these things were understood could be the subject of intense debate and mutual denunciation. The vast majority of Jews, however, did not belong to any of the named parties and were content simply to be Jews.

A few first-century texts outside the NT mention Jesus or individual Christians. Interestingly, none identify the Christians as a distinct group alongside the Pharisees, Sadducees and Essenes. Most Jewish groups were distinguished from one another by their mutually exclusive approaches to the interpretation of the law. The Christians, however, became an identifiable group because of their conviction that Jesus is the risen and soon-to-return messiah. It was therefore possible to be both a Christian and a member of at least one of the other groups. There were, for example, a number of men in the Jerusalem church who were

Pharisees (Acts 15:5). The apostle Paul continued to identify himself as a Pharisee as well (Acts 23:6), though he no longer found it something to boast about (Phil. 3:4–7).

D. Christian Jews and Gentiles

After Jesus' ascension his followers quickly established the centre of their activities in Jerusalem. Within twenty-five years Christian communities could be found in most major cities of the eastern Mediterranean as well as Rome itself. Christianity was initially established outside Palestine by Jewish pilgrims who had travelled to Jerusalem for one of the pilgrimage festivals and heard the gospel while they were there. Acts records one instance of this happening on the day of Pentecost (Acts 2:1–41). It is likely that diaspora Jews responded to the Christian message during subsequent festivals as well, though perhaps not in such numbers as on that initial Pentecost. The Christian message was taken to new regions when these pilgrims returned to their homes.

Within a few years Christian missionaries began to take their message to Jewish communities outside Palestine. Key to their success was the synagogue. It is not known when or where the first synagogues were built (they are not mentioned in the OT), but by the first century AD they were an important institution in Jewish society. They served as a place for the Jewish community to assemble on the Sabbath for prayer and study of the Torah. The formal service included prayer, Scripture reading, exposition and a benediction. The men then had opportunity for open discussion about the text. At this time any travelling teacher who might be present could share their ideas (e.g. Acts 13:15–16). Jesus had regularly proclaimed his message in the synagogues of Galilee. Sometimes this took place as part of the formal service (Luke 4:16–21), at other times probably during the discussion period. Early missionaries utilized Jesus' technique in diaspora synagogues.

Gentile God-fearers could be found in a few Palestinian synagogues, but not in as large numbers as in diaspora synagogues. Christian missionaries often found God-fearers to be more receptive to their message than their fellow Jews. While already associated with the Jewish community, these God-fearers had not been circumcised and thus were not Jews. This gave rise to a theological problem. The natural Jewish assumption was that any Gentile would need to be circumcised and keep the Mosaic law in order to be a full member of the Christian community. The apostle Paul insisted that Gentiles did not, in fact, need to be circumcised or keep most aspects of the law in order to be equal with Jews in the church. Moreover, Paul and his associates did not confine their proclamation to the synagogues. They also shared their message with Gentiles fully immersed in pagan culture and with no prior association with Judaism or its moral standards. This served to exacerbate the theological issue and led to many pastoral problems in the churches they founded. It also served as the bridge that allowed Christianity to fully enter the Gentile world and eventually transform it.

Most of the opposition Paul faced in his ministry came from Jews, both Christians and non-Christians, who vigorously opposed his teaching that Gentiles did not need to be circumcised. To them it was highly counter-intuitive to think that God would save Gentiles *as Gentiles*. Surely, they reasoned, Gentiles had to become part of Israel to experience the benefits of Israel's God and his messiah. This controversy dominated much of Paul's ministry, and many of the central themes of his letters, such as justification by faith, are directly related to the issues involved in the debate. Eventually a meeting was held in which the apostles and elders of the mother church in Jerusalem debated the issue. They determined that OT prophecy supported Paul's basic position (Acts 15:1–30; cf. Amos 9:11–12). In theory this settled the issue for the Christian community, but Paul's teachings were still subject to misunderstanding (cf. Acts 21:17–26). Of course, opposition also continued from non-Christian Jews who did not recognize the authority of the Jerusalem council. Nonetheless, his message won the day and by the middle of the second century the majority of Christians were Gentile converts. It is then, a generation after the last books of the NT were written, that it begins to make sense to think of Christianity and Judaism (i.e. Rabbinic Judaism) as truly separate from one another.

E. Jewish literature

Roman Catholic editions of the Bible include several Jewish works not found in Protestant editions. Catholics classify these books as Deuterocanonical ('second canon') while Protestants generally refer to them as the Apocrypha ('hidden books' – see ch. 1, D.2). Among these books are pious tales of courage and virtue (Tobit, Judith), wisdom literature similar to the book of Proverbs (Ecclesiasticus, Wisdom of Solomon) and historical narratives that describe events that took place in the intertestamental period (1 & 2 Maccabees). Protestants don't consider any of these books to be Scripture, but can cherish them for their devotional value in addition to the information they convey about Second Temple Judaism.

Other Jewish works have also been preserved that help us better understand the NT. The writings of Flavius Josephus recount the history of the Jewish people with a special focus on the events leading up to the Jewish revolt against Rome. Josephus mentions several people named in the NT, including Jesus, his brother James and John the Baptist. The works of Philo of Alexandria, a Jewish philosopher, inform us about Judaism in the diaspora and, to a lesser extent, Palestine. Philo is also important because later the Church Fathers utilized his philosophical ideas in their theology. The Dead Sea scrolls were produced by a dissident group living at Qumran near the Dead Sea, mostly in the second and first centuries BC. They are especially helpful because they give us a direct window into some of the issues debated by first-century Jews in Palestine. They have also helped scholars to better appreciate the Jewishness of several NT teachings that had previously been thought to have come from Greek philosophy. Insight into first-century Jewish beliefs, practices and scriptural interpretation can also be found in the motley assortment of narratives, apocalypses, letters, wisdom literature and other texts that modern scholars have grouped together under the (only partly accurate) title of Pseudepigrapha.

F. The New Testament

The books of the NT are simultaneously Jewish, Christian and Greco-Roman literature. They describe aspects of Jewish society and clearly utilize the conceptual categories of Second Temple Judaism. They address problems particular to Christian communities and develop Jewish ideas in light of what God had done through Christ. They also employ Greek language, literary forms and rhetorical techniques. In addition, there are numerous passages in the NT that assume knowledge of ancient Jewish, Greek or Roman customs. Scholars often find that other literature produced during the same period can enlighten our understanding of the NT. Greco-Roman literature is most useful for understanding the meaning of words, grammar and rhetorical techniques. Jewish literature informs us about most of the relevant history of the period as well as Jewish beliefs, practices and attitudes. We also know that some of this other Jewish literature is alluded to in the NT. So, reading other Second Temple Jewish literature along with the NT can be especially fruitful.

The reader of the NT should keep in mind that most people in the first century were illiterate. Those who could read nearly always read aloud. When authors wrote, they were concerned about how their work would sound when it was read. In addition, the books of the NT were written specifically to be read in the churches. Modern readers can draw closer to the world of the NT if, on occasion, they listen to the text rather than read it from the page. (Audio versions are now widely available.)

And when they listen to the words read, they should be mindful to listen for what God is saying to his people through the NT – and not merely to hear it, but also to do it (Jas 1:22).

NEW TESTAMENT THEOLOGY

A. What is New Testament theology?

New Testament theology is part of *biblical theology*, which may be defined as the progressive revelation of God through particular persons and periods. Biblical theology is distinct from *systematic theology* in that the former concerns truth from the perspective of the individual biblical writers while the latter concerns the systematization of truth based on the complete revelation of God. Systematic theology is at heart a *philosophical* discipline, asking the question 'What is truth?' Biblical theology is fundamentally *historical*, asking 'What is truth from the perspective of individual authors and periods?' In this sense biblical theology focuses on the progress of revelation and the diversity of Scripture, asking 'What did Isaiah believe?' 'What did Paul believe?', etc. It then seeks an internal unity behind these authors' diverse expressions of faith.

Any systematic theology that claims to be biblical should have biblical theology as its foundation. This is because biblical theology is simply 'theology done in context'. For example, exegesis of the Pauline letters produces theological conclusions which may be developed into a 'Pauline theology'. This Pauline perspective is then compared to other biblical authors to analyse differences and similarities and integrate them into a broader NT theology. Since evangelicals affirm the ultimate unity of biblical truth, there is an assumption that the integration of the Bible's diverse expressions will result in a theology that is complementary and consistent rather than contradictory.

Based on our definition above, we can see that the goals of NT theology are threefold: (1) to discern the theological themes and emphases of each biblical author; (2) to compare and contrast these perspectives with other books and authors; and (3) to seek to integrate these theologies into a comprehensive and coherent unified theology. In our discussion of NT themes and theology below, we will first suggest a common theme of integrated theology, and will then identify some of the diverse expressions of that theme throughout the NT.

Certain limitations of NT theology should also be noted. First, the NT documents are all occasional in nature, written to address specific needs and concerns. No biblical author set out to write a systematic theology or a comprehensive statement of faith. We must therefore expect gaps in our understanding of each author's theological perspective. It is unsafe to draw conclusions based on silence, assuming what an author must or must not have believed. Similarly, all the theology of the NT is *task theology*, truth brought to bear on real-life situations. Caution must be exercised before assuming that every statement is intended to be universal in application. For example, are Paul's commands related to the role of women in 1 Tim. 2:11–15 meant to apply to the church of all time? This is a question outside the scope of biblical theology. It must be dealt with in the larger context of biblical interpretation and the present-day application of the text.

B. Salvation history

Does NT theology have a central theme from which all other categories emerge? While a variety of themes have been proposed, perhaps the most appropriate is *salvation history* – the idea that God is acting through human history to deliver his people and to bring them back into relationship with him.

Salvation history in the OT. It is impossible to comprehend the theology of the NT without the foundation laid in the OT, the Hebrew Scriptures. The OT recounts that God created a perfect universe, but this world became fallen through the rebellion and disobedience of Adam and Eve (Gen. 1 – 3). The rest of Scripture is the account of God's redemptive purpose for his creation. Through a series of covenants – with Abraham (Gen. 12, 15, 17), the nation of Israel (Exod. 19 – 31), David (2 Sam. 7), and finally a promised 'new covenant' (Jer. 31:31–34) – God gradually brings redemption to sinful humanity and restoration to his creation. (See ch. 2.)

Salvation history in the NT. NT writers assume this OT background and announce that with the coming of Jesus the Messiah, God has inaugurated the final redemption and renewal. Through Jesus' life, death and resurrection, the judgment on humanity has been reversed and the end-time resurrection has begun. God is now creating a new people of God – the church – whose mission is to proclaim the message of salvation to the whole world. All who respond in faith by confessing Jesus to be the Saviour receive salvation from their sins and a renewed relationship with God.

While this framework of salvation permeates the NT, it is expressed differently by different authors. Some of the clearest expositors of salvation history are Luke, Paul and the unknown author of Hebrews. Luke's grand scheme throughout Luke–Acts, his two-volume work, is to demonstrate that the coming of Jesus and the establishment of the church represents the fulfilment of the promises to Israel and the culmination of God's purpose for the world. For Luke, Jesus is the centrepoint of human history; 'all the Scriptures' point to him (Luke 24:27). For Paul, God's sending of his Son represents the 'fullness of time' (ESV), and leads to the redemption of God's children (Gal. 4:4–5). With Jesus, the fulfilment of the ages has come (1 Cor. 10:11). The writer to the Hebrews draws a strong dichotomy between the old and the new. While the revelation given through the prophets was partial and preparatory, the revelation through Jesus the Son of God is complete and perfect (Heb. 1:1–4). The sacrificial and atoning death of Christ on the cross is more than the fulfilment of the promises. It is the only true reality. The OT temple and sacrifices were a mere shadow for what was to come, and could never take away sins. They pointed forward to the true salvation accomplished through Jesus' high-priestly service and sacrificial death on the cross (Heb. 10:1–18).

C. Jesus Christ: God's agent of redemption

Throughout the NT Jesus is presented as God's agent of salvation. Yet different aspects of his person and work are developed by different authors. The following are some of the more important Christological categories of the NT.

Jesus the Messiah. The most common title for Jesus in the NT is *christos* ('Christ'), a Greek translation of the Hebrew *mashiach* ('Messiah'), meaning 'anointed one'. To be anointed meant to be set apart by God for a special task. In the OT period, priests, kings and prophets were anointed for service. Most commonly, 'the Lord's anointed' means Israel's king, chosen and appointed by God. By the first century AD the term was used of God's agent of end-time salvation – 'the Messiah'. First-century messianic expectations took on a variety of forms, but focused especially on the Davidic Messiah, the king from David's line who would re-gather Israel, defeat the nation's enemies, and reign in righteousness and justice in Jerusalem, the city of God.

Jesus' identity as Israel's Messiah is most prominent in the Synoptic Gospels. Matthew identifies Jesus as the royal Messiah, the son of David born in Bethlehem who fulfils the promises made to Israel. For Luke, Jesus is also the Davidic Messiah (Luke 1:32–35), but with special emphasis on the theme that Jesus is the Saviour of all people everywhere. The salvation which began in Israel is now going forth to the whole world. Mark presents Jesus as a mysterious and enigmatic figure. He is the mighty Messiah and Son of God who challenges and defeats the forces of Satan. But his task is not the military conquest of Rome, as many in Israel had hoped. It is to suffer and die as a ransom payment for sins (Mark 10:45). Victory over sin and Satan comes through suffering and death.

Son of Man. All four Gospels affirm that Jesus' favourite self-designation was 'Son of Man', from a common Hebrew term for 'human being' (*ben adam*). Jesus seems to have used this as a title both to affirm his solidarity with the human race, and as a veiled allusion to Dan. 7:13–14, where an exalted messianic figure – one 'like a son of man' (i.e. having human form) – comes before God and is given authority, glory and an eternal kingdom. In the Synoptic Gospels, the title appears predominantly in three key contexts: affirming Jesus' authority on earth (Mark 2:10; 2:28), predicting his coming death (Mark 8:31; 9:31; 10:33), and describing his return in glory (Mark 13:26; 14:62).

Son of God. Closely related to the title Messiah is 'Son of God'. In the OT a variety of figures are called sons of God – from angels, to Israel as a nation, to the coming king from David's line (Pss. 2:7; 89:26; cf. 2 Sam. 7:14). In some NT contexts 'Son of God' is practically synonymous with 'Messiah'. and carries the sense of God's representative ruler (Mark 3:11; 14:61; Matt. 16:16; John 1:49). Elsewhere the title carries a deeper significance as the divine Son in unique relationship with God the Father (Matt. 11:27 // Luke 10:22; Rom. 1:3; 8:3; Gal. 4:4; Heb. 1:1–14, etc.). John presents Jesus as the divine Son who came from heaven to bring glory to the Father and eternal life to all who believe (John 3:16–18).

Second Adam. Jesus' unique role in salvation history is especially evident in his role as the second 'Adam', a portrait explicit in Paul and implicit elsewhere in the NT (cf. Luke 3:38; Heb. 2). Just as sin and death entered the world through the disobedience of one man, Adam, so forgiveness and resurrection life came through the obedient sacrifice of one man, Jesus Christ (Rom. 5:12–21; 1 Cor. 15:21–22).

High priest and once-for-all sacrifice for sins. The portrait of Jesus as eschatological high priest is the unique contribution of the author of Hebrews. Writing to a Jewish–Christian community in danger of reverting back to the social and political safety of Judaism, the author affirms the superiority of Christ and the new covenant. Jesus is a high priest according to the order of Melchizedek, a priestly order greater than the OT order of Aaron and Levi. Yet Jesus is more than a priestly mediator, offering sacrifices to God on behalf of human beings. He is also the *means* of atonement, who offers himself as a single sacrifice for sins for all time and all people. Jesus' death on the cross inaugurates the new covenant and achieves eternal salvation for those with a persevering faith.

God in human form. While Jesus is explicitly identified as 'God' in only a few passages (John 1:1; 20:28; Titus 2:13; 2 Pet. 1:1), throughout the NT divine attributes and titles are attributed to him. John's prologue presents Jesus as the pre-existent 'Word' (*logos*), who was 'with God' (i.e., distinct from the Father) and yet 'was God'. He is the creator of all things, and the 'Word made flesh' who came to earth to reveal the invisible God (1:1–18). Elsewhere in John, Jesus says that to know him is to know the Father (14:7–9), and he claims to have existed before Abraham (8:58). Here Jesus seems to be identifying himself as the 'I am', God's self-revelation to Moses in Exod. 3:14–15.

Other authors take up similar language. Hebrews describes Jesus as the creator of all things, 'the radiance of God's glory and the exact representation of his being' (Heb. 1:2–3). For Paul, Jesus is the one Lord 'through whom all things came and through whom we live' (1 Cor. 8:6). He is 'the image of the invisible God', and in him 'all the fullness of the Deity lives in bodily form' (Col. 1:15; 2:9). In Revelation Jesus is called 'the Alpha and the Omega, the First and the Last, the Beginning and the End' (Rev. 22:13; cf. 1:17; 2:8), titles elsewhere attributed to the Lord God (Rev. 1:8; 21:6; Isa. 44:6; 48:12). The title 'Lord' (Greek *kyrios*), commonly used in the Greek OT (Septuagint) to translate the divine name Yahweh, is applied to Jesus throughout the NT, often with divine connotations (e.g. 1 Pet. 3:15). Similarly, quotations referring to God in the OT are sometimes applied to Jesus (Acts 2:20–21; Rom. 10:13; Heb. 1:10). These references confirm that the early church viewed Jesus as more than God's agent or spokesperson. He is the real presence of God with his people.

D. Salvation: the goal of redemptive history

Various images and metaphors are used in the NT to describe the nature of the salvation achieved through Jesus Christ.

The kingdom of God. The Synoptic Gospels affirm that Jesus' central message concerned the coming of the 'kingdom of God'. The OT concept of God's kingdom was dynamic and multi-dimensional. It could refer to God's sovereignty over the cosmos *in the present*, or the consummation of that reign *in the future*. Jesus' proclamation of the kingdom included both dimensions. He spoke of entering the kingdom in the present, but also the final establishment of the kingdom at the end. At its heart, receiving the kingdom means submitting to God's reign – his sovereign purpose and plan for the world. It means faith in Jesus the Messiah, who is both herald and executor of God's final salvation. It also means embracing the kingdom ethic: love for God and unconditional love for human beings – even one's enemies.

Eternal life in the present. While the Synoptics speak of salvation especially with reference to the kingdom of God, John's Gospel emphasizes *eternal life.* Eternal life in John is more than a future condition; it is true spiritual life in the present. Jesus says, 'I have come that they may have life, and have it to the full' (John 10:10). While he will raise the dead to eternal life on the last day (6:40), Jesus is already the resurrection and the life, bestowing eternal life on those who believe (11:25). This is because eternal life is equivalent to *knowing God,* a relationship with the Father through the Son (17:3).

A future inheritance kept in heaven. While the Gospel of John emphasizes the present, other writers stress the future dimensions of salvation. This is especially important since the church is experiencing suffering and longs for future deliverance. Writing to persecuted believers in Asia Minor, Peter encourages perseverance and hope in 'an inheritance that can never perish, spoil or fade ... kept in heaven for you'. Through faith believers are 'shielded by God's power until the coming of the salvation that is ready to be revealed in the last time' (1 Pet. 1:3–5). The writer of Hebrews speaks of a Sabbath rest which believers must strive to enter through perseverance and enduring faith (Heb. 4:11; 10:36; 12:1–3).

Reconciliation through justification. For Paul salvation means especially reconciliation with God, the restoration of a right relationship with him (2 Cor. 5:17–21; Rom. 5:1). Though all people are sinners who fall short of God's righteous standards, God 'justifies', or declares righteous, those who have faith in Christ's atoning death on the cross. Justification is a free gift of God, bestowed on all who believe (Rom. 3:23–26). Salvation comes through identification with Christ in his life, death and resurrection. Believers are now incorporated 'in Christ', dying with him to their old life of sin and being raised with him to new resurrection life (Rom. 6:3–4). Now adopted as children of God, believers receive the Spirit of God as the seal and assurance of their future glorification (2 Cor. 1:22).

E. The Holy Spirit: God's power and presence with his people

While the OT speaks of the 'Spirit of God' primarily in the sense of the manifestation of God's power and presence, in the NT the Holy Spirit is identified more specifically as distinct from the Father and the Son. The most developed theologies of the Holy Spirit appear in Luke, John and Paul.

In Luke–Acts the Holy Spirit is associated especially with the fulfilment of prophecy, the evidence of the arrival of God's end-time of salvation. In Luke's birth narrative, the Spirit-inspired renewal of prophecy after some 400 years of silence confirms that God's final deliverance is about to arrive. Elizabeth and Zechariah are filled with the Spirit when they break into prophetic utterance (Luke 1:41, 67), and the Spirit rests upon righteous Simeon, granting guidance and revelation (2:25–27). During Jesus' public ministry, the Spirit is identified uniquely with him. In fulfilment of OT prophecy (Isa. 42:1; 61:1–2), the Messiah is 'anointed' by the Spirit at his baptism and 'filled with the Spirit' to accomplish the messianic task (Luke 3:22; 4:1, 14, 18; 10:21). Following his resurrection, Jesus ascends to the right hand of God and – as promised (Luke 24:49; Acts 1:4–5) – pours out the Spirit upon his disciples (Acts 2:16–21; Joel 2:28–32). Throughout Acts the Spirit guides and empowers the church to take the gospel to the ends of the earth.

John shares with Luke–Acts a special interest in the work of the Spirit. Here also the Spirit represents the continuing presence of Jesus in his church, guiding and directing the disciples on their mission. Yet while Luke emphasizes the role of the Spirit as sign of the new age, John presents the Spirit as *another* counsellor (paraclete), who will act in Jesus' place to mediate the presence of the Father. As Jesus imparted life, light and knowledge of the Father to the disciples, so now the Spirit will do the same thing. He will guide them into all truth, testifying to Jesus and reminding them of all he taught them (John 14:26; 15:26).

The most comprehensive theology of the Holy Spirit comes from the letters of Paul. For Paul, life 'in the Spirit' represents all that believers are and have by virtue of their reception of the salvation available through Jesus Christ. The Holy Spirit is the agent of redemption who washes, sanctifies and justifies the believer (Rom. 15:16; 1 Cor. 6:11; 12:13; 2 Thess. 2:13; Titus 3:5). He is the very presence of God (2 Cor. 3:17–18), who indwells, fills, guides, enlightens and empowers believers (Rom. 8:9–14; 15:19; 1 Cor. 2:10–14; 3:16; Gal. 3:5; 5:18). He is the bestower of spiritual gifts, providing unity and spiritual vitality to the church (1 Cor. 12:7–13; Eph. 4:3–4). He provides peace and assurance of salvation, and is the seal and guarantee of our final salvation (Rom. 8:13–16, 23; 2 Cor. 1:22; 5:5; Gal. 4:6; Eph. 1:13; 4:30). Life 'in the flesh' (fallen human life apart from God) leads to death; while life 'in the Spirit' leads to peace and life.

F. The church: the Spirit-filled community of salvation history

Throughout the NT, the community of salvation is the church, the people of God indwelt and guided by the Spirit of God in the new age of salvation. The Greek term *ekklesia* means a congregation or assembly, and in the NT usually refers to a congregation of believers in a particular place. At times, however, it carries the universal sense of believers everywhere (Matt. 16:18; Gal. 1:13; Eph. 1:22; 3:10, 21; Col. 1:18, 24). The church's task is to manifest the presence of God in the world and to take the message of salvation to all people everywhere. While this portrait of the church permeates the NT, certain themes and metaphors are emphasized by particular authors.

For Luke the church is the end-time people of God, the restored remnant of Israel together with the Gentiles who have been incorporated into the people of God. The church is established on the day of Pentecost, when Jesus, now ascended to the right hand of God, pours out the Spirit on his disciples, who then boldly proclaim the message of salvation. The church's strength and vitality comes from the power and guidance of the Spirit, and from unity based on the apostles' teaching, fellowship, breaking bread, and prayer (Acts 2:42–47). Its success and phenomenal growth confirms that this is no human endeavour, but is truly the work of God (Acts 5:39).

Paul uses a variety of metaphors for the church (temple, household, etc.), but the most important is that of the body of Christ. This metaphor emphasizes both the unity and diversity of the church. As one body filled with one Spirit and serving one Lord, the church strives together for the common goal of the gospel. Like the individual parts of a body, each member exercises unique Spirit-bestowed gifts for the common good (Rom. 12:4–8; 1 Cor. 12 – 14; Eph. 4:1–16).

Peter develops a number of metaphors for the church from OT descriptions of Israel. The church is 'a chosen people, a royal priesthood, a holy nation, God's special possession', and all this with the purpose 'that you may declare the praises of him who called you out of darkness into his wonderful light' (1 Pet. 2:9).

Baptism. Throughout the NT, incorporation into the church comes through baptism, the outward sign of an inward cleansing and renewal by the Spirit. For Paul in particular, baptism is symbolic of incorporation in Christ and identification with him in his death, burial and resurrection (Rom. 6:3–4).

The Lord's Supper. In worship the church celebrates the Lord's Supper (eucharist/communion), a rite inaugurated by Jesus on the night before his crucifixion. The Lord's Supper is a remembrance of Christ's sacrificial death on the cross and an anticipation of his return in glory. The bread represents his body, given up as a sacrifice of atonement. The wine represents his shed blood and the inauguration of the new covenant (Luke 22:17–20; 1 Cor. 11:23–26).

Leadership in the church. Leaders in the church are identified by a variety of titles: apostles, elders, overseers, deacons, pastors, etc. No specific model of church governance is established, since the NT documents are occasional in nature and were written before patterns for such offices were codified. What *is* normative throughout the NT is that church leaders must be Spirit-filled people of integrity, with a good reputation in the community and behaviour that is above reproach.

G. The goal: consummation of redemptive history

Throughout the NT, the completion of salvation history is the second coming of Christ to judge and to rule. The Synoptic Gospels identify Jesus as the Son of Man who will return on the clouds of heaven to gather the elect and to judge the wicked. Believers are called to be watchful and prepared, because they do not know the day or the hour when he will return (Matt. 24 – 25; Mark 13; Luke 17, 21). Although the Gospel of John emphasizes eternal life as a present possession, Jesus also teaches that he is going away to prepare a place for his people, and will return to gather them to himself (John 14:1–3, 28; 21:23).

Paul speaks of the return of Christ as our hope of deliverance from enemies and from the wrath of God coming against the world (1 Thess. 1:10). Christ will descend from heaven with the voice of the archangel and with the trumpet call of God. Believers who have died will be raised in glorified bodies and those who are still alive will be instantly transformed into incorruptible, immortal bodies (1 Cor. 15:50–57; 1 Thess. 4:13–18).

The book of Revelation presents the most developed description of the end-time (Greek *eschaton*, from which we get 'eschatology'). At its climax, Christ returns on a white horse with the armies of heaven. He defeats the wicked nations, binds Satan in the abyss, raises the righteous dead, and reigns on earth for a thousand years. Following the thousand years, Satan is released and instigates a final revolt against God. He is defeated and cast into the lake of fire, the 'second death'. God creates a new heaven and a new earth, and the new Jerusalem, the holy city, descends from heaven. God will dwell with his people; he will wipe every tear from their eyes; death and suffering will be no more (Rev. 19 – 21). Salvation history concludes with the restoration of all things to a relationship with the creator God. While the nature of the thousand years (the 'millennium') is debated – whether present or future, literal or figurative – the message of the book is clear: God is the sovereign Lord of all, who will right every wrong and bring history to its destined conclusion.

Throughout the NT the final state of the wicked is most commonly referred to as 'hell' or 'Gehenna' (Greek *geena*; Matt. 5:22, 29; 10:28; 18:9; 23:15, 33; etc.). Gehenna is a Latin term derived from the Hebrew *ge'hinnom*, 'Valley of Hinnom' – originally an OT place of pagan sacrifices. A variety of images are used to describe this final state: eternal fire and torment (Matt. 25:41, 46; Mark 9:43–48; Jude 7); outer darkness (Matt. 8:12); the pit or Abyss (Rev. 9:1–2, 11); the lake of fire and sulphur (Rev. 20:10); and the second death (Rev. 21:8). Interpreters are divided on whether these images are literal or figurative and, especially, what they denote. Some suggest that they depict the eternal conscious torment of the wicked. Others claim such torture would be unjust punishment for temporal sins, and that the images rather represent utter destruction – the annihilation rather than the unending torture of the wicked. In either case, the primary characteristic of hell is the agony of separation from our creator God, who is the only source of life, joy and fulfilment.

The final state of the righteous is in the presence of God (Rev. 21:3), usually referred to as 'heaven', but also with terms like 'paradise' (Luke 23:43; 2 Cor. 12:4; Rev. 2:7) and 'the new Jerusalem' (Rev. 3:12; 21:2). Heaven is described as a place (and a state) of security, rest and bliss, where believers will experience complete fellowship with the Father and the Son for all eternity. Sorrow, evil and death will be no more (John 14:2–3; 1 Thess. 4:17; Heb. 4:9–11; Rev. 21:3–4). Apart from these generalities, little is said about the details of life in the eternal state. The reason, no doubt, is that it is so qualitatively different from our own that finite minds are incapable of comprehending it. As Paul writes, 'What no eye has seen, what no ear has heard, what no human mind has conceived – these things God has prepared for those who love him' (1 Cor. 2:9).

NEW TESTAMENT INTERPRETATION

A confident and appropriate reading of any text recognizes its key features and considers its stated purposes. This is just as true of a novel, an engineering manual, a poem or a TV guide as it is of the Bible. Essentially, the NT is three things: *literature*, *history* and *theology*. These three aspects correspond to its impulses to engage, record and teach respectively. To bring us into relationship with God through Jesus Christ is its overriding purpose.

A. The New Testament as literature

The NT consists of three main types of literature, or genres. The Gospels and Acts are narrative, the book of Revelation is apocalyptic and the rest is letters. Subtypes appear within these, including genealogies, parables, miracles, sermons, proverbs, vice-lists, hymns and confessions. Whereas some are more straightforward than others, each has unique features that the interpreter must bear in mind. The best interpreters notice the details of the passage they are reading without losing sight of the overall thrust of the book, and they also respond to the impact of the text on our senses and emotions. Rather than merely reading to gain information, the literary nature of the NT encourages us to 'stop and smell the roses'. As good literature, the NT does not merely inform but unnerves, enthrals, inspires and transforms.

Two of the Gospels tell us their purpose. Luke wrote that Theophilus might 'know the certainty of the things' he had been taught concerning Jesus (Luke 1:4), and John 'that you may believe that Jesus is the Messiah, the Son of God, and that by believing you may have life in his name' (John 20:30–31). Thus the main purpose of the Gospels is to lead people to put their trust in Jesus as their Lord and Saviour and then to follow him in discipleship. This can be easily illustrated with reference to the Gospels' major features.

The many miracle stories in the Gospels are clues or 'signs' (John 20:30) to the identity of Jesus. They demonstrate his power over nature, evil and sickness and the extent of his dominion and authority. Our main response is not to look for similar experiences but to mimic the disciples' reaction: 'The men were amazed and asked, "What kind of man is this?"' (Matt. 8:27). Other actions of Jesus equally point to his unique identity. His entry into Jerusalem on a donkey with the adulation of the crowds (Matt. 21:1–11, etc.) stamps him as a king, but the humble beast on which he rode marks his agenda as distinct from that of military liberation.

Parables are among the Gospels' most puzzling yet alluring features. These are stories Jesus told to describe his kingdom, his return, future judgment, and how disciples should behave. They can pack a punch like a good political cartoon, as in the Good Samaritan (Luke 10:25–37), where the hero isn't the religious worker but the despised foreigner. Parables dress profound truths in memorable and provocative garb. Instead of merely stating that finding God is supremely valuable, Jesus said, 'The kingdom of heaven is like treasure hidden in a field. When a man found it, he hid it again, and then in his joy went and sold all that he had and bought that field' (Matt. 13:44).

In terms of application when reading the Gospels, an important task is to distinguish between what was unique to Jesus' context and what is exemplary for all believers. We should not expect every chapter in the Gospels to contain specific instructions for our daily lives; application is not as simple as doing what Jesus told the disciples to do. Clearly, some of the commands are situation-specific. Even within one Gospel not everything applies uniformly. For example, in Matt. 10:5–6 Jesus told the Twelve to minister only to fellow Jews, but in 28:19 they are to go to all ethnic groups. The promise in John 14:26 that the Holy Spirit will remind the disciples of everything Jesus had said to them obviously does not include us. We should also take care not to take the many figures of speech literally. The command to gouge out your eye in Matt. 5:29 is a vivid way of recommending drastic action to avoid temptation. Similarly, the call in Matt. 6:3 not to 'let your left hand know what your right hand is doing' when you give to the poor concerns the motives of seeking human praise rather than being an attack on keeping financial records.

This is not to say that the distinctiveness of Jesus' life limits its relevance. In John 3 and 4 Jesus has conversations with a religious leader and a woman on the fringes of society. If the former, Nicodemus, finds Jesus perplexing, the latter, the Samaritan woman, responds in faith and becomes a witness to her people. Such narratives invite readers to consider the great reversal of the kingdom of God, its universal appeal and the surprising nature of God's grace. To give another example, while Jesus' death and resurrection are obviously unique, his followers are called to give up their lives in imitation, dying to self-centredness (Luke 9:23).

Acts narrates the progress of the gospel from a small gathering of Jewish disciples of the earthly Jesus in Jerusalem, across formidable boundaries, to Paul's bold and unhindered preaching of the risen and ascended Jesus to Gentiles in Rome. Hence its main purpose is to report the progress of the faith and to show how this is in continuity with both the time of Jesus and the time of Israel. What God is doing through the apostles in the early church is the activity of Jesus and the Spirit, and the climax of salvation history. The consistent message to which we are still called to respond is that salvation is to be found in Jesus (e.g. Acts 4:12; 16:31).

The question for application with reference to much of Acts concerns whether what is narrated is prescriptive for the church today or merely descriptive of the early church and its experience. Like the Gospels, the narrative of Acts provides clues as to its correct appropriation. The sharing of goods in the community in 2:44–45 and 4:32–35 is a case in point. Acts records that the practice led to positive results, including the expansion of the church, but also to the judgment of Ananias and Sapphira (5:1–11). So in general, sharing of possessions is strongly commended. Should we then set up comparable communities of shared goods? Since in 6:1–7 and 11:27–30 different approaches are used to make provision for those in material need, the model of communal sharing in chs. 2 and 4 is not to be adopted in all circumstances.

Revelation, like Matt. 24 – 25, represents apocalyptic literature. Prone to major misunderstanding, such texts are not meant to be read as code for interpreting contemporary events or predicting the second coming. Rather, in this genre, past, present and future events are presented in symbolic garb to bring encouragement to God's people in difficult times. As the letters to the seven churches show, the setting of Revelation includes persecution by the emperor (2:3, 10, 13; 3:10), harassment by the synagogue (2:9; 3:9), compromise urged and practised by false teachers (2:2, 6, 14, 15, 20), and complacency related to excessive wealth (2:4–5; 3:1–3; 3:15–17). The eschatology of Revelation calls its readers to alert resistance to the seductive powers of the present age and an active obedience to a merciful God who will make all things new.

A major feature of the literary nature of the NT is its wide use of figurative language. For example, 1 Corinthians compares the church to a cultivated field in 3:5–9, a temple in 3:10–17 and a body in 12:12–27. The right approach to such metaphors is to discern the relevant comparison, and the danger is over-interpretation. In all likelihood, the author is only drawing on a small range of possible resemblances. In 1 Cor. 3:5–9, using the analogy of the church as a garden with servants, Paul points out that it makes no sense to venerate your favourite minister, because they are just serving God who assigned them their tasks (v. 5); it is God who causes the church to grow (v. 6). In comparison with God who gives the growth, church leaders are nothing (v. 7) and God, not the Corinthians, is the one who assesses the workers, giving the appropriate reward for their toil (v. 8). Metaphors carry an affective impact and create a mood and tone for the passage. They cue the reader as to how to feel as much as what to think. The base character of the image in question, with unskilled farm labourers and a common field, impresses upon the readers the unimpressive and menial nature of the work of Christian ministers and add weight to Paul's case for 'no more boasting about human leaders' (3:21).

B. The New Testament as history

1. The NT and its historical context

The NT was written two thousand years ago, in Greek. So it is foreign to most modern readers in terms of culture, customs and geography. As on London Underground platforms, we do well to 'mind the gap'. An understanding of the historical background is sometimes crucial to its interpretation and application. For instance, the words of Jesus to turn the other cheek (Matt. 5:39) are not a recommendation to put up with physical abuse, but a call not to retaliate when mistreated; a 'slap on the cheek' in the ancient world was a form of insult rather than an act of violence. Changed social conditions may also blunt the impact of the NT's teaching today. The NT's consistent advocacy of humility as a virtue was revolutionary in its day. To 'value others above yourselves' in humility (Phil. 2:3) was unheard of in a society obsessed with preserving one's status and honour and avoiding shame. Until God's Messiah took the form of a servant and was crucified, humility was thought of negatively as servility, the domain of the pitiful and weak. The more we know about life in the days of Jesus and the apostles, from washing feet to forms of travel, conditions of work to building materials, the better equipped we are to understand it accurately.

The fact that all the NT letters arise out of and are intended for specific situations makes them trickier to interpret than at first sight. Initially, they were each addressed to one Christian congregation or individual. Who wrote, to whom and to what ends, are questions that must be answered if these letters are to be read aright. As to be expected when reading someone else's mail, some imagination is required to reconstruct what is going on. In 1 Corinthians, for example, it is clear that Paul had planted the church in Corinth and that problems had arisen since his departure. The precise nature of their faults may never be known, but some sense that Paul is correcting them is needed in order to put his words in context.

The next step is to work out which commands in the letters are timeless in nature and which apply only under certain circumstances. Some statements are clearly ageless, such as Paul's conclusion that 'all have sinned and fall short of the glory of God' (Rom. 3:23), where 'all,' in the context of Rom. 1:18 – 3:20, means every human being. Sometimes, however, the rationale for a particular command does not work in other cultures. The reason Paul insists on head coverings for women in church in 1 Cor. 11 was that a covered head suggested sexual fidelity. Since in our culture a hat carries no such symbolism, we should look for other ways to be true to his instructions.

2. The NT as a historical record

The NT is not only historical in the sense that its origins lie in the distant past, it is also history in terms of its subject matter: it purports to record historical events. The Gospels, for instance, are examples of a recognized category of Greek historical writing, namely, the biography.

And most of the letters are pages from chapters in the lives of real churches.

A fair assessment of the available evidence supports the reliability of the NT documents. Obviously, the NT does not follow the conventions of modern historiography with its attention to full documentation and precise quotation. Nonetheless, what the NT depicts fits well with the chronology and geography of ancient history, and archaeology has confirmed some of the details, such as the description of the pool of Bethesda in John 5:2 and the existence of 'Pontius Pilate, Prefect of Judea'. Only a few pagan and Jewish sources refer to Jesus and the early church, but this is not surprising since Christianity was only a small movement in the context of world history at the time of its beginnings.

Some people object to reading the NT as history on the grounds that it contains accounts of Christ's miracles. Science, they say, has removed the need for appeal to the supernatural to explain things. However, if God exists then miracles cannot be excluded in principle. Whereas science operates in the realm of the predictable and repeatable, miracles are by definition unique events. Concerning the miracles of Jesus, such as those surrounding his birth, the nature miracles, exorcisms and healings, his own resurrection is the linchpin. Here the evidence has been scrutinized to the nth degree and no one has come up with a better explanation for the empty tomb and the transformation of the disciples from frightened deserters to fearless proclaimers than that he was raised from the dead by the power of God.

3. The NT and biblical history

The fact that the NT records history is something it shares in common with the OT. The OT recounts the history of Israel as the chosen people of God, from the covenant promises to Abraham, the conquest, kingship, exile and return, and the NT continues the story at a later period. Reading the NT with no knowledge of the OT would be like reading a later volume of a fiction series with no knowledge of the earlier ones. Although not impossible, it would hardly be satisfying.

Matthew opens with a genealogy that demonstrates continuity of 'Jesus the Messiah the son of David, the son of Abraham' (1:1) with the story of Israel. He gives more than sixty OT quotations, forging links between the life and death of Jesus and what God did to save his people in the past. For Matthew, the OT is a book of prophetic predictions: 'this took place to fulfil' punctuates the Gospel. More allusively, through typology (i.e. patterns or analogies in history), Jesus is depicted as a new Moses, who demands a 'higher righteousness' and a new Israel, who recapitulates the nation's history (rescued from Egypt, tempted in the wilderness, etc.), but without failure, and fulfils her destiny.

The use of the OT in the rest of the NT is no less profound. Mark describes the good news in terms of the fulfilment of Isaiah's prophecy of a new exodus (1:2–3; cf. Isa. 40:3; Mal. 3:1). OT passages and themes frequently underlie Mark's narrative. Jesus' messianic identity is made clear at his baptism in words which echo Ps. 2:7: 'you are my Son, whom I love; with you I am well pleased' (1:11). Luke emphasizes that God has bound himself to Israel with words of promise (e.g. to David, 1:30–32, 68–71, cf. 2 Sam. 7:14; to Abraham, 1:54–55, 72–73, cf. Gen. 12:1–3, etc.), which are accomplished in Jesus. Jesus is also depicted as the interpreter of Scripture himself (24:25–49), for 'everything must be fulfilled that is written about [him] in the Law of Moses, the Prophets and the Psalms'. The story of the inception and growth of the early church in Acts is likewise depicted as a continuation of biblical history.

OT antecedents also define the shape of the Messiah and his mission in John. The final revelation from God which Jesus embodies is contrasted with that received and mediated by Moses. The signs he performs, recalling the 'signs and wonders' of Moses, point to a new exodus. Jesus eclipses the great Jewish feasts and institutions which marked God's saving work in the past. As the 'light of the world' and 'living water' he fulfils the torch-lighting and water-pouring ceremonies of the feast of Tabernacles. He replaces the Jerusalem temple and, by dying during Passover week, is the ultimate Jewish Passover sacrifice. He is also seen as the long-awaited 'prophet like Moses' (6:14; 7:40; cf. Deut. 18:15).

In Paul's letters, God's dealings with Israel recorded in the OT lead to Christ who is the turning point of history. History divides into two epochs, the old age of sin, death and the Torah, and the new which eclipses it. The decisive act is the ending of Israel's exile and the restoration of God's people which has now taken place in Christ.

The other books of the NT are equally intertwined with the OT. Gathering together many of its major themes, the NT closes in Rev. 21 – 22 with a vision of a new Jerusalem and temple (21:2; 21:9 – 22:5), a new covenant (21:3–4), and even a new Israel; both the 'names of the twelve tribes of Israel' (21:12) and 'the names of the twelve apostles of the Lamb' (21:14) are found on the gates and walls of the city.

It is no accident that the two parts of Scripture are usually bound together in one 'Holy Bible'. Considering the ways in which the NT relates to the OT is one of the main tasks of biblical interpretation. In one sense the only compulsory prerequisite for NT interpretation is to have read the OT. In Matthew Jesus asks six times with reference to the OT, 'have you not read?'

C. The New Testament as theology

Although essential, neither literary nor historical analyses suffice. There is a sense in which reading the NT is *unlike* reading any other book. We read it to answer life's most fundamental questions: Who am I? Why am I here? Where is the world heading? Above all, who is God? In particular, what has he done? What are his plans for the future? Where do I fit in? Notwithstanding the historical distance and the literary unfamiliarity of the NT to modern readers, we share with the first readers the conviction that God has changed the world forever through Jesus Christ. As Peter writes: 'Though you have not seen him, you love him ... you believe in him and are filled with an inexpressible and glorious joy' (1 Pet. 1:8).

The best way to read the NT is to allow it to shape all our faith, life, worship and service. This includes everything from our private prayers to our political engagement. It can be a subversive and unsettling document, as well as comforting and reassuring. At root, the NT wants to transform all our relationships, not only with God, but also with ourselves, our families, our enemies and friends, and with society as a whole.

The task of reading the NT for all its worth is a challenging endeavour. It takes the sensitivity of a literary critic, the skills of an historian and the vision of a theologian. On the other hand, 'the word is very near you' (Deut. 30:14), especially if you heed the advice to 'smell the roses' and 'mind the gap'. Such readers will always find not only things to believe, but also reasons to trust God and ways to obey him. Ultimately Scripture is clear because God is light (1 John 1:5), Christ is the light of the world (John 8:12), and his word is like a lamp in a dark place (2 Pet. 1:19). The radiance of God is not a mystery of metaphysics but a matter of fellowship between himself and those he enlightens through his Word.

While it is true that the NT handsomely repays careful study, it can be read by anyone with profit. The biggest obstacle to right reading is not a dull mind, nor the absence of specialized knowledge, but a hard heart. As God's word to the world the message of the NT is accessible to all who come to it in faith.

Further reading

Good general introductions to the New Testament include:

John Drane, *Introducing the New Testament* (Lion, 2nd edn 1999) – excellent, well-illustrated summary of the NT's story and early Christian faith.

Don Carson and others, *Introduction to the New Testament* (Apollos, 2nd edn 2005)
- more detailed standard textbook for evangelical theological study.
David deSilva, *Introduction to the New Testament* (Apollos, 2004)
- another more detailed standard textbook for evangelical theological study.

Other useful books include:
Ben Witherington, *The New Testament Story* (Eerdmans, 2004) – well-presented summary of 'the story of' and 'the stories in' the NT.
Ben Witherington, *New Testament History: A Narrative Account* (Baker, 2001) – more detailed description of the history of the whole NT period.
Leon Morris, *New Testament Theology* (Zondervan, 1986) – clear presentation of the teaching of the whole NT and its individual books.
Howard Marshall, *New Testament Theology* (IVP, 2004) – good, more detailed, exposition of NT theology.

9. Gospels

Howard Marshall

Four accounts of the life of Jesus open the NT. They were the earliest such books to be written and come from people closely associated with Jesus or his first followers. Other accounts of Jesus were written later but are often legendary, and written to further the purposes of various groups generally considered heretical. They have not survived except in fragments.

THE GOSPEL OF MARK

A. *The earliest Gospel*

Although some early Christian scholars (such as Augustine c. AD 400) thought that Matthew was the first Gospel to be written, and some still do, the majority opinion is that Mark was the earliest writer. If he was not, it is difficult to see why Mark would have written a shorter work that leaves out much that is in Matthew. Various signs indicate that it is the earlier composition. Matthew, Mark and Luke are compositions with individual features and characteristics but also with so much material in common, often expressed in passages with the same basic structure and wording, that it is universally agreed that there is some kind of common basis behind them. That is not surprising; within the comparatively limited and closed group of followers of Jesus it is likely that one basic version of the story would quickly develop and be told with individual variations. When we compare the three Gospels, for the most part it is Mark who seems to have formed the basis for the other two writers, and the majority view is that Matthew and Luke had access to copies of Mark (or something extremely like what has been handed down to us as his work) and used it as their main source. Such a procedure is perfectly natural, especially if the tradition is correct that Mark was associated with Peter and wrote down what he remembered.

B. The storyline

Mark's Gospel begins with a scene that brings together two men. There is John, nicknamed the Baptizer, who felt called to prepare a people, currently in danger of divine judgment, to repentance and to readiness for when the Lord himself would come among them. And there is Jesus, who joins the crowds flocking to John in the desert, and indicates his personal association with them by taking part in the ceremony of washing with water. This was a symbol of consecration to God and of the way in which God would give them the gift of the Holy Spirit. But, whereas the people experienced forgiveness, Jesus experienced the Holy Spirit, and heard a heavenly voice assuring him that he was God's Son and commissioning him for his own task (1:1–13).

Thus begins a mission in which Jesus announces the arrival of God's rule over his people (the kingdom of God), and calls them to turn in their tracks and accept this good news with all its implications. He gathers a group of young men to be his companions in the task – in the social and cultural setting of Judaism it would have been unheard of and counter-productive to include young women, although Jesus certainly encouraged women also to respond to his message. And he sets out on an itinerant mission mainly in the small towns and villages of Galilee (1:14–20).

In the story as Mark tells it, there are two fairly explicit stages (1:1 – 8:30; 8:31 – 16:8), in both of which there are three interwoven strands of plot. These three storylines can be seen as the relationships of Jesus with the crowds, with the people who responded positively to him, and with those who developed hostility.

The two stages are concerned with the figure of Jesus himself. Although his own message was concerned with the coming of the kingdom of God (1:15), it was impossible to separate this from the question of his own status and role. His announcement of the kingdom was accompanied by his own remarkable deeds: he quickly acquired a reputation for healing diseases and disabilities and for other remarkable deeds. This naturally raised the question of his own role in relation to the kingdom of God. This could have been that of a prophet who simply announced what God was doing (or about to do) without actually bringing it about. But under the influence of prophetic statements in the OT many Jews believed that there would be an agent of God, the Messiah, who would act as king in God's kingdom (like the Israelite kings, especially David). The first part of Mark's Gospel is essentially the telling of a story which raises the question of Jesus' identity and gives the evidence to enable people to answer it. The readers, of course, already know what the right answer is, because they have read the opening sentences, but Mark takes us along the journey of discovery.

So Jesus spoke and acted with an impressive appearance of authority, and did his mighty works in the presence of the people, constantly moving around to fresh audiences. He did not tell people who he was, and when he referred to himself he often used the strange phrase 'Son of Man'. This reflects an Aramaic form of modest self-reference; it also reflects the reference in Dan. 7:13 to a heavenly figure who receives authority from God as the representative of his people.

From the start his activity aroused opposition because he said and did things that went against the teaching and practices of the Pharisees, who were sticklers for the minutiae of God's law as they understood it. He quickly became *persona non grata* with them, and disqualified himself for being an agent of God in their eyes. Mark records several stories of conflict between them.

At the same time there were people who responded to him positively, out of whose number he enlarged his group of companions. To this group he gave deeper insights into his teaching. The first part of the Gospel culminates in Jesus putting to them the question that was being widely discussed (8:27–30): Who am I? What do you make of me? At various points in Mark's story people under the control of evil spirits cried out that Jesus was the Son of God or the Holy One of God, but Jesus tried to silence them. Now his close companions (the disciples), led by Peter, recognized that Jesus must be the Messiah, although he could hardly be said to have acted like a traditional king.

But they were in for a greater surprise. If the first part of Mark identifies Jesus as the Messiah, the second relates a story in which he is seen to be a rejected, suffering Messiah who would give his life to set people free (10:45). The same activity of responding to the crowds continues, but the relationships with his companions and his opponents intensify. There is more teaching for the companions on two main issues when they are alone with him. The first was his repeated revelation to them that he must suffer rejection and be put to death, but would return to life (8:31; 9:31; 10:33–34). This was probably totally beyond their comprehension, for how could God's agent be overcome and defeated like that? The second was a lengthy session on what was going to happen after his departure, including the demolition of the temple and the fulfilment of the picture in Daniel of the coming of the Son of Man as God's agent on earth (ch. 13). In line with Jesus' own prophecy regarding himself, the opposition of the Jewish religious leaders came to a head in a series of verbal battles that led to the decision to get rid of him. A major part of Mark's story is thus taken up with the events leading to the trials and execution of Jesus.

Then the story, as we have it, ends quite abruptly with accounts of his burial and a subsequent visit by some of his women followers to the tomb. They found it to be empty, save for a young man who told them that Jesus had come back to life and they would see him if they returned to Galilee. (Note that 16:9–20 is missing from the oldest manuscripts of the Gospel and is written in a different style, so it was not part of the original Gospel. It is unclear whether Mark intended to conclude at v. 8, or whether the original ending has been lost.)

C. The character of the story

Such a brief sketch of the story has inevitably left out most of the detail and some of the main points as well. As Mark tells it there is a sense of movement and hurry, one of Mark's favourite words being 'immediately'. His Greek is somewhat rough and homespun, as in his frequent use of the present tense to tell the story (Matthew and Luke generally replace it by the more usual past tense). The story is a compilation of brief vignettes rather than lengthy narratives. Much of Jesus' teaching is given in the form of soundbites, brief and memorable sayings, apart from the longer stories (parables) and the two or three places where there is something more like a connected discourse (the collection of parables in ch. 4; the dialogue about aspects of the law in ch. 7; and the look into the future in ch. 13).

At the same time there is a sense of mystery and wonder conveyed by the story. There are demonic powers inhabiting human beings who recognize who Jesus really is. The things that Jesus does, both in the presence of the crowds and when alone with his companions, have a numinous quality about them, and the vocabulary of wonder and amazement is common. There is constant misunderstanding or lack of understanding, as if Jesus' identity and teaching are beyond the grasp of his hearers.

D. The evangelist

The book is anonymous, like the other Gospels, purely in the sense that the narrator does not name himself within the story. But it is hard to believe that the first readers did not know who the author was, or were unable to find this out. Our earliest information comes from Papias very early in the second century; he names the author as John Mark (known as a companion of Paul, Acts 13:5, 13; Philm. 24), an associate of Peter and dependent on him for much of his information. Despite the rigorous scrutiny of sceptical scholars, there is no solid reason to reject his statement.

Dating the Gospel is less certain. The considerable amount of space devoted to the hardships and suffering of people, culminating in the destruction of the temple in Jerusalem in AD 70 (referred to in coded language in 13:14) leads most scholars to conclude that the Gospel was written around that time, and that one purpose of the writer was to help people to understand what was going on around them in the light of what Jesus had said. Nevertheless, the primary purpose of Mark seems to have been to enable Christian believers to know the important features of the earthly life of the One whom they now knew as their heavenly Lord, and to provide them with a book that would be of great value in their evangelism.

Attempts have been made to identify the audiences and origins of the individual Gospels with specific places or Christian communities. A number of features suggest that, though Mark belonged to Jerusalem, his Gospel may have been composed and first used in Rome. The fact that it was written in Greek, not Hebrew or Aramaic, makes it unlikely that it was meant for a Jewish audience whose first language was not Greek. However, Greek was the common language of the eastern Mediterranean world, and writing in Greek would give the book a wide circulation and readership.

THE GOSPEL OF MATTHEW

A. Matthew and his predecessors

The first thing that we observe about the Gospel of Matthew is that it is considerably longer than Mark (c. 18,300 words in Greek, compared to 11,200 words). This is not due to its author being more expansive in his style, for in fact where he relates the same incidents as Mark he does so in briefer fashion. Rather, it is because he has more information to include, and the effect of his additions (together with some rewriting of the common passages) is to cast fresh light on the story of Jesus and bring out some significant new features. The generally accepted view is that Matthew has produced what is in effect a revised and augmented version of Mark.

A considerable amount of the fresh material is shared with Luke, and the symbol 'Q' is commonly used to refer to this shared material. The majority of scholars hold that Q existed as an earlier collection of (mainly) sayings of Jesus, and was utilized independently by the two evangelists. Those who postulate the existence of this earlier collection can be sure of its contents only when they are found in both Matthew and Luke. But both Gospels contain other materials peculiar to themselves, and we cannot rule out the possibility that in each case some of this material may be items taken from Q that the other evangelist did not take over. Yet another problem is whether the basic minimum of Q material common to Matthew and Luke was taken from one comprehensive collection of sayings (and some stories) of Jesus, or whether it came from two or more independent collections. In the absence of firm evidence a good deal of speculation is involved.

The postulation of this source (or sources) may thus seem to put a lot of uncertainty into attempts to trace the line from Jesus to the completed Gospels. There has been much scepticism regarding the reliability of the transmission of the material; some more radical critics insist that we cannot be sure that any sayings, as they stand, go back to Jesus unless they survive various tests of their authenticity. We cannot be sure (it is said) that the early Christians did not create fresh sayings and attribute them to Jesus (possibly through prophets who claimed to speak in his name), or that sayings were not substantially modified as they were handed down by word of mouth.

Over against such scepticism it is fair to make a number of points. First, the postulation of collections of sayings earlier than Matthew or Luke shows that the sayings were not invented by the evangelists but were in circulation at an earlier stage. Second, various parallels from semi-literate societies (including Middle-Eastern ones) show that, despite individual variations in telling stories, the main substance was handed down with considerable fixity, and the presence of people who had good memories for what we might call the authorized form of the tradition prevented wild deviations. Third, putting arguments of this kind together, it is fair to say that the Gospels give us an accurate picture of 'Jesus Remembered' (the title of a recent detailed defence of this view), and that the onus of proof is on those who claim that this collective memory was faulty or that it deliberately skewed the evidence.

B. Matthew's story of Jesus

Back then to Matthew! His Gospel differs from Mark at the outset by containing an account of the birth of Jesus preceded by a genealogy which links him back to Abraham (as a Jew) and to David (as the starting point of the kingly line). Alongside the genealogy of his earthly pedigree, however, there is the narrative of the conception and birth of Jesus by the Holy Spirit. This shows that he is more than a human being or even a human king, and is rightly understood as 'God with us' (chs. 1 – 2). This extended prologue thus identifies Jesus at the outset in the same way as the statement in Mark 1:1.

After this the story unfolds in a way that follows Mark fairly closely, but can be the better appreciated by noting the similarities and differences. The basic similarity is that it is the same story, virtually all of the incidents in Mark being included in it. Like Mark, it has the same two-part structure in which the companions of Jesus come to recognize him as the Messiah and then accompany him on a journey to Jerusalem. During this journey they learn that the Messiah must suffer and rise again, and then see these things actually happen (3:1 – 16:20; 16:21 – 28:20; note the parallel wording of 4:17 and 16:21). The same essential picture of Jesus emerges.

Although Matthew contains the same stories about Jesus as Mark, there is quite a bit of difference, at least in the earlier chapters, in the order of the material. This shows that, while the evangelists give the same broad picture of the historical course of his mission, many individual stories contained no means of identifying when they happened in relation to one another, or where. So the evangelists were free to arrange them topically rather than chronologically. We cannot expect a day-by-day account of what happened, and we lose nothing of significance by being unable to reconstruct one.

Second, Matthew is much fuller on the sayings and teaching of Jesus than Mark. And where Mark had relatively few connected accounts of Jesus' teaching, Matthew has several extended accounts, clearly structured round particular themes. There is no reason to doubt that Jesus gave an extended 'Sermon on the Mount' (chs. 5 – 7), perhaps repeating the same basic teaching in more than one location. Matthew's account may well incorporate sayings from a number of occasions, and the structure may be partly due to him. Compare how the teaching in 10:17–22 is found in Mark 13:9–13. Such editorial rearrangement and compilation is a fact that is there to be observed. It demonstrates that the evangelists were real authors, not simply annalists recording everything in the precise order and the original wording.

With this emphasis on Jesus' teaching, Matthew brings out more clearly a number of features:

1. The new way of life that Jesus put before his hearers, combining both the blessings that come from the kingdom of God and the demands placed upon its members (chs. 5 – 7).
2. The call to discipleship and mission that he gave them, both for when he was with them on earth and for later (ch. 10).
3. The way in which Jesus used parables to describe how the kingdom of God will grow, and how it will lead to a final consummation in which those who refuse to enter the kingdom will be excluded from its blessings and will suffer unutterable loss (ch. 13).
4. The way in which the followers of Jesus form a community (Matthew alone of the evangelists uses the word 'church') and must relate to one another in love (ch. 18).
5. The need for his followers to be faithful in service of their Master while waiting for his return (chs. 24 – 25).

Interwoven with such themes as these is the way in which the Gospel deals particularly with the attitude of Jesus to the Jewish people, warning their religious leaders against a form of religion which concentrated on trifling matters of ritual while ignoring the great issues of justice and mercy (ch. 23). Running through the Gospel is the tragedy of a people who failed to recognize the Messiah and leaders who failed in their stewardship. Matthew is the Gospel most concerned with the Jewish people, and this may well reflect something of the situation of its author and primary audience, who faced the continuing opposition of many Jews to the Christian church. At the same time it fully recognizes the calling of followers of Jesus to bring the gospel to Gentiles as well as Jews.

C. The origins of the Gospel

Early Christian tradition refers to Matthew, a follower of Jesus (9:9), as the composer of the 'logia' (oracles), and one possibility is that this notice identifies him as the writer of this Gospel. This identification makes the author of the Gospel somebody who had been in the close circle of companions of Jesus. A major difficulty is that the Gospel betrays little or no evidence of being written by somebody personally involved with Jesus. Another possibility is that these oracles were a compilation of teachings of Jesus (perhaps Q – see above on Mark). In this case the Gospel is associated with Matthew less directly, and we simply do not know who the author was. There is insufficient evidence to come to a firm decision.

Nor can a firm date or place of composition be identified. If our reasoning above is correct, it is later than Mark. There is some evidence to connect the Gospel with Antioch in the north of Syria, where there was a substantial Christian presence from an early date.

The special value of Matthew is as a more systematic collection of the teaching of Jesus. It was the most popular Gospel in the early church, if the number of early citations is any guide. Matthew gives the impression of being more of a Gospel for those who are already believers. It is much more concerned than Mark with the ongoing life of the followers of Jesus, as regards both their personal behaviour and their community life. And it is particularly focused on the situation of Christian believers who are Jews, living alongside other Jews and yet standing under the command of Jesus to make disciples from all nations. This is very much a churchy Gospel.

THE GOSPEL OF LUKE

A. *The Gospel and the book of Acts*

The third Gospel differs significantly from the two that we have already considered by the fact that it is the first volume in a two-part work. It is unclear whether Luke intended a two-volume work from the outset, or wrote the Gospel and then later decided (or was persuaded) to write a second volume telling 'what happened next'. In any case the present form and wording of the two books shows that a unified, single whole has resulted. Consequently, the Gospel and Acts each need to be read in the light of the other, and of the whole of which they are parts. Those who later created the NT chose to place Luke alongside the other Gospels and to separate off Acts so that the latter occupied the bridge position between the Gospels and the Epistles. Although the order of the Gospels varies in our earliest manuscripts, none of them keeps Luke and Acts together.

B. *The storyline*

What distinguishes this Gospel from the others? As in the case of Matthew, we appear to have a work that incorporates Mark and expands the story by numerous additions. Like Matthew this Gospel has an account of the birth of Jesus, a rather different story from that in Matthew, told more from Mary's point of view than from Joseph's. It is also interwoven with the story of John the Baptist, who had the role of preparing the people for the coming of Jesus. But it has the same function of letting the readers know the real identity of the main character (chs. 1 – 2).

Thereafter the story follows the now familiar course, keeping to the thread of Mark, but with significant sections of new material and (unlike Matthew) with two lengthy omissions of material (Mark 6:45 – 8:26; 9:42 – 10:12). This was probably sacrificed for the sake of including additional matter from Luke's other sources. (He may have been constrained by the practical consideration of how much could be included in a single scroll or codex.) Where Matthew tended to combine materials from his different sources, Luke's policy was more to alternate between them. It is not inconceivable that the material from Q and Luke's other stories and sayings were combined before Luke then incorporated this material with his revision of Mark.

The resulting Gospel tells the same story but does so in its own distinctive way. What happens is that Luke really gets going in ch. 3 (in a way that might suggest that what preceded was prologue to the main story). Where Matthew places the Sermon on the Mount up front, Luke begins with the scene in Nazareth (brought forward from its position in Mark) because it epitomizes so aptly several key themes: the role of Jesus as the bringer of good news and salvation, the opposition that he (like earlier prophets) faced, and the threat of action against him that would not prevent him from accomplishing his purpose. After this we read the same stories as in Mark and Matthew: Jesus' deliverance of people from diseases, disabilities, demonic possession and the power of sin itself, and his conflict with the Jewish religion and customs of the day. We read a shorter version of the Sermon on the Mount, with the same promises of God's goodness to those in his kingdom, the same demands for a radical ethic of love, the same appeal for self-examination and repentance, and the same choice between acceptance and rejection of his appeal for discipleship.

Luke notes how the theme of Jesus' 'departure' (i.e. his death and resurrection) already surfaces in the story of the transfiguration, following which Jesus sets himself resolutely to go to Jerusalem. But, whereas in Mark and Matthew the departure from Galilee and the arrival in Jericho en route are separated by a comparatively short piece of narrative, in Luke this is expanded to some ten chapters. Here the real interest is the teaching of Jesus to the usual three audiences (followers, crowds and opponents), always set against the foreboding background of what will happen in Jerusalem (9:51 – 19:27). Thereafter the story is again close to Mark, but is noteworthy for the fuller account of what Jesus said to his companions at the last supper (22:14–38) and for the fresh details in the account of his crucifixion. Like Matthew, Luke follows up the account of the discovery of Jesus' empty tomb with narratives of his appearances to various groups of his followers, and lays particular stress on the reality of his resurrection and the call to mission.

C. Some highlights in the Gospel

The way in which Luke handles the story brings out several significant aspects of it. These are not absent from the other Gospels, but they stand out more emphatically in Luke.

(1) Luke brings out more fully the role of Jesus as a prophet, even though this term expresses only part of his role and status as the Messiah. As Messiah he is the Son of God in a way that transcended the relationship of the previous kings of Israel to God. The term 'Son of Man' also expresses his authority as God's agent. And where Matthew and Mark use 'Lord' simply for people addressing Jesus with some respect (cf. our use of 'sir' or 'madam'), Luke also uses the term to convey Jesus' high authority as the exalted Lord, in the way which became normal in the early church (e.g. 'the Lord saw', Luke 7:13; 10:1; cf. Acts 2:36; 10:36).

(2) Again, Luke lays more stress on the role of the Holy Spirit as the empowerer of Jesus (similar to the later experience of his followers), and he draws more attention to the place of prayer in both Jesus' personal practice and his teaching.

(3) Luke's Gospel also depicts more clearly the way in which the proclamation of the kingdom of God and the accompanying mighty works of Jesus brought the benefits of salvation to marginalized people, including women and non-Jews (such as Samaritans).

(4) Finally, Luke highlights the concern of Jesus for the materially poor, and the duty of his followers to be free from love of possessions and to give generously to those in need.

For Luke the story of Christian beginnings is not confined to the story of Jesus on earth. This Gospel is summed up as being about 'all that Jesus began to do and to teach' (Acts 1:1), and it leads on to the story of how Jesus continued to work through his witnesses. Thus the account of his death and exaltation became the basis for a declaration of his roles as saviour and judge; the missions of his followers during his lifetime became the models for the wider mission of the church; and the pattern of Jesus' own life set the pattern for the way of his followers.

D. Theophilus and the author

The formal occasion for this Gospel lay in the further instruction of an otherwise unknown individual called Theophilus. He was probably a

Christian believer already, but needed a written account of what he had been taught orally. This would provide confirmation through careful historical research that made use of material handed down by those involved in the story from its beginning (1:1–4). Luke thus presents his account in a self-consciously historical kind of way. But it is highly important to note that his predecessor, Mark, and his opposite number, Matthew, evidently wrote their Gospels in the same kind of way, so much so that Luke was happy to utilize the work of the former as a major component of his own work. Mark and Matthew's works are no less historical than is Luke's.

Much attention has been given to trying to establish the particular genre or type of writing to which the Gospels belong, and there is a growing consensus (but not a universal recognition) that they are closest to the ancient kind of biography. Biographical writing could be used in the service of commending the particular virtues of a subject (or drawing attention to vices to be avoided). The Gospels partly reflect this, but are more concerned with persuading the readers to believe in Jesus or with strengthening their belief.

It is patently obvious that Theophilus would have known who was the author of the two books sent to him, even if the author is not named within the narrative. In the second volume there are passages in which the author lapses into writing in the first person plural ('we'), thereby identifying himself as a companion of Paul on some of his missionary travels. An undisputed second-century tradition has identified this companion as Luke, referred to by Paul as a physician and missionary colleague (Col. 4:14; 2 Tim. 4:11). This tradition has been questioned for various reasons. In particular, the picture of Paul presented in Acts is said to be sufficiently different from that given by Paul's own writings as to make it doubtful whether a close companion could have written thus about him. For further discussion see the section on Acts in this book. But in summary, the evidence against Luke's authorship is not compelling, and there is no good reason to reject the traditional ascription.

The circumstances of composition are obscure. The preface to the Gospel (which also covers Acts) makes clear that it is written to enable Theophilus, and people like him, to have a reliable basis for their faith. Various suggestions that the books were written to provide evidence for Paul's defence at his trial before the Emperor, or to rehabilitate him against opposition within the church, thus fall from consideration. We should take Luke at his word and see in his work a more comprehensive and more deeply researched account of Jesus and the early church than previously existed. The very fact that Luke tells the story of the early church makes his work fuller than that of any other author – there is no reason to believe that he had any predecessors in this part of his composition.

The date of the finished work clearly cannot be any earlier than the last event recorded, and there is a case that Luke brought his story up to the point at which he was writing. So he did not record the death of Paul, for example, because it had not yet happened. A date somewhat later, to allow time for the development of some perspective on the events recorded, is also possible.

THE GOSPEL OF JOHN

A. The 'different' story

To turn to John from the three Gospels that we have considered so far is to enter what appears to be new territory. There is a considerable degree of resemblance between Matthew, Mark and Luke, in that the general character of their contents, whether shared by two or more of them or peculiar to any one of them, is broadly similar. John's Gospel, however, stands somewhat apart.

It begins with a prologue that is more like a theological meditation interwoven with some historical reference (1:1–18). Its main purpose is to identify Jesus as the human incarnation of the Word of God, a phrase that might seem abstract but refers rather to a personal being sharing the nature and functions of God. Then a story begins, commencing (like the other Gospels) with the activity of John the Baptist as a witness to Jesus. As a result various people come into contact with Jesus and believe in him as the Messiah (1:19–51). The action shifts from Judea, where John was active, to Galilee, where Jesus makes an impact at a wedding (ch. 2). Then he goes to Jerusalem for the Passover, makes a demonstration in the temple (contrast the placing of such an incident at the end of his life in the other Gospels), and has a significant interview with Nicodemus and a conversation about new birth (ch. 3).

Jesus returns to Galilee via Samaria, where he has another significant scene with an individual, this time a woman. Some time afterwards he revisits Jerusalem for an unnamed festival, at which he heals a paralysed man. This incident becomes the occasion for an extended discourse by Jesus (chs. 4 – 5). Then he is back in Galilee where he feeds the large crowd who came to hear him in the desert, and again there is a lengthy dialogue (ch. 6). Although he wanted to stay in Galilee because opposition to him was mounting in Judea, he nevertheless went up to Jerusalem for another feast (Tabernacles), where his public teaching in the precincts of the temple led to further controversy, largely concerned with whether he was the Messiah (chs. 7 – 8). A blind man is healed in Jerusalem, and again the incident becomes the occasion for a series of dialogues (chs. 9 – 10).

Jesus spends some time away from Jerusalem east of the Jordan, and then returns to the neighbourhood of Jerusalem where he raises Lazarus from his tomb. The effect of this is to reinforce the determination of the Jewish authorities to do away with him (ch. 11). Once again he leaves Jerusalem but does not go far away, and then returns to ride into the city. Some Greeks attending the festival meet up with his followers (ch. 12). He gathers with his close companions for a meal at which he, the host, washes their feet. Then comes a long dialogue in which he tries to prepare them for a future time without his physical presence with them, when they will experience severe opposition but must continue to be his witnesses and will have the help of the Advocate, i.e. the Holy Spirit (chs. 13 – 16). A lengthy prayer by Jesus is recorded (ch. 17). This is followed by Jesus going to a garden where he is arrested and taken for examination before the high priest. There is a lengthier examination before the Roman governor Pilate, which issues in his condemnation to death and crucifixion (18 – 19). The story of the discovery of his tomb is told, but in this version the resurrected Jesus appears to his follower Mary in the vicinity of the tomb, and there are accounts of his appearances to his followers as a group in Jerusalem (ch. 20; cf. Luke's account). The Gospel appears to come to an end, but a further story of an appearance by the shore of Galilee is added (ch. 21).

B. Explaining the differences

This outline story is clearly different from the one found in the other Gospels, in that it has repeated visits by Jesus to Jerusalem for Jewish festivals (perfectly credible for a pious Jewish male in the light of Jewish customs), and a good deal of the action takes place there. Nevertheless, the two accounts can be slotted into each other. Jesus also acts and teaches in different ways. The list of mighty works performed by him is different (except for the feeding of the crowd and his walking on the water of Galilee), although they are of the same general kind. The way in which the mighty works often become the starting point for teaching and dialogue goes well beyond what happens in the other Gospels.

It is possible to find many individual sayings of Jesus in this Gospel that are very similar to the things he says in the other Gospels. Nevertheless, there are no examples of the parables that are so characteristic of the other three Gospels, apart from some brief similes that look like undeveloped parables. The vocabulary of John is smaller than that of the other Gospels (roughly 1,000 words, compared with 2,000 in Luke), but the principal theological terms employed are somewhat different. Where the 'kingdom of God/heaven' is a major term in the other Gospels, in John it is almost absent.

Some points that receive greater emphasis in this Gospel are:

1. There is much more open discussion of Jesus' identity. Jesus speaks about his personal relationship to God as his Son and this is challenged by his audience.
2. There are extended passages in which Jesus' significance is explained in terms of physical images like bread, a vine, the gate of a sheepfold and the shepherd with his flock, and abstract images such as resurrection, life and truth. All this goes well beyond the traditional concept of the Messiah and represents the new understanding of Jesus and his followers.
3. Correspondingly, this Gospel emphasizes the need for faith in the dual sense of believing what Jesus says and committing oneself to him.
4. The teaching of Jesus about humanity is structured by a more conspicuous dualism of light and darkness, righteousness and sin, life and death. Salvation from judgment consists positively in eternal life, and this life is essentially a personal relationship with God and Jesus expressed in terms of people being in fellowship with one another.
5. There is much fuller teaching on the role of the Holy Spirit as the Counsellor and Helper ('Advocate', TNIV) in helping the followers of Jesus after he has left them.
6. There is less emphasis on the final return of Jesus (though it is not absent) and more on his spiritual relationship with his followers here and now.

The basic storyline certainly remains the same. The earlier part of the Gospel is concerned with Jesus' identity and teaching to the people in general, and the latter part with his teaching to his committed followers. There is no difficulty in principle in holding that this writer told the story from a different angle to the other evangelists. One group of artists might paint broadly similar pictures of a particular scene, while another artist (an Impressionist perhaps) might produce something extraordinarily different which nevertheless expresses what was there all along. Hence we have the famous statement of Clement of Alexandria (c. AD 200) that 'last of all John wrote a spiritual gospel'.

Two extreme positions exist. One is that Jesus literally said and did everything recorded in all the Gospels and was capable of speaking and behaving in two rather different idioms. The other is that the Gospel of John is simply untrue and contradicts the picture gained from the other more realistic Gospels. In between there is the view that John has written a Gospel based on sources with the same level of ascertainable historical reliability as the other Gospels, but has cast it in his own unique idiom to present the true significance of Jesus.

C. The origin of the Gospel

The identity of the author is much disputed. No name is given in the Gospel itself, but there are several references to a follower for whom Jesus had a particular affection and a concluding note that he wrote the Gospel, followed by an attestation of reliability by his associates (21:24). Internal evidence suggests that he was John, the son of Zebedee, and this was the view taken in the early church. Other less plausible identifications have been made, e.g. Lazarus. It is also often argued that, while John was the authority behind the Gospel, somebody else may have written up his testimony.

The occasion for writing the Gospel of John is unknown. There have been many speculative reconstructions of a Christian community in which the material in the Gospel was gradually put together in the form that we now have, but these remain hypothetical. As with the other Gospels, John's expressed purpose should be taken seriously: to persuade people to believe in Jesus as the Messiah and Son of God (20:30–31). This purpose is broad enough to challenge non-believers and to strengthen the faith of believers by enlarging their knowledge of Jesus.

Many readers have had the same impression as Clement, that this Gospel presupposes the existence of the other three and was in fact the latest to be written. Others have argued that it was composed independently by a writer with information about Jesus (whether personal memory or community traditions) unknown to or not used by the other evangelists. In this case there is no necessary reason for dating his Gospel later than theirs. We don't know, and it doesn't really matter.

READING THE GOSPELS

What are we to do with the Gospels? One thing is clear at the outset. Over the centuries people with little or no knowledge of Christianity have read the Gospels and come to living faith in Jesus. Possibly the Gospel of John has been most used in this way. These books retain their comprehensibility and their power to change lives. Yet this basic fact should not mask the various difficulties of reading them.

First, there is the fact that the Gospels were originally written in Greek and have been translated into many other languages – just as in its own time the teaching of Jesus needed to be translated from Aramaic into Greek. But translation may need to be accompanied by some explanation, to put later readers as far as possible into the position of the original readers. They understood not only Greek, but also what kind of people were named Pharisees, or what the Jewish regulations about clean and unclean foods were, or what was meant by the phrase 'Son of Man'. Reading through the parable of the vineyard, for example, we may not get the point because we do not know that a vine or vineyard was a long-standing symbol for the Jewish people, whereas Jewish hearers would easily get the point that their rulers were failing in their responsibilities towards the 'owner' of the nation, God himself. Commentaries exist to provide readers with such basic background material. We should not be surprised that the Gospels need to be read within an interpretative community, and it is a myth that we can understand everything in them by ourselves.

One very important case of this background knowledge is that much of Jewish religious teaching was naturally taken from their Scriptures, our Old Testament. All the Gospels contain citations from the OT and other less obvious allusions to it. Matthew in particular has a series of quotations to show how the story of Jesus corresponds in important details with patterns and prophecies in the OT. It is essential to recognize when this is happening, and the use of a Bible which indicates quotations and verbal allusions is very helpful.

Second, there are some statements whose meaning was largely self-evident to those who understood the language and concepts involved. Jesus told a story about some tenant-farmers left in charge of a vineyard who failed to behave responsibly and maltreated the owner's agents. Mark comments that the Jewish leaders who heard the story 'looked for a way to arrest him because they knew he had spoken the parable against them' (Mark 12:12). They got the point!

But there were also occasions when Jesus spoke cryptically and even the people of his time were puzzled:

> 'I am with you for only a short time, and then I go to the one who sent me. You will look for me, but you will not find me; and where I am, you cannot come.' The Jews said to one another, 'Where does this man intend to go that we cannot find him . . . ? What did he mean when he said . . . "Where I am, you cannot come"?' (John 7:33–36).

In some cases we know the meaning because we have fuller knowledge in light of what subsequently happened, and we know that Jesus was speaking about his return to be with his Father. At other times it may not be so easy. When Jesus told one story about farming, even his closest friends could not understand what he was getting at and asked him what it meant (Mark 4:10). Jesus seems to have expected them to understand, but needed to supplement this and other such stories with an explanation (Mark 4:33–34). We might compare the way in which the Bible contains several accounts of dreams that were believed to have a meaning, but the dreamers could not get the message and had to find an interpreter. In the Gospels there are some texts that were expected to convey a clear message, and others that were meant to make people think about their significance.

And, third, there is the question of whether what Jesus says is credible and should be accepted. He said, 'I am the light of the world. Whoever follows me will never walk in darkness, but will have the light of life' (John 8:12). The Pharisees responded, 'Here you are, appearing as your own witness; your testimony is not valid' (John 8:13). Clearly they did not accept his affirmation. And throughout the Gospels there are many instances of people not believing what he said.

It has been said that 'A Gospel is more of a creed than a biography; it is a proclamation of faith.'[1] While a Gospel is partly biography, it is more like the statement 'I believe that Jesus is the Son of God', which challenges me to consider whether I could make the same affirmation. John makes this clear when he sums up what he has been doing in his Gospel:

> Jesus performed many other signs in the presence of his disciples which are not recorded in this book. But these are written that you may believe that Jesus is the Messiah, the Son of God, and that by believing you may have life in his name. (John 20:30–31)

It is because of this faith perspective that many wonder whether the evangelists were tempted consciously and unconsciously to play around with the facts and put a spin on them to make their narratives more persuasive. The question is crucially important because so much is at stake. On a humbler level a political party may aim to win an election and attempt to do so by making promises that cannot be kept. The Gospels are concerned with belief about what matters most in human life, the identity of Jesus as the Messiah and his role as the Saviour of the world – and our own Saviour. The question of truth is at stake.

There are two questions that are sometimes confused. One is whether Jesus' recorded words and actions show that he understood himself to be the Messiah. The other is whether such a self-understanding was correct. The problem may be seen by thinking of some contemporary person who is said to suffer from delusions because he claims to be the Messiah. We would need reliable evidence that he actually made these claims, but we would also need to ask whether he was in fact the Messiah. Concerning the former, we would like to have reliable evidence of what he said, for example, the testimony of trustworthy witnesses. In theory at least it should be possible to find these, although there may be many difficulties, and we might have to be content with less than absolute certainty. We might not have much difficulty in deciding that he was deluded (e.g. because he showed other signs of abnormality), but there might always be the niggling trace of doubt that maybe our judgment is mistaken and perhaps that person is actually what he claims to be.

Similarly, it is one thing to enquire historically into what lies behind the narratives in the Gospels; it is another to decide whether the narrative conveys ultimate truth. To answer the first question is a historical enquiry; to answer the second is to take a step of faith. And unfortunately it is difficult to separate the two questions from one another. Many a historian has examined the narratives on the basis of a set of beliefs that exclude the possibility of (say) a dead person being resurrected, and the result of the enquiry is therefore foreclosed in advance. Others, whose beliefs include that possibility, may too easily accept the historicity of the narratives or adopt a certain interpretation of the evidence without sufficiently careful examination. Complete objectivity is difficult, if not impossible.

This book is written from a standpoint of faith by people who have been persuaded by the kind of things written by John in his Gospel. Nevertheless, we have to tackle the historical questions in a responsible manner, in order to help people who cannot believe that things happened just as they are narrated simply because (in the words of an old hymn) 'the Bible tells me so'. An introduction to the Gospels, therefore, has to provide information that will help contemporary readers to decide whether they can trust the story. But in the end they must make their own response to that story.

USING THE GOSPELS TODAY

There are two broad types of approach to Christian use of the Gospels. One is to read the Gospels as presumably they were intended to be read, right through from start to finish, as complete works. It doesn't take that long: they are much shorter than the Oxford series of 'Very Short Guides'! What is the total impression made by the story? How do the various parts contribute to the meaning of the whole, and how do they become more comprehensible in light of the total account? The other approach is to read the Gospels in short sections and ponder their meaning closely. Each section needs close investigation to get the full effect of the details.

From an early date Christians divided up the Gospels into short sections for consecutive reading Sunday by Sunday, and thus achieved something of a compromise between the two approaches. Another type of reading consisted in weaving together the texts of the four Gospels to produce a single account (called a 'harmony') in which everything in each Gospel was included – although differences in the recording of the same incidents or sayings would tend to be ironed out in favour of one version. This type of composition is not without its value, but it is open to the obvious criticism that it flattens out the four distinct accounts of Jesus, each with their own individual artistry, into one rather bland narrative.

We have noted that the Gospels were written for slightly different audiences and situations. Mark and John are both concerned with presenting the story of Jesus in a way that will especially help not-yet believers, although they are also intended to be of value to believers. Luke is part of a larger work aimed at strengthening the faith of a believer who has so far had to reply on oral accounts, and who wanted a coherent written record of what he had heard piecemeal. And Matthew looks more like an orderly textbook for the instruction of the Christian congregation and its workers as they lead the congregation and engage in evangelism and face controversy. Each of the Gospels could be used for any of these purposes, but each has its own special angle on the story of Jesus.

Similar audiences have existed ever since then, and readers today have the same kind of needs, although their actual situations are different. Few of us today live in direct contact with Jewish groups who would question whether Jesus is the Messiah or would argue that the Messiah is still to come. In the western world few of us live in situations where religion and politics are so closely associated as in ancient Judea, although it is different for people in, say, a Moslem or Hindu setting. Many of us live in urban and global settings rather different from the rural world in which Jesus and his followers lived, although we should not underestimate the degree of 'globalization' that had already taken place. Alexander the Great had conquered much of the known world and imposed Greek language and culture upon it, and the Romans had then set up their imperial system all round the Mediterranean Sea. We have to do some transposition in order to think ourselves back into the ancient world and apply to ourselves the teaching given then. It is therefore important that we learn to recognize the basic principles of living under the rule of God taught by Jesus in ways appropriate to his first-century context, and then learn to apply these basic principles to ourselves in our different situations.

One key question is how we apply the teaching given to individuals in their personal relationships to ourselves in our social relationships: what does loving my neighbour (never mind my enemy!) mean if I am the director of a commercial company and my neighbour is the director of a business rival (Matt. 22:39)? Or how do I 'turn the other cheek' if I am a soldier engaged in a war for the defence of my country (Matt. 5:39)? And how do I act in the spirit of 'Do not judge, or you too will be judged' (Matt. 7:1) if I am a magistrate? These questions have often been ignored, despite the fact that they are of crucial importance for what people do with the major part of their time, and despite the fact that they arise in the Gospels (see Luke 3:10–14). Reading the Gospels is going to be challenging, and perhaps upsetting!

Note

[1] J. Ashton, *Understanding the Fourth Gospel* (Oxford, Clarendon, 1991), p. 432.

Further reading (see **Introduction** for good commentary series)

Steve Walton and David Wenham, *Exploring the New Testament 1. The Gospels and Acts* (SPCK 2001) – excellent introduction, with panels highlighting themes and points to ponder.

Richard Burridge, *Four Gospels, One Jesus?* (SPCK, 2nd edn 2003) – lively, lucid exposition of the four portraits of Jesus.

Craig Blomberg, *Jesus and the Gospels: An Introduction and Survey* (IVP, 1997) – well-written guide to all the key points.

Craig Blomberg, *The Historical Reliability of the Gospels* (IVP, 1987) – clear, carefully reasoned defence of this important issue.

10. Acts

Mark Strauss

As a companion volume to the Gospel of Luke, Acts continues the story of the Christian movement from the ascension of Jesus and the coming of the Spirit on the day of Pentecost, to Paul's arrival in Rome – a period of about thirty years. While the Gospel records what Jesus 'began to do' through his life, death, resurrection and ascension, Acts records what he continues to do as the risen head of the church through the Holy Spirit he has poured out (1:1; 2:33).

A. Unity and purpose of Luke–Acts

The Gospel of Luke and the book of Acts were written by the same author. This is evident in that they are addressed to the same recipient (Theophilus), share similar style and vocabulary, have common themes and theology, and are cross-referenced ('my former book', 1:1). Yet Acts is more than just a second book written by Luke. It is the second part of a two-volume work ('Luke–Acts'). When Luke wrote the Gospel he probably already had the book of Acts in mind. The two form a *literary and theological* unity.

    This conclusion has important implications for the way we approach both books. (1) Luke and Acts should be read as a single narrative. The story that begins in the first chapter of the Gospel does not come to its conclusion till the end of Acts. (2) Luke and Acts share common themes and theology which should be progressively followed through both volumes. (3) Luke and Acts were written with a common purpose.

The prologue of the Gospel, which probably serves as an introduction to both volumes, states Luke's purpose. He is writing so that Theophilus might know 'the certainty of the things you have been taught' (Luke 1:4). Luke's overall purpose is *the confirmation of the gospel*, i.e. the veracity of the gospel *message* and the gospel *messengers*. He writes to show that God's great plan of salvation has come to fulfilment in the events of Jesus' life, death, resurrection and ascension, and continues to unfold in the growth and expansion of the church.

B. Central message of Acts

How does the book of Acts fit into this broader purpose of Luke–Acts? The first chapter gives us the key to Luke's central theme. Following his resurrection and before his ascension, Jesus commands his disciples to remain in Jerusalem until they receive the Holy Spirit:

> But you will receive power when the Holy Spirit comes on you; and you will be my witnesses in Jerusalem, and in all Judea and Samaria, and to the ends of the earth (1:8).

The rest of the book tells how the church, filled and empowered by the Holy Spirit, takes the message of salvation from Jerusalem to the ends of the earth. Throughout Acts the gospel advances despite strong opposition and apparent setbacks. Persecution and imprisonment only strengthen the church (4:23–31; 5:41–42; 8:4; 12:24; 16:16–40; 28:30–31). In an ironic episode, the Pharisee Gamaliel warns the Sanhedrin that if the Christian movement is not from God, it will surely fail; but if it is from God, they will not be able to stop it (5:33–40). The unstoppable progress of the gospel confirms that the church – including both Jews and Gentiles – represents the true people of God in the new age of salvation.

C. Occasion of Acts

Luke writes at a time of increasing challenges for the church. While many Gentiles have responded positively to the gospel message, most Jews are rejecting it. This raises many questions: (1) How can Jesus be the Messiah if he died on a cross like a criminal? (2) How can the salvation have arrived if the Messiah is not reigning in Jerusalem? (3) How can Israel's promises be fulfilled if most Jews are rejecting the gospel? (4) How can the church be the people of God if it is increasingly made up of Gentiles who are uncircumcised and do not keep the OT law?

Luke's narrative provides answers to these questions. (1) Jesus is indeed the Messiah, as confirmed through signs and wonders which God performed through him (2:22; 9:22). Furthermore, Scripture predicted that the Messiah would die and rise from the dead (2:30–31; 3:18; 17:3; 26:23; Luke 24:26, 46). (2) God's great salvation has indeed arrived, as evidenced by Jesus' exaltation to the right hand of God as Messiah and Lord, and his pouring out of the Spirit of God (2:17, 33–35). (3) While many Jews are rejecting the gospel, a remnant is being saved (2:41; 4:4; 6:7; 21:20). Furthermore, this rejection was predicted in Scripture, and is part of Israel's history as a stubborn and resistant people (7:51–53; 13:40–41, 46). (4) The mission to the Gentiles was also predicted in Scripture as part of God's end-time salvation. It was not instigated by any human being, but by God himself (10 – 11:18; 13:47; 15:1–29; 28:28–29). Paul of Tarsus – the apostle to the Gentiles – is not a renegade Jew preaching against the traditions of Judaism, but is God's faithful instrument to bring salvation to the Gentiles (9:15–16; 13:46–48; 22:21; 26:20).

In addition to these Jewish challenges, the infant church is facing increasing hostility from the Gentile world. Luke seeks to show that Christians like Paul are not renegades and troublemakers, but law abiding citizens with a message of hope and salvation for the world (16:37–40; 18:12–15; 19:35–41; 22:22–29; 23:27–30; chs. 24 – 28).

D. Structure of Acts

An outline of Acts can be derived from its theme verse, 1:8. The book progresses outward geographically, from Jerusalem to Judea, to Samaria, and beyond. It climaxes in Rome, the symbolic 'ends of the earth', with Paul freely proclaiming the gospel message to Jews and Gentiles alike (28:30–31). The book also progresses ethnically, as first Jews, then Samaritans, and finally Gentiles received the message. Much of Luke's purpose is to show that the salvation of the Gentiles was all along part of God's purpose and plan.

1:1 – 8:3	The gospel to Jerusalem
8:4 – 12:25	The gospel to Judea, Samaria and Syria
13:1 – 28:31	The gospel to the ends of the earth

E. Themes and theology

1. The Holy Spirit as sign of the new age

For Luke the coming of the Spirit marks the dawn of the new age. The OT prophets predicted that in the last days God would pour out his Spirit on all humanity (2:17–21; Joel 2:28–32). Now resurrected and ascended to God's right hand, Jesus pours out the Spirit to fill, empower and guide the church (2:33). In many ways the Spirit is the leading character of Acts, referred to over sixty times. Throughout Acts reception of the Spirit marks entrance into the people of God (2:38; 8:17; 11:17; 15:8; 19:6). The Spirit fills and empowers believers (2:4; 4:8, 31; 6:3, 5; 7:55; 9:17; 11:24) and guides the progress of the gospel (8:29, 39; 10:19; 11:28; 13:2, 9; 16:6, 7; 21:4). The Spirit of God is the Spirit of Christ, his presence among his people (Acts 16:6, 7).

2. God's purpose and plan

The theme of divine sovereignty and purpose permeates Luke's narrative. God ordained not only the death and resurrection of Jesus, but also that salvation would now go to the ends of the earth. Throughout Luke, there is the overriding concern that what is happening is the work of God – the Greek term *dei*, meaning 'it is necessary', occurs forty times in Luke–Acts. Though wicked men put Jesus to death, this was God's plan, accomplishing salvation by raising him from the dead (2:23–24; cf. Luke 24:7, 26–27, 44–47; Acts 3:18; 4:28).

3. To the Jew first

Luke strongly stresses the theme of promise and fulfilment, and the continuity between the old and new covenants. Though writing from a Gentile perspective, he firmly grounds the Gospel in its Jewish roots. Jesus is the Jewish Messiah who fulfils the promises of the Hebrew Scriptures (Luke 1:32–35; 2:11; Acts 2:36). The birth narrative at the beginning of the Gospel plunges the reader into the world of first-century Judaism (Luke 1 – 2). The characters we meet represent the faithful remnant of Israel eagerly longing for the Messiah (2:25–26). In Acts the original disciples are all Jews who continue to worship in the temple and proclaim Jesus to be Messiah, the fulfilment of Israel's hopes. The salvation Jesus accomplishes is the 'consolation of Israel' (Luke 2:25), the fulfilment of the promises made to the Jewish nation (2:39). The gospel finds huge initial success in Jerusalem as thousands respond

(2:41; 4:4; 6:7; 21:20). When Paul enters a city, he preaches first to the Jews and then turns to the Gentiles. Salvation comes forth from Israel and goes first to Israel.

4. The Gentile mission

Despite this emphasis on salvation for Israel, the key theme of Acts is the outward expansion of the gospel, both geographically and ethnically. As many Jews reject the message, the church increasingly becomes a Gentile entity. Luke writes to justify the Gentile mission by showing that the mission to the Gentiles is not a departure from God's purpose for Israel, but is its fulfilment, predicted in Scripture (15:15–18). Paul, God's apostle to the Gentiles, is not unfaithful to his Jewish roots, but is fulfilling God's purpose for Israel: to be a light of revelation to the Gentiles (13:47; Isa. 49:6).

F. Authorship, date and audience

Both the Gospel and Acts have been traditionally ascribed to Luke, a physician and part-time missionary companion of the apostle Paul (Col. 4:14; 2 Tim. 4:11; Philm. 24). Col. 4:11–14 implies that Luke was a Gentile, which would fit well with the author's strong emphasis that the good news is for all people everywhere.

The tradition of Lukan authorship can be traced back to the middle of the second century, and there are no statements in the early church that would point to any other author. Considering Luke's relative obscurity in the NT, it is unlikely that a Gospel would have been attributed to him had he not been the author. There is also the internal evidence of the 'we' sections in Acts, which confirm that the author was at times a companion of Paul (16:10–17; 20:5–21; 21:1–18; 27:1 – 28:16). Though Paul had other companions (Mark, Timothy, Titus, Silas, Barnabas, etc.), when this internal evidence is placed beside the strong and unanimous external testimony, there seems no reason to doubt Luke's authorship. While authorship by Luke remains the most likely option, other scholars opt for an unknown author – perhaps drawing on sources compiled by a companion of Paul – writing in the last decade of the first century AD. In any case, it should be noted that Lukan authorship is part of church tradition rather than the inspired text. Like the other Gospels, Luke and Acts are anonymous, strictly speaking, and their inspiration and authority do not depend on the traditional view of their authorship.

The date of Acts is uncertain. Since Paul is alive and in prison in Rome at the end of Acts (about AD 60), some believe that Luke finished writing before Paul's release and later martyrdom. This would place its writing sometime around AD 60–62. The Gospel of Luke would then be dated sometime prior to this, perhaps in the late 50s.

On the other hand, if Mark was the first Gospel written (as seems likely), and was composed in the late 60s shortly before the destruction of Jerusalem (see Mark 13:14), Luke's Gospel must have come later, perhaps in the 70s or later. In this case, Luke would have had a different reason for ending his Gospel with Paul alive in Rome, perhaps to show that the gospel message was reaching 'the ends of the earth' (1:8).

Luke addresses both his books to Theophilus, who was probably the patron who sponsored their writing (1:1; Luke 1:1–4). Yet Luke clearly writes to a larger audience, probably mostly Gentile churches who are wrestling with their identity as the true people of God. Luke assures believers of the historical foundation for their faith. The coming of Jesus and the growth of his church represents the culmination of God's purpose and plan for the salvation of the world.

G. Reading Acts today

The reader of Acts should first recognize what it is *not*:

1. It is not an 'Acts of the Apostles' in the sense of a history of the twelve apostles. The Twelve appear in the early chapters and then mostly disappear from the narrative. Peter shows up again in chs. 10 – 12 and 15, but we learn nothing about the later ministries of the other eleven apostles or their ultimate fate. The second half of the book (chs. 13 – 28) mostly concerns the ministry of another apostle, Paul, rather than that of the Twelve.
2. Nor is Acts a history of the early church. While it provides an account of the church's growth in Judea, Samaria and Syria, and then through Paul's ministry into Asia Minor, Greece and Rome, these accounts are highly selective and little is said about the church's outreach into many other regions (Egypt, Libya, Arabia, Cappadocia, etc.).
3. Further, Acts is not a manual on church polity and order. Many readers come to Acts for direction on how to administer the church. Yet not everything that happens in Acts is meant to establish the pattern for the church today. Many critical issues of church order and function are barely addressed in Acts, or do not follow a consistent pattern. This includes things like church governance (rule by elders, bishops or congregation?), baptism (immersion or sprinkling? infants or believers?), the Lord's Supper (frequency of observance? spiritual significance?), the reception of the Spirit (at

conversion? following baptism? accompanied by tongue-speaking?). The point is that Luke was not intending to write a handbook on how to run the church. Rather, his purpose was to demonstrate how the church, filled and empowered by the Holy Spirit, crossed geographical and ethnic boundaries to take the good news of Jesus Christ from Jerusalem to the ends of the earth.

Acts should therefore be read for what it is: *historical narrative motivated by theological concerns*. Luke's stated purpose is historical: to give Theophilus an authoritative account of the origin of the Christian faith (Luke 1:1–4). This historical purpose continues in Acts (1:1) with the account of the growth and expansion of the church. Functioning on this level, Acts give us a (limited) glimpse of the early church and provides the historical background for the letters of Paul.

Yet Luke writes not merely as an historian, but also as an evangelist and theologian, seeking to convince his readers of the spiritual significance of these salvation-bringing events. His account is therefore selective, focusing on key persons and events which are meant to confirm that the coming of Jesus and the growth of the church represent God's purpose for the world.

What has been said above confirms the abiding relevance of the book of Acts for the church today. The book is not dry and dusty ancient history; it is *our* history and *our* heritage. Acts tells us who we are as a Christian movement and how we came into being. It reminds us what it means to be the church: a Spirit-filled and Spirit-directed body of believers whose purpose is to cross every ethnic and geographical boundary to take the message of salvation to the ends of the earth. The same Jesus Christ whose death and resurrection the early church proclaimed still reigns at God's right hand as head of his church. The same Spirit who was poured out on believers on the Day of Pentecost is still empowering and guiding the church today.

Further reading (see **Introduction** for good commentary series)

Steve Walton and David Wenham, *Exploring the New Testament 1. The Gospels and Acts* (SPCK 2001) – excellent introduction, with panels highlighting themes and points to ponder.

Craig Blomberg, *From Pentecost to Patmos: An Introduction and Survey* (IVP 2006) – well-written guide to the key issues.

11. Letters

Ian Paul, Brian Rosner and Carl Mosser

INTRODUCTION

A. *Letters in the New Testament*

A significant proportion of the NT – something like 40% – consists of letters. The simplest classification would be to group them as 'written by Paul' (the majority) and 'the rest'. But in fact the letters are of several types:

- Those written by one or more individuals to a church. This includes most of Paul's letters and 2 John.
- Those written by an individual to several churches as a kind of circular. This includes Galatians (written to the churches in a region), probably Ephesians, 1 and 2 Peter and Jude.
- Those written by an individual to other individuals. This includes Philemon, 1 and probably 2 Timothy, Titus and 3 John.
- Those called 'letters' but lacking some of the formal features of written letters, and apparently with a wide audience in mind. This includes Hebrews and James.

In addition, Revelation has many of the formal features of a letter, but is clearly something more, and the texts of two letters are included within Acts (in chs. 15 and 23).

Sections in this chapter were written as follows – Ian Paul: Introduction, 1 & 2 Timothy and Titus, James to Jude; Brian Rosner: Paul's letters, Romans to 2 Thessalonians, Philemon; Carl Mosser: Hebrews.

B. Letters in the ancient world

Letter writing developed in the ancient world whenever information needed to be recorded or when face-to-face communication was not possible. Letter writing only flourished under certain social and cultural conditions, notably the existence of a reliable network of communication. But for letter writing to become important, there had to be a consistent need, and this primarily arose from the administration of empires.

From as far back as the eighteenth century BC we have evidence of regular letter writing from empires in Mesopotamia. By NT times letter writing was an important part of the administration of the Roman empire, aided by the development of the road network which was first designed to allow rapid movement of troops. The Emperor Augustus had developed a postal system that allowed official letters to travel on horseback at a rate of fifty miles a day. Private letters would use the same network of roads, but would have to be carried by a slave, friend or trusted stranger going to the right destination.

C. Letter format

As today, ancient letters followed a conventional pattern and this remained constant for several centuries:
* *Opening*, containing the names of sender and recipient, a greeting, and usually some form of wish for good health.
* *Thanksgiving*, thanking the gods for some aspect of good news about the recipient.
* *Body of the letter*, with the main message to be conveyed.
* *Closing*, with final greetings, possibly from other people connected with the sender, and a final wish for good health.

The letters of the NT mostly show this conventional pattern, but often adapt and extend it.

In the *opening* the NT writers frequently add some form of self-designation. For example, Paul usually calls himself 'apostle' but sometimes 'servant' or 'prisoner'. Paul also frequently adds the names of others as co-writers. This was unusual in Greek letter writing, so we must assume that these others made a real contribution to the contents and construction of the letters.

Paul's letters in particular develop the *thanksgiving* section. His letters are regularly marked by praise for the faithfulness of the church and a reminder of God's faithfulness, and often include a report of the way Paul prays for the church. Sometimes these thanksgivings flow into the body of the letter so that it is hard to see where one finishes and the other begins. In 2 Corinthians, Ephesians and 1 Peter the (Greek) thanksgiving is replaced by a (Jewish) blessing of God. Galatians is notable for omitting the thanksgiving altogether.

The *body* of the NT letters varies widely. In 1 Corinthians we have perhaps the best example of conventional letter-like correspondence, as Paul answers questions he has been asked in a letter from Christians in Corinth (see 1 Cor. 7:1). The body of Romans appears to be a much more general statement of Paul's understanding of the gospel, in preparation for asking support for the next stage of his missionary work. But some 'letters' read much more like written sermons (e.g. Hebrews), and others consist of general exhortations (e.g. James). Throughout the body of their letters, NT authors deploy a whole range of rhetorical techniques.

The *closing* section also involves developments from the standard pattern, while still retaining the basic shape. Paul often includes (sometimes extensive) greetings from others in leadership with him. He ends with a blessing rather than a farewell, and this at times develops into a short piece of liturgy, suggesting that Paul expected his letters to be read to the community in the context of a meeting for worship.

This all shows the range of purposes that the NT letters have – something mirrored, in fact, in secular letter writing. For example, the Roman philosopher Seneca (also writing in the first century) wrote a large number of letters to a friend which were, in effect, essays on questions of ethics.

D. Significance of letters in the New Testament

We are so used to having letters in the NT – and for many Christians, some letters are the part they are most familiar with – that we might not have reflected on how unusual this is. The correspondence of an individual to another individual or small group at a particular time and place has become recognized as God's word, in some way or other, to all Christians at all times and in all places. This highlights two key issues.

First, it reminds us that these documents are *acts of communication* between people. All too often, the Bible is treated as an object to be studied which sets out certain doctrines to be believed – and the pastoral implications are somehow seen as detached and secondary. But in the NT letters we find belief expressed in the context of pastoral relationships, doctrine interleaved with the consequences for individuals and their relationships.

As a spin-off, this also reminds us how interconnected the communities of the early church were. The communications network of the Roman empire meant that the traffic of both individuals and theology flowed relatively freely between one community and another. It is now less and less sustainable to argue that there were distinct Christian communities with their rival theologies battling it out for influence in the young church.

Secondly, we need to recognize the *particular circumstances* that each letter was written for. Most of the letters are 'occasional'; that is, in contrast to stories of historical events or collections of wise sayings, or gatherings of the praise songs of God's people, letters were written for a specific purpose to address a particular situation. In reading the letters, we are wanting to hear *God* speak *to us* in the *here* and *now* through what (say) *Paul* said to the *Corinthians* in the *there* and *then*. We are eavesdropping, as it were, on the conversation of another, and we need to bear this in mind as we think about interpreting the letters, that is, as we seek to make sense of them as God's word to us.

Of course, these two factors are true to some extent for every section of the Bible and every kind of writing in it. But the letters serve to offer a particular reminder of these features, which we need to bear in mind whenever we open the Scriptures.

E. Interpreting the letters

A helpful way to approach any text of the Bible is to ask three questions: 'what?', 'why?' and 'how?' What was the author saying to the first hearers of this text? Why was this said in this way at this time? How does this relate to our own situation and speak into it? Problems arise when we move too quickly from the 'what?' to the 'how?', and the particularity of each letter makes it especially important that we reflect on all three questions.

We need to be aware that the letters were written in a particular *cultural context*. So we might read Rom. 1 differently when we realize that Paul's critique of the secular world parallels closely the kind of critique that Jews offered of Greek culture – something Paul then turns on its head in Rom. 2. It will shape our reading of 1 Cor. 11 if we know something about the assumptions made in the first century about human anatomy, and in particular the significance of hair. 1 Cor. 8 makes much more sense when we are aware of the availability of meat and its relation to pagan temple worship.

We also need to be aware of *questions of vocabulary* and the use of language. Much ink has been spilled concerning the meaning of 'head' in 1 Cor. 11:3f.; the use of 1 Tim. 2:12 will depend on what we think the unusual word 'to take authority' meant to Paul's first-century readers.

The *occasional nature* of the letters will also guard us against thinking that these are systematic guides to Christian belief and practice. If the Corinthians hadn't had problems with celebrating the Lord's Supper together, making it necessary for Paul to write a few paragraphs in 1 Cor. 11:17–34, we would know little about the importance of this in the early church, aside from the brief reference in Acts 2:42 and evidence from the second century. It is difficult to know exactly what Paul is referring to in some of the spiritual gifts he mentions in 1 Cor. 12, so we must exercise some caution in making too quick a link with modern phenomena.

An important element will be to follow the *structure* of the argument before us. Whatever the meaning of 'head' or 'because of the angels' (1 Cor. 11:10), the point of Paul's argument here is to allow women to pray and prophesy in the assembly (1 Cor. 11:5), in a context where Paul sees prophecy as the pre-eminent gift of the Spirit (1 Cor. 14:1).

It is sometimes thought that interpretation is the art of making the Bible say something different when you don't like what it appears to be saying! But really it is recognizing that what *we* think the text appears to be saying may not be what *the author* or the *first readers* would have thought it was saying. And it is what would have made sense to *them* which must have controlling influence over any responsible claim as to how it should make sense to *us*.

F. Pseudonymity

It has been suggested that some letters were written not by those to whom they have been attributed, but by others using their name (i.e. pseudonymously). The questions have been especially persistent in relation to 2 Peter, the Pastoral Letters (especially 2 Timothy) and Ephesians. Discussions on authorship can be found in the sections on these letters, but two general points are worth making.

Letter writers often used a secretary ('amanuensis') whose role could vary from simply taking down dictation, to composing under direction, to freely composing a letter under the author's general instructions. This makes the task of identifying authorship slightly different from the modern context, where we would think of an author as the person who wrote every single word.

On the other hand, the practice of writing under the name of someone else, living or dead, was a common feature in the ancient world. However, there is no evidence that it was ever thought acceptable in the Christian community, and apostolic authorship was one important criterion in determining what was included in the emerging canon that was added to the Jewish Scriptures.

PAUL'S LETTERS

Letter	Date	Origin
Galatians	Probably (a) 49 – after first missionary journey (Acts 13:2 – 14:28)	(a) Syrian Antioch or Jerusalem
	Possibly (b) 53 or 55 – during third missionary journey (Acts 18:23 – 21:17)	(b) Ephesus or Macedonia
1 Thessalonians	50–51 – during second missionary journey (Acts 15:40 – 18:22)	Corinth
2 Thessalonians	50–51 – during second missionary journey	Corinth
1 Corinthians	55–56 – during third missionary journey (Acts 18:23 – 20:3)	Ephesus
2 Corinthians	55–56 – during third missionary journey	Macedonia
Romans	57 – during third missionary journey	Corinth or Cenchrea
Ephesians	60–61 – first Roman imprisonment[1] (house arrest; Acts 28:16–31)	Rome[1]
Colossians	60–61 – first Roman imprisonment[1]	Rome[1]
Philemon	60–61 – first Roman imprisonment[1]	Rome[1]
Philippians	62 – first Roman imprisonment, near the end[1]	Rome[1]
1 Timothy	63–65 – some time after the first Roman imprisonment[2]	Philippi[2]
Titus	63–65 – some time after the first Roman imprisonment[2]	Macedonia[2]
2 Timothy	67–68 – second Roman imprisonment, near the end of Paul's life	Rome

[1] Possibly written in earlier imprisonment in 57–59 in Caesarea (Acts 23:23 – 26:32), or earlier still in 53–55 in Ephesus (Acts 19:1 – 20:1).

[2] Possibly written later, after a trip to Spain.

Destination	Contents	Issues scholars discuss
(a) Churches in south Galatia (b) Churches in north-central Asia Minor	The gospel of the grace of God	Date, origin, destination
Christians in Thessalonica	Encouragement for new Christians	
Christians in Thessalonica	Comfort for a church in distress	Author, date, relationship to 1 Thessalonians
Christians in Corinth and Achaia	Problems of a Gentile church	Chronology of Corinthian correspondence and Paul's visits
Christians in Corinth and Achaia	The heart of an apostle	Literary unity (2:14 – 7:1; chs. 8 – 9; chs. 10 – 13)
Christians in Rome	The righteousness of God revealed in the gospel	Literary unity (chs. 15 – 16)
Christians in Ephesus and surrounding region	The church of Christ	Author, date, origin, destination
Christians in Colossae and Laodicea	The supremacy of Christ	Author, date, origin, nature of heresy
Philemon and the Christians in Colossae	The dilemma of Christian slave ownership	Origin
Christians in Philippi	The joy of knowing Christ	Origin, literary unity (3:2 – 4:3)
Timothy and Christians in Ephesus	Teachers and leaders in the church	Author, date, origin, destination, nature of heresy
Titus and Christians in Crete	The grace of God and Christian living	Author, date, origin, destination, nature of heresy
Timothy and Christians in Ephesus	Encouragement to be faithful	Author, date, origin, destination, nature of heresy

ROMANS

Described by Samuel Coleridge as the most profound book in existence, of all Paul's letters Romans presents the most comprehensive exposition of his gospel. Probably no book in the NT has exerted more influence in the history of the church.

A. Occasion and purpose

Rome was the centre of a vast empire that encompassed all the countries around the Mediterranean Sea. With a population of around one million people, the city included a sizeable Jewish population. In the mid 50s AD there were probably several groups of Christians composed of both Jews and non-Jews meeting in different places. The greetings in ch. 16 mention a number of people and the churches that met in their homes. Reading between the lines of 14:1 – 15:13, it seems that the Roman Christian community was split between Jewish and Gentile factions.

Paul wrote Romans on his third missionary journey from Cenchrea or nearby Corinth. He had never visited the city and we do not know how the gospel first came there. Why did he write such a weighty letter to them? Three related reasons are evident. These are of a missionary, apologetic and pastoral nature.

First, Paul wrote to inform the Roman Christians of his desire to visit them on his way to Spain (15:23–24) and to enlist their interest, prayers and support. Just as Syrian Antioch was Paul's home base for his first three missionary journeys in the east, Paul apparently hoped that Rome would become a base for his missions further west. In this sense Romans is a letter of introduction in which Paul explains himself, both his message and agenda, fairly comprehensively (see 15:14–24). The letter serves this same purpose for us too, as the first in the sequence of Paul's letters in the NT.

Secondly, familiar with opposition, Paul wrote to defend both himself and his message. Romans functions as an apologia for Paul, the sort he would soon be giving in Judea when he brought the money he had been collecting from the Gentile churches to Jerusalem for the poor Jewish believers (see 15:25–33).

Thirdly, Paul had apparently heard of a split in the church between Jewish and Gentile believers. The first part of Romans presents a theology that bolsters his plea that the two groups 'accept one another' (15:7). The issue of Jew–Gentile relationships is evident throughout the letter and reaches centre stage in chs. 9 – 11.

B. Content and structure

The letter opens with a good summary of Paul's identity and task. Paul is an authoritative messenger charged to spread the good news, especially to Gentiles, about Jesus Christ, who is God's Son, promised in the OT (1:1–7). The conclusion (15:14 – 16:27) expands on Paul's role in God's plans as apostle to the Gentiles, notes that he intends to visit Rome in connection with this commission, warns against 'those who cause divisions' (16:17), greets those Paul knows who have an active part in the life of the church, and ends by praising God in terms that recall the main ideas of the letter.

In 1:16–17 Paul gives a brief statement of the gospel, which he goes on to expound in the rest of the letter. The gospel offers salvation to all, both Jews and Gentiles, is received by faith, and reveals the righteousness of God.

In the first main section, 1:18 – 3:20, Paul establishes the sinful condition of all human beings with the relentless drive of a trial lawyer. Jews and Gentiles alike are under the guilt and power of sin and deserve God's wrath. Next, in 3:21 – 4:25, Paul announces that God has done what is needed for us to be right with him through Jesus Christ and his sacrificial death. Our acceptance with God is not our own achievement and is not dependent on keeping the law; it is by faith. However, it is not contrary to the law, but rather upholds it, as the examples of Abraham and David attest.

In 5:1 – 8:39 Paul explains that the new situation of the justified person brings peace, hope, freedom and life. Believers have a sure hope of final salvation; have been set free from sin as an enslaving power and from law as a condemning power; and are indwelt by the Holy Spirit, who leads them onward to a life of righteousness.

In 9:1 – 11:36 Paul defends God against the charge of unrighteousness in the light of Israel's substantial failure to respond to the gospel and his consequent rejection of them. What of his pledge to Abraham and the patriarchs? Paul explains that, despite Israel's rejection of the righteousness of God by faith, God still remains faithful to his covenant promises.

The last major section lays out the practical implications of the righteousness of God. In 12:1 – 13:14 believers are called to obedience and faith in their daily attitudes and actions. In the light of the coming consummation of salvation they are to live in humility and love towards each other and in submission to civil authorities. Finally in 14:1 – 15:13, in what many see as the climax of the letter, Paul seeks to calm quarrels in the church by urging Jewish and Gentile believers to act responsibly towards each other in matters of social custom.

1:1–7	Opening greeting
1:8–15	Thanksgiving
1:16–17	Theme: God's righteousness revealed in the gospel
1:18 – 3:20	God's righteousness in his wrath against sinners
3:21 – 4:25	God's saving righteousness: justification by faith
5:1 – 8:39	The effects of God's righteousness: freedom and life in the Spirit
9:1 – 11:36	The rejection of God's righteousness: the problem of Jewish unbelief
12:1 – 15:13	God's righteousness in everyday life
15:14–33	Paul's past, present and future plans
16:1–27	Closing greetings

C. Reading Romans today

Romans is not an easy read. One problem can be losing the thread of Paul's argument. When reading the letter, it is always worth asking, where am I in the major divisions of the book? These are chs. 1 – 4, 5 – 8, 9 – 11, 12 – 15 and 16. Individual sections must be read in the context of the big picture. To this end, it is important to read Romans both slowly, verse by verse, and rapidly, covering whole sections and even the whole book in one sitting.

Attention to Paul's extensive use of the OT in Romans, which boasts as many as fifty quotations, is essential to appreciating the nuances of Paul's message. Key examples are Hab. 2:4 quoted in 1:17 ('The righteous will live by faith'), several psalms in 3:10–18, Gen. 15:6 in 4:3, Hos. 2:23 in 9:25 and Isa. 11:10 in 15:12.

In expounding the gospel in depth, Romans uses technical language that can be confusing. So vast are the blessings of salvation that Paul draws on terms from different realms of life, such as courts of law for justification, the temple for propitiation and family relations for reconciliation. Bible dictionaries and modern English versions provide assistance with these concepts.

For all its difficulty, the theological and practical significance of Romans is immense. There has never been written a more compelling exposition of the way of salvation, which defends the character of God at every turn, and of the nature of holiness and Christian obedience.

1 CORINTHIANS

1 Corinthians gives an insight into a church struggling to apply the lofty truths of the gospel to the problems of everyday life. It was not in fact Paul's first letter to the Corinthian Christians, nor was it his last. Paul's

relations with the Corinthian church spanned several years in the 50s AD and produced some of Paul's most profound teaching on the Christian life.

A. Occasion and purpose

The capital of the province of Achaia, Corinth was the seat of its governor and a major trading route between the east and west of the empire. Corinth was cosmopolitan and religiously pluralistic, accustomed to visits by impressive, travelling public speakers. It was obsessed with status, self-promotion and personal rights.

Paul laid the foundation for the church of God in Corinth on his second missionary journey, and spent eighteen months there building it up (Acts 18:1–18). Most of its members were former Gentiles (cf. 12:2: 'when you were pagans...') and had turned to God from idols. Sent from Ephesus on his third missionary journey a few years later, 1 Corinthians mentions a previous letter of Paul to the church (1 Cor. 5:9–11). In it he had warned them not to associate with those who were guilty of serious sins, such as sexual immorality, greed and idolatry. Since these were the typical faults of the Gentiles, Paul was effectively exhorting them not to be conformed to the world. Unfortunately, some in the church mistook Paul to be saying they should shun not just fellow believers who behaved in such ways, but their non-Christian friends also. The book which we call 1 Corinthians is in part Paul's attempt to correct this misunderstanding. Paul was prompted to write it in response to disturbing news from the church. This included both oral reports, from Chloe's people (1:11) and from Stephanas, Fortunatus and Achaicus (16:17), and a letter from the church (7:1) consisting of a series of questions posed by the congregation.

As far as we can reconstruct the situation, after Paul had left, Apollos, and possibly Peter, visited Corinth. As well as bringing various benefits, this caused unintended problems. The congregation was now divided based on loyalty to their favourite Christian leader (1:12). Further, Paul learned that they were in considerable disarray with civil litigation between members (6:1–11), sexual immorality (5:1–13; 6:12–20), marriage problems (7:1–40) and questions concerning food offered to idols (chs. 8 – 10) and spiritual gifts (chs. 12 – 14).

The common element in all the problems in the church is that the Corinthians were 'worldly', 'acting like mere human beings' (3:3). The social values of secular Corinth had infiltrated the church. Paul's attempt to sort out the serious problems within the largely Gentile church in Corinth consists primarily of a confrontation over two particular vices: sexual immorality and idolatry.

Paul wrote 1 Corinthians to tell the church of God in Corinth that they are part of the fulfilment of the OT expectation of worldwide worship of the God of Israel. Therefore, as God's end-time temple, they must act in a manner appropriate to their pure and holy status by becoming unified, shunning pagan vices, and glorifying God as they reflect the lordship of Jesus Christ.

B. Content and structure

In 1:2 Paul refers to the Corinthians as those 'sanctified in Christ Jesus and called to be his holy people, together with all those who call on the name of our Lord Jesus Christ [literally] in every place'. The last phrase echoes Mal. 1:11, which predicts a future time when God would be worshipped by Gentiles all over the world: ' "My name will be great among the nations, from where the sun rises to where it sets. *In every place* incense and pure offerings will be brought to me, because my name will be great among the nations," says the LORD Almighty.' For Paul, the Corinthians are part of the fulfilment of God's plan to be worshipped among all the Gentiles and he wants them to help fulfil this worldwide eschatological vision by glorifying God.

In chs. 1 – 4 Paul urges the Corinthians to be united in the proclamation and service-oriented lifestyle of the cross, for they have entered the new eschatological age of salvation. There is a negative treatment of the wisdom of the world, which asserts that God has outsmarted and overpowered human powers and authorities (1:10 – 2:5), followed by a positive section that proclaims the Christ-centred wisdom of the cross (2:6 – 4:17). In 4:18 – 7:40 Paul deals primarily with issues related to sexual immorality, first in a negative treatment of its manifestations in the church in Corinth (4:18 – 6:20) and then in a positive treatment of marriage (7:1–40).

Chs. 8 – 14 deal with the issue of idolatry, beginning again with a negative treatment of its manifestations in Corinth (8:1 – 11:1) and then moving to a more positive treatment of the proper worship of the one true God (11:2 – 14:40). 1 Corinthians comes to a climax in ch. 15 with a discussion of the resurrection as it relates to the ultimate triumph of Christ over all adversaries and the final transformation of our corruptible humanity into a humanity that fully reflects God's glory. Ch. 16 closes the letter with instructions for the collection, some personal requests and Paul's final greetings.

Paul's use of the key words 'flee' and 'glory' reveal his main concerns in the letter. In concluding the negative section on sexual immorality, Paul exhorts the Corinthians to 'flee from sexual immorality' (6:18) and to 'glorify God' with their bodies (6:20, literally). In concluding the negative section on idolatry, Paul exhorts them to 'flee from idolatry' (10:14) and to do everything 'for the glory of God' (10:31).

1:1–9	Letter opening
1:10 – 2:5	Division and false wisdom of this world
2:6 – 4:3	True wisdom of the cross and the Spirit
3:5 – 4:17	Nature of Christian leadership
4:18 – 6:20	Condemnation of illicit sexual relations and greed
7:1–40	Affirmation of sexual purity in marriage and singleness
8:1 – 11:1	Condemnation of idolatrous practices
11:2 – 14:40	Affirmation of edifying worship
15:1–58	The resurrection of the body
16:1–24	Letter closing

C. Reading 1 Corinthians today

Reading Paul's letters can be like listening to one end of a telephone conversation; unfortunately we are left to guess what the party on the other end of the line is saying. Called mirror reading, this strategy is especially pertinent to the interpretation of 1 Corinthians. In each section attentive readers gain from Paul's responses some sense of what had been said and was going on in Corinth. Read this way, the letter is far from dry moral discourse, but is a vital conversation. It is possible to speculate too much about the situation in Corinth, but English versions usually give a starting point by indicating where Paul is quoting the Corinthians, as in 1:12: 'I follow Apollos'; 6:12: 'I have the right to do anything'; 7:1: 'It is good for a man not to have sexual relations with a woman'; and 8:1: 'We all possess knowledge.'

As well as supplying concrete answers to many problems which have comparable manifestations today, on subjects as diverse as preaching, sexual ethics and worship, 1 Corinthians models how to approach complex ethical problems of Christian living with the resources of the OT and the example and teaching of Jesus. Above all, it shows the importance of asking, how does the gospel of the death and resurrection of Jesus, which envelop the letter in chs. 1 and 15, teach us to live?

2 CORINTHIANS

If 1 Corinthians reveals the heart of a church, 2 Corinthians shows us the heart of an apostle. In it Paul expresses not only his anguish, distress and sorrow but also his deep desires, hopes and joys as he struggles to secure the Corinthians' sincere and pure devotion to Christ.

A. *Occasion and purpose*

Following the writing of 1 Corinthians, a number of developments took place between Paul and the church in Corinth. 2 Corinthians refers to a 'painful visit' (2:1), a tearful letter (2:4), and visits by Timothy (1:19; cf. 1 Cor. 16:10–11) and Titus (7:6–7). It also mentions Paul's own plans to visit being changed (1:15–16). Further, Paul had experienced great hardship in Ephesus (1:8–10) and had instigated a major collection of financial aid for famine-stricken believers in Jerusalem to which he hoped the Corinthians would contribute. How this all fits together in the story of the Corinthian correspondence is not entirely clear.

What is clear is that 2 Corinthians was written after some of the problems in the church had been resolved, and when visiting preachers threatened to undermine Paul and his gospel in Corinth. Paul's rivals were evidently Jewish Christian missionaries (11:22), some of whom claimed to be apostles (11:5, 13; 12:11). Apparently they disparaged Paul as being a lousy speaker (11:6) and lacking in personal presence (10:1, 10; 13:3–4). They boasted of their own eloquence and erudition (11:6), visions and revelations (12:1, 7), pure Jewish lineage (11:22) and impressive letters of recommendation (3:1). In short, they commended themselves as in every way superior to Paul (10:12). In response Paul accused them of preaching another Jesus, a different spirit and a different gospel (11:4).

In Macedonia, on his way to Corinth, Paul wrote 2 Corinthians to express his relief that the church had responded well to his 'tearful letter' and to the visit of Titus (2:6, 9, 12–14; 7:5–16), and to encourage them to reaffirm their allegiance to him and to complete their contribution to the collection for the saints in Jerusalem (8:6–7, 10–11; 9:3–5). His defence to those who accused him of personal weakness was to agree with the accusation, but to counter that in this very weakness God reveals *his* power. To prepare the church in Corinth for his upcoming visit, Paul exhorted them to examine themselves in the light of his teaching (12:14; 13:1, 5, 11) and save him from having to exercise discipline in the community when he arrived (10:2, 5–6, 11; 11:3; 12:19–21; 13:10).

B. *Content and structure*

The letter has three main sections. The main theme of chs. 1 – 7 is 'comfort in the midst of troubles' (cf. 1:4). Paul tells of his own suffering in 1:3–11, 6:4–10 and 11:23–29. Throughout we learn that suffering endured patiently deepens our appreciation of God's character, drives us to trust in God alone, leads us to identify with Jesus Christ (cf. 1:5: 'the sufferings of Christ'), is met by comfort from God and is ultimately eclipsed by eternal glory. All this leads Paul to reflect directly on death and resurrection in ch. 5, where death brings deepened fellowship with Christ and a spiritual body. The prospect of being accountable to Christ prompts the believer to seek to please the Lord in every circumstance (5:9). Other teaching in this section covers church discipline (2:5–11), the old and new covenants (3:7–18), reconciliation (5:11–21) and holiness (6:14 – 7:1).

Chs. 8 – 9 highlight several features of genuine Christian giving, as Paul encourages the Corinthians to finalize their contribution to his collection for the 'the poor among the Lord's people in Jerusalem' (Rom. 15:26). Generous giving is motivated by the example of other believers, by a desire for spiritual excellence and supremely by the example of Christ. An equal sharing of burdens and voluntary mutual sacrifice are endorsed. Christian giving is to be voluntary, enthusiastic and sensible and is an evidence of God's grace.

Finally, in chs. 10 – 13 Paul defends his authority as an apostle against the intruders from Palestine, who were 'false apostles, deceitful workmen, masquerading as apostles of Christ' (11:13). His main theme is 'strength in the midst of weakness' – paradoxically, the power of God finds its full scope and potency only in acknowledged human weakness (12:9; 13:4).

1:1–2	Opening greeting
1:3–11	Thanksgiving for Paul's deliverance
1:12 – 2:13	The rift with the congregation
2:14 – 7:1	Gospel ministry: divine power and human weakness
7:2–16	The joy of reconciliation
8:1 – 9:15	Arrangements for the collection
10:1 – 13:10	Paul's apostleship: Christ's 'fool' versus the 'super apostles'
13:11–13	Closing greetings

C. Reading 2 Corinthians today

Paul's robust response to a church in turmoil models the proper concern of a pastor for the congregation. Paul was willing 'to spend and be spent' for the benefit of his spiritual children (12:14–15). He calls them to 'open wide' their hearts to him (6:13). Indeed, throughout the letter his paternal affection for them is obvious: 'If I love you more, will you love me less?' (12:15). 2 Corinthians is punctuated by desire, compassion, joy, tears, courage, shame, anxiety, fear, sorrow and regret. This dimension of the letter can make it frustrating to interpret; it lacks the order and logic of a less emotive text like Romans. However, readers today should beware of favouring cognition over emotion and filtering out the affective elements of the letter. Feelings play an essential role in Christian faith.

Theologically, 2 Corinthians develops a profound and yet practical truth introduced in 1 Corinthians: God's power is revealed in the midst of human weakness (cf. 1 Cor. 1:17 and the power of the cross). Just as the power of God was revealed in the death of Christ, so the power of the resurrection is revealed in the ministry of those who recognize their own weakness and therefore trust in God (like Paul) and not in themselves (like the false apostles). The crucifixion of Christ appeared on the surface to be a manifestation of his weakness, but in fact it revealed God's power. Likewise the weakness of the Christian is the key to experiencing the power of God.

GALATIANS

As one of Paul's earliest letters, if not his first, Galatians provides invaluable information about the apostolic age. Written in response to a serious crisis in the church, the letter defends our full acceptance and freedom in Christ alone. Strident and even intimidating in tone, Galatians has been a cornerstone of our understanding of the gospel of the grace of God for two thousand years.

A. Occasion and purpose

While there is some debate over the destination and date of Galatians (see chart), the setting is clear. Jewish Christians had come from Jerusalem to the church that Paul had planted in central or northern 'Asia' (now Turkey). They then told Paul's Gentile converts that, in order to be accepted by God and be fully integrated into his family, they needed to be circumcised and to keep the Jewish festivals and food laws. These so-called Judaizers questioned the adequacy of Paul's gospel and his credentials as an apostle. Evidently, some in the church were buying their arguments.

This scenario can be reconstructed from clues scattered throughout the letter:

- The Galatians were Gentile believers who had gladly received Paul and his message (4:8–9, 13–15)

- They were now confused and turning to a 'different gospel' (1:6–7)
- They were considering circumcision and keeping the Mosaic law (3:2–5)
- Some visitors were trying to compel them to be circumcised (6:12–15)
- Paul warns: 'if you let yourselves be circumcised, Christ will be of no value to you' (5:2).

Paul wrote to the Galatians to call them to remain firm in the gospel message he had preached to them on three grounds: his law-free gospel is of divine origin; their experience and the Scriptures show that they have become full members of God's new people by faith in Christ and not by works of the law; and the Spirit is the true remedy to the problem of the sinful nature.

B. Content and structure

In Paul's view, the solution to the Galatian crisis is to remember what time it is. The coming of Christ has brought about a radical transformation. The promises to the Jewish forefather Abraham (3:7–8, 16–17, 29; 4:22–23), the giving of the law (3:17, 19; 4:24–25), the execution of the curse of the law in Israel's exile (3:10, 13; 4:24–25) and the prophetic promise regarding the future salvation and restoration of God's people (3:6–9) are all part of a unified historical drama which climaxes in the coming of Jesus, his death for sins and his resurrection from the dead. In Jesus Christ, God has pierced the barrier between the divine and human (1:12), heaven and earth (4:25–26), spirit and flesh (5:16–17), new and old creation (6:15). A new age has dawned in which God the Father deals with humanity as sons, not slaves (4:3–5); where humans relate to God not by law, but by faith working through love (3:23, 25; 5:6).

Related to this, Galatians trumpets the grace of God as the fundamental basis of Christian existence (1:3, 6; 2:21; 5:4; 6:18). Our standing with God rests entirely on his undeserved favour. Justification, leading to acquittal on the day of judgment, is not gained by keeping the law, by living according to a set of community standards or by performing good deeds, but is experienced now by those who simply have faith in Jesus.

Galatians is the only letter of Paul to a church that does not begin with some kind of thanksgiving. With so much at stake, Paul launches immediately into a defence of his apostleship, since his person and message are inseparable. He then defends justification by faith and Christian liberty against his opponents' attempt to impose adherence to the Mosaic law on the church.

1:1–5	Opening greeting
1:6–12	Setting: the message of the Judaizers is not the gospel of Christ
1:11 – 2:21	Autobiography: Paul's gospel and apostleship is of divine origin
3:1 – 4:31	Doctrine: justification by faith and not by works of the law
5:1 – 6:10	Practice: walk in the Spirit
6:11–18	Final plea

C. Reading Galatians today

Since Paul's opponents were basically urging Gentile believers to become Jews, many of Paul's arguments are based on the OT. He quotes Gen. 15:6 in 3:6, Gen. 12:3 in 3:8, Deut. 27:26 in 3:10, Hab. 2:4 in 3:11, Lev. 18:5 in 3:12, Deut. 21:23 in 3:13, Gen. 12:7 in 3:16, Isa. 54:1 in 4:27, Gen. 21:10 in 4:30 and Lev. 19:18 in 5:14. We need to read these in their OT contexts, along with the other texts he cites less explicitly, to appreciate the full impact of Paul's rejoinder.

Galatians answers abiding questions of fundamental importance: How do you know you are a child of God? How do we decide who else is a member of the family? How do we live out our family life? Paul's letter warns against limiting our fellowship with fellow believers because of any cultural, racial or social differences.

The letter also acknowledges that our freedom in Christ is open to abuse (5:13); rather than indulging the sinful nature we are to serve each other in love. Walking in the Spirit is put forward as the solution to gratifying 'the desires of the flesh' (5:16, literally). If the flesh is the weakness of the human nature living on the resources of this age (4:23), promoting corruption and disunity (5:19–21), life in the Spirit represents the presence and power of the age to come (4:29) with its supernatural ability to manifest love and promote good in the community (5:22–23).

EPHESIANS

Ephesians expounds the nature of Christian salvation and the character of the new life that flows from it. The letter bears many similarities to Colossians, though the latter concentrates on the person of Christ. Ephesians presents Paul's most mature thought on the church in God's purposes.

A. Occasion and purpose

Ephesus was the capital of the province of Asia (now Turkey) and a major city of the Roman Empire situated on a busy trade route. Its theatre had a seating capacity of 24,000 people. Not surprisingly, then, it became a focus of Paul's missionary labours over many years. He visited Ephesus at the end of his second missionary journey (Acts 18:18–21) and spent most of his third missionary journey there (Acts 19:1 – 20:37). According to 1 Tim. 1:3, he later appointed Timothy to oversee the work in Ephesus.

Paul wrote Ephesians from prison (3:1; 4:1; 6:20). The letter is fairly general in content and may even have been a kind of circular letter intended for several congregations in Western Asia Minor since some early manuscripts do not have 'Ephesus' as the specific destination in 1:1.

However, certain emphases in the letter do suggest some of Paul's reasons for writing. The emphasis on the unity of Jewish and Gentile Christians may well be intended to address tensions in the church. Additionally, the fact that the devil and various 'powers' are mentioned sixteen times in the letter suggests a concern to encourage believers in their struggle with pernicious spirit-forces. Acts 19 associates demonic activity with Ephesus, and archaeology has uncovered ancient Ephesus as a centre for magical practices, the Artemis cult, a variety of Phrygian mystery religions and astrological beliefs. Paul wrote Ephesians to celebrate God's mighty work of redemption, which includes the forgiveness of sins and raising up of believers, both Jews and Gentiles, to new life in the power of the Spirit.

B. Content and structure

The letter has a basic two-part structure, with chs. 4 – 6 setting out conduct appropriate to the gospel which Paul expounded in chs. 1 – 3. The transition comes in 4:1: 'I urge you to live a life worthy of the calling [to salvation] you have received.'

Ch. 1 opens with an inspiring thanksgiving for the gift of salvation, planned from eternity past and now being realized in the lives of believers. Paul then prays for the spiritual progress of his readers in light of Christ's supreme power in the universe. Ch. 2 recalls the readers' hopeless situation of death and condemnation and God's astounding deliverance. The barriers between Jews and Gentiles have now been demolished and their reconciliation through the cross has been achieved. Those who believe in Jesus are now united in one body on an equal basis. Ch. 3 explains the way in which this truth (of God bringing diverse people into one church) had been hidden for ages, but has now been made known to the Christian apostles and prophets and especially to Paul. The apostle then prays again for the readers, that they may know the love and power of God.

In 4:1–16 Paul exhorts them to express this unity through the rich variety of gifts which Christ has given to the church. The rest of chs. 4 – 6 offer practical instruction for appropriate Christian living. Most readers were former Gentiles, whose way of life before their conversion needed to be replaced by new patterns of behaviour: 'put on the new self ... in true righteousness and holiness' (4:24). The letter closes with a call to spiritual vigilance in 6:10–20.

1:1–2	Opening greeting
1:3–14	Thanksgiving for salvation in Christ
2:1–22	Reconciliation of both Jews and Gentiles to God
3:1–21	The mystery of Jews and Gentiles in one body
4:1–16	Appeal to live in unity
4:17 – 5:20	Moral exhortation: new life/new lifestyle
5:21 – 6:9	Christian relationships in the household
6:10–20	Appeal to spiritual warfare: the armour of God
6:21–24	Closing greetings

C. Reading Ephesians today

Ephesians presents a vision of the love and power of God as comprehensive as that found in Romans. A number of features stand out. The letter's teaching on reconciliation being both vertical (with God) and horizontal (with people unlike ourselves) is an important lesson to those of us in Western societies that are riven by individualism and often xenophobia.

The preponderance of 'power' language in the letter reminds us that people need not only forgiveness, but also deliverance from the evil forces that enslave them and control their destiny. Ephesians announces both God's power and Christ's supremacy over these forces, along with the believer's access to that power. We have been transplanted from one sphere of power, or 'kingdom', to another. The role of faith for obtaining God's strengthening is stressed (1:19; 3:17; 6:16) and the purpose of this power is to show love following the example of Christ (3:16–17; 5:2).

Finally, worship and praise dominate the letter. People filled with the Spirit speak to one another 'with psalms, hymns and songs from the Spirit' (5:19). This reminds us of the celebration of God's work of salvation in chs. 1 – 3. In talking about God we must avoid the trap of reducing everything to arguments and propositions. Ephesians expresses the profoundest theology in dazzled worship.

PHILIPPIANS

Although written from prison, Philippians contains some of the most encouraging passages in the NT. In it Paul writes of his passion for knowing Christ, his joy in the midst of adversity and his confidence in the face of death.

A. Occasion and purpose

Paul and Silas arrived in Philippi in Macedonia (mainland Greece) from Asia (now Turkey) on Paul's second missionary journey, having received a summons in a vision from God (Acts 16:9–10). A small but important city on a busy overland trade route, Philippi was named after Philip of Macedon, the father of Alexander the Great. It was a Roman colony with the privileges of self-government and freedom from taxation, and many of its inhabitants were proud to be Roman citizens. The account of Paul's visit in Acts 16:11–40 tells of the conversion of Lydia, an encounter with a slave girl who told fortunes, and Paul's subsequent arrest and miraculous escape from prison. The apostle and his associates made a number of visits in the years to follow.

A close relationship between Paul and the church developed, and they supported him financially. When Paul ended up in prison, probably in Rome (cf. Acts 28), they sent Epaphroditus with another gift and enquired about his welfare. Several things about the church concerned Paul. As well as facing the general hostility regularly met by Christians in the ancient world (cf. 1:29–30), the church was experiencing quarrels among prominent members (cf. 4:2) and was in danger from Judaizing Christian missionaries who, as in Galatia, held that the gospel must be supplemented by circumcision and the Jewish law. Additionally, Epaphroditus had fallen severely ill (cf. 2:25–30).

Paul wrote Philippians for a number of reasons: to inform the Philippians that his current troubles are reason to rejoice (1:12–26); to thank them for their support (1:3–7; 2:25; 4:14, 18); to urge unity (1:27 – 2:18; 4:2–3); to warn of threats to the church (3:2–18); to reassure them that Epaphroditus is now well (2:25–30); and to inform them of his intention to send Timothy to help them out (2:19–24).

B. Content and structure

Although addressing some serious concerns, Philippians maintains a mood of confidence and optimism based on what God is doing with respect to Paul and the church: the word 'joy' occurs sixteen times in the letter. In ch. 1, even in the midst of what seem to be tragic circum-stances, Paul is upbeat and chiefly concerned with the progress of the gospel and the welfare of the church.

Ch. 2 urges meekness and unity in the church and a good witness to the world. The ground for this appeal is the example of Christ himself, whose own humiliation in becoming human and dying on the cross was vindicated by God. The magnificent hymn about Christ in 2:6–11 shows that it is not the nature of God to seize and to grasp, but rather to share and to give at great personal cost.

According to Paul in ch. 3, progress in the Christian life is not about keeping rules. Rather, it involves concerted effort toward the goal of knowing Christ (cf. 'I press on' in 3:12, 14). Likewise, Paul's warning against false teaching includes a description of holiness in terms of an ever-increasing understanding of the surpassing value of Jesus Christ.

Ch. 4 addresses directly some of those members causing problems in the church (Euodia and Syntyche), gives some general exhortations to positive Christian living, and thanks the Philippians for their financial support.

1:1–11	Opening greeting and thanksgiving
1:12–26	Paul's imprisonment and prospects for Paul and the gospel
1:27 – 2:18	Appeal for humility and unity in the church
2:19–30	Future plans for visits to Philippi
3:1 – 4:1	Warning about Judaizing missionaries
4:2–9	Encouragement to unity, prayer and Christian virtues
4:10–23	Thanks for personal gifts and closing greetings

C. Reading Philippians today

Philippians contributes much to our understanding of Christian doctrine and practice, and demonstrates the secure connection between the two. A prime example is the teaching about Jesus Christ in 2:6–11; Paul recounts that Christ renounced the privileges of deity in order to be a servant of others. Strikingly the profound truth of the incarnation is used by Paul for the practical end of urging humility and unity in the congregation (2:1–5).

At the same time, the letter contains some of the most personal reflections in the NT. In wrestling with the prospect of his own death the apostle takes a remarkably positive view. It is the gospel that imbues him with such confidence: 'to live is Christ and to die is gain' (1:21). Central to Christian experience is knowing Christ and sharing in his sufferings and resurrection (3:10).

In relation to church and society, without diminishing civic responsibility, Paul exploits the status of Philippi as a Roman colony to teach that Christians belong to a higher and more important commonwealth: since 'our citizenship is in heaven' (3:20) we are to 'live in a manner worthy of the gospel of Christ' (1:27).

COLOSSIANS

Although one of the shortest of Paul's letters, Colossians expresses more fully than his other letters what he believes about Jesus Christ. Writing in response to false teaching in Colossae, Paul offers a profound exposition of the supremacy of Christ and the completeness of the believer's new life in Christ.

A. Occasion and purpose

Colossae was a small town on a Roman road in the Lycus valley, about 100 miles/160 kms east of the provincial capital city of Ephesus. Paul had not visited Colossae (2:1), but the church was probably planted as a result of his wider ministry. Paul spent three years in Ephesus on his third missionary journey and, as Luke reports, 'all the Jews and Greeks who lived in the province of Asia heard the word of the Lord' (Acts 19:10). It was probably during this time that Epaphras, one of Paul's fellow workers, evangelized Colossae and established the church (1:7; 4:12–13).

Along with general encouragement (1:4, 6; 2:5), Colossians is sharply focused on a particular problem in the church. It appears that while in prison (4:3, 10, 18) Paul received news of dangerous teaching that had infiltrated the region. This teaching was Jewish and ritualistic in nature (2:16–17) and philosophical in approach (2:8, 18), advocating the worship of angels and harsh treatment of the body (2:18, 20–23). In Paul's view it was a denial of the sufficiency of Christ.

Paul wrote to the Colossians to provide a refutation of this false teaching and to commend a truly Christian way of life. Col. 2:6 sums up his message: 'Just as you received Christ Jesus as Lord, continue to live your lives in him.'

B. Content and structure

The letter opens with Paul's thanksgiving for the Colossian Christians and his prayer for their future. They are characterized by faith, hope and love (1:4–5), and their goal ought to be to live a life befitting the people of God.

The hymn-like description of Christ in 1:15–20 sets the tone for the rest of the letter. Two 'stanzas' proclaim him as supreme in creation, as the uncreated image of God (1:15–17), and supreme in redemption, as the first to rise from the dead and as the reconciler of the universe (1:18–20). But Christ has a unique relationship not only to God, the universe and the cross, but also to the Colossian believers (1:21–23). Anticipating his rebuttal of false teaching, 1:24 – 2:5 explains Paul's authority to teach as a servant of the church. Paul devotes all his energy to sharing the fullness of wisdom that comes from Christ.

In 2:8–23 Paul insists that all the knowledge they need is contained in Christ. Consequently, any teaching that seeks to supplement this is effectively a denial of the truth. In 3:1 – 4:6 the Colossians are told to be what they really are, those who have died to the sinful world and now live to God. Far from impractical or merely theoretical, being 'raised with Christ' (3:1) has radical implications for personal relationships and for the shape of family life.

1:1–14	Opening greeting and prayer for the Colossians
1:15–23	The pre-eminence of Christ in creation and redemption
1:24–29	Paul's ministry in Christ
2:1–5	Paul's ministry to the Colossians
2:6–7	The theme of the letter: continue in Christ
2:8–23	Attack on false teaching: the sufficiency of Christ
3:1 – 4:6	Moral exhortation: new life in Christ
4:7–18	Further news and final greetings

C. Reading Colossians today

While the 'Colossian heresy' is long gone and is not a threat to us, Paul's response to it contains numerous insights into genuine faith and spirituality, and continues to serve as a warning against substitutes. Counterfeit faiths range widely, but all foolishly underestimate Christ (2:8–9), while counterfeit spiritualities naively underestimate sin and 'lack any value in restraining sensual indulgence' (2:23). Paul's answer in both cases is to point to the sufficiency of the believer's relationship with Christ (3:3: 'your life is now hidden with Christ in God').

Colossians addresses the most profound questions of human existence and points to Christ as the answer to them all: What is God like? Why are we here? How can the world be put right? How can I be put right?

1 THESSALONIANS

One of Paul's earliest letters, 1 Thessalonians provides an insight into the deep affection Paul felt for people and the manner in which he worked with and helped young Christians. Since every chapter ends with a reference to the second coming of Christ, 1 Thessalonians also contains vital teaching on the end of the world.

A. Occasion and purpose

Paul's crossing into Europe on his second missionary journey, in answer to the call of 'a man of Macedonia' in a dream (Acts 16:6–10), was a major step forward in the progress of the gospel. The new campaign consisted of two phases, in the north and then the south of modern-day Greece. The first was in Macedonia, in the cities of Philippi and Thessalonica, and the second in the region of Achaia, where Paul visited Athens and Corinth. Trouble in Thessalonica meant that Paul had to leave in a hurry (Acts 17:1–10). Even if his initial stay was only three weeks, it was long enough for the formation of a small congregation of mainly Gentile believers ('you turned . . . from idols', 1:9; cf. 2:14).

However, after Paul left, the situation in the church was one of instability. Paul had sent Timothy to strengthen them in the faith (3:2), and it seems that he wrote this letter to support Timothy's ministry and to encourage them to live a life pleasing to God (4:1). Apparently the Thessalonian believers were disturbed by opposition and by the death of some members of the church (4:13–18). They wanted to know when the Lord would arrive and how those who died would fit into the divine plan regarding the second coming.

Paul wrote this letter to encourage the Thessalonian believers not to be shaken by the opposition they were experiencing or by the death of their fellow members, but rather to be strengthened in their faith and to grow in Christian character (see Paul's prayer for them in 3:12–13). To do this he offers them some doctrinal instruction, and corrects some errors in living.

B. Content and structure

Paul reminds the Thessalonians that, having turned to God from idols, they are under his protection and are to live holy lives befitting their new status (4:3; 5:23). The Father has called them, Jesus is their Lord, and the Spirit is active in the powerful proclamation and joyful reception of the gospel that gave them new life. The letter reminds the church that they are 'in God' (1:2) and 'in Christ Jesus' (2:14; 3:8; 4:1, 16; 5:12, 18).

The warm relationship between Paul and this church is also a highlight (2:17, 20; 3:6).

The teaching about the second coming serves a pastoral rather than speculative purpose. Paul writes to reassure the Thessalonians that Jesus will certainly return, and that all believers, living and dead, will be taken up to be with the Lord forever (4:13–18). Confidence in our own resurrection rests on God having raised Jesus from the dead (4:14). The Day of the Lord will come like a thief in the night (i.e. when we least expect it). In the meantime the children of light must remain vigilant (5:1–11).

1:1–10	Opening greeting and thanksgiving
2:1–16	The apostles' ministry in Thessalonica
2:17 – 3:13	Paul's plans to revisit, and his continuing concern
4:1–12	Living to please God
4:13 – 5:11	The return of Christ
5:12–24	Life in the church
5:25–28	Closing greetings

C. Reading 1 Thessalonians today

1 Thessalonians offers comfort and encouragement to young Christians experiencing opposition to their faith, feeling the pressures of temptation to sexual immorality, or losing confidence in the future following the death of a loved one.

The two millennia since Christ first came have not altered the character of Christian hope. In the face of undeniable evil in the world, the resurrection of Jesus from the dead guarantees that the God of love and justice will ultimately triumph. Being ready for the return of Jesus (5:23–24) is a good summary of the Christian life.

2 THESSALONIANS

2 Thessalonians offers comfort to a church in distress. The letter testifies to powerful spiritual opposition to God and the gospel. God's control over the course of history, including a final victory over evil, is affirmed as an integral part of Christian faith.

A. Occasion and purpose

After receiving their first letter from Paul the Thessalonians began to panic, thinking that the countdown to the end of the world was already far advanced and that the end times were upon them. This error seems to have arisen because of the immaturity of the persecuted church and a mistaken interpretation of Paul's first letter with its references to trials and persecution (1 Thess. 1:6; 3:3–4, 7) and 'wrath' (1 Thess. 1:10; 2:16; 5:9). Further, the exhortations to be ready at all times and to be vigilant until that day (intended to encourage them to live holy lives) may have led them to neglect daily responsibilities such as work, and to devote themselves exclusively to waiting for the return of Christ (3:6–14).

These misunderstandings of his first letter came to Paul's attention while he was still in Corinth and prompted him to write 2 Thessalonians. Some scholars doubt the letter's authenticity, presuming that it is a pseudonymous work by a later Christian writer. The primary objection to Pauline authorship is the striking similarities between the two letters, thought to suggest imitation by a follower of Paul. However, the overlap between the letters is best explained by assuming that they really are by the same author, on the same subjects, to the same audience, and written one shortly after the other.

Paul wrote to tell the Thessalonians that the Day of the Lord had not yet come (2:1–12) and to encourage them to remain firm, hold fast to the teachings that Paul had passed on to them (2:15), and live orderly lives (3:6–10) worthy of their calling by God (1:11; 2:14).

B. Content and structure

If 1 Thessalonians expresses a lively hope in the imminent coming of the Lord (e.g. 1 Thess. 4:17), 2 Thessalonians counsels that the end of the world cannot happen before the Satanic opposition to God has reached a climax. Other NT texts, such as Mark 13 and Revelation, likewise stress that evil will increase before the final showdown with God. Before the day of Christ, there will be rebellion and 'the man of lawlessness' (2:3), who will exalt himself as if he were God and will deceive many (cf. Dan. 11:3–36). The identification of who or what is 'holding him back' (2:6) is beset with difficulty. It may be that God himself restrains him with the purpose of providing opportunity for the gospel to be heard everywhere. What is clear is that the glory of Christ's coming will most certainly defeat the forces of wickedness (2:1–12).

The final part of the letter addresses the practical problem of the laziness of some believers in the church. Paul appeals to his own example of hard work as a model to imitate.

1:1–22	Opening greeting, thanksgiving and prayer
2:1–12	Lawlessness will precede Christ's return
2:13–17	Exhortation to stand firm

| 3:1–16 | Exhortation to pray and work |
| 3:17–18 | Closing greetings |

C. Reading 2 Thessalonians today

Given its particular teaching about 'the man of lawlessness', 2 Thessalonians is among the most difficult of Paul's letters. As strange as this teaching on the second coming and the last days may seem to some, it brings comfort to those overwhelmed by forces hostile to God, a common experience in the twenty-first century AD. In emphasizing the sovereignty and goodness of God, 2 Thessalonians continues to bring consolation to Christian people in all kinds of distress.

1 & 2 TIMOTHY AND TITUS

The Pastoral Letters of 1 & 2 Timothy and Titus belong together and are distinctive amongst the NT letters. They are the only ones written to individuals in church leadership, and generally focus on the personal lives and activity of those leaders (or 'pastors' – hence the title 'pastoral' letters). They also have a common literary style, but one which is quite different in a number of respects from other Pauline writings. This raises sharply the question of their origin.

Of a vocabulary of 901 words in the Pastoral Letters, 335 are not found elsewhere in Paul. Every letter has its own distinctive vocabulary, but this proportion is about twice that of the other Pauline letters. The Pastorals also omit many terms that are characteristic of Paul's other writings, including 'free', 'to work', 'to preach the gospel', 'heaven', 'spiritual', 'wisdom', 'body', 'son' and 'soul'. There are a number of other points of style that differ. Further, there is a distinct lack of Paul's theological emphases, with little mention of the fatherhood of God, of being 'in Christ', or of the work of the Spirit in the believer.

If Paul is the author, then these differences are due to changes of situation for him and the churches, and his writing to individuals rather than groups of believers. But if we conclude that Paul was not the author, then there are serious problems with the integrity of these letters in the Bible – and we are also faced with the challenge that Pauline authorship was never doubted in the early church.

A. Occasion and purpose

Titus appears to have travelled with Paul for part of his missionary work, and was Paul's companion at Jerusalem during the controversy about circumcision (Gal. 2:1, 3). Later he made several visits to Corinth and reported back to Paul (2 Cor. 7:6–7, etc.).

Timothy joined Paul on his second missionary campaign (Acts 16:1–3) when Paul visited his home town of Lystra. He appears to have worked closely with Silas, and travelled with Paul to Thessalonica, Philippi and Corinth. He is listed as co-writer with Paul in the letters to the Thessalonians, Colossians, Philippians and the second to the Corinthians, and was with Paul when he wrote Romans.

2 Tim. 1:17 places Paul firmly in Rome, but in rather different circumstances from those depicted in Acts 28:30–31. Although we have no record of what happened after the end of Acts, it seems probable that Paul was released and engaged in further missionary activity. If so, then this is the most likely time for him to have written Titus and 1 Timothy. Eusebius (c. AD 300) records the tradition that Paul was again imprisoned in Rome and executed under Nero, and that he wrote 2 Timothy at that time. The personal nature of the letter accords with this. So all three letters are likely to have come from the 60s.

B. Content and structure

1 Timothy and Titus contain many practical instructions, while 2 Timothy is more like a 'testament' of Paul as he faces death. Nevertheless, there are common themes in Paul's description of the opposition facing the churches:

- A recurrent theme is of 'myths and genealogies' (1 Tim. 1:3–4; Titus 1:14; 3:9), probably esoteric interpretations of Jewish tradition.
- Related to this are various debates and arguments (2 Tim. 2:23; Titus 3:9); Paul's reference to 'knowledge' (1 Tim. 6:20) may suggest the development of a kind of rational intellectualism.
- Some were engaging in ascetic practices, i.e. abstaining from food and sexual relations, as part of a claim to spiritual superiority (1 Tim. 4:2–3).
- There was some debate about whether the resurrection of the dead had passed (2 Tim. 2:18).
- There was also moral laxity or licence (1 Tim. 1:19; 2 Tim. 3:1–9; Titus 1:15–16).

There are signs of these debates in Paul's earlier letters, especially to the Corinthians and Thessalonians. It may be that these challenges to Christian faith were growing and eventually fed into the second-century development of Gnosticism, with its emphasis on special knowledge and secret ritual.

1 Timothy

1:1 – 3:16	Teachers and leaders in the church
1:3–11	Warning against false teachers
1:12–20	Paul's testimony
2:1–15	Prayer and worship when meeting together
3:1–16	Qualifications for overseers and deacons
4:1 – 6:21	Instructions to Timothy
4:1–16	How Timothy is to respond to the threat of heresy
5:1 – 6:2	Different groups in the church
6:3–21	False teaching, love of money, and the call to godliness

2 Timothy

1:1 – 4:5	Timothy's role as leader
1:3–18	Encouragement to be faithful
2:1–13	Encouragement to be strong in the face of suffering
2:14–26	Encouragement to purity in the face of pressure
3:1–9	Warning of godlessness in the 'last days'
3:10 – 4:5	Encouragement to give mature leadership
4:6–22	Paul's personal experience and greetings

Titus

1:1–4	Opening greeting
1:5–9	Appointment of elders/overseers
1:10–16	Warnings about false teachers
2:1–15	Different groups in the church
3:1–11	Peaceful living, through God's grace
3:12–15	Closing instructions and greetings

C. Two key issues for today

1. Church order

The Pastoral Letters are the only place in the NT where there is a sense of developed church order in leadership. But there appears to be some interchangeability of terms (e.g. 'elder' and 'overseer', Titus 1:6–7) and the structure has the fluidity seen elsewhere in the NT, rather than the rigidity and hierarchy which emerged in the second century.

2. The place of women

1 Tim. 2:11–15 has probably caused more debate and upset than any other paragraph in the whole NT! Any credible interpretation needs to take account of the following issues of text and context:

- 'Quietness' (v. 11) has to do with demeanour and is not the same as 'silence'; 'submission' is the quality that elsewhere Paul commands of all believers to all others (Eph. 5:21).
- Inviting women to participate in worship and learn alongside men would have been a radical challenge to some first-century religious traditions.
- 'I do not permit' (v. 12) is an unusual expression, better translated 'I am not permitting', i.e. current practice rather than permanent ruling.
- The word for 'to have authority' is an odd one and used only here in the NT. In other literature it means 'taking power to oneself', often with overtones of violence.

All this needs to be read in the context of Paul's other statements about the status of men and women in Christ (such as Gal. 3:28) and his particular concern that women should participate fully in worship through praying and prophesying (1 Cor. 11:5), and through exercising spiritual gifts which are given 'to each one' (1 Cor. 12:7).

PHILEMON

The shortest and most mundane of Paul's surviving letters, Philemon is a potent illustration of the breaking down of social and cultural barriers in Christ. In it we see not only the intriguing story of an errant slave, but also the essence and power of the gospel.

A. Occasion and purpose

Two reconstructions of the letter's background are possible. Either Onesimus had stolen from his master Philemon and run away (18), or the two had simply fallen out and Onesimus had gone to Paul for help. In either case, once they had made contact, Paul led Onesimus to Christ (10). Philemon is also a Christian and is faced with the dilemma of Christian slave ownership.

Paul wrote to effect reconciliation between Onesimus and Philemon, by encouraging Philemon to forgive Onesimus and welcome him back as a dearly-loved Christian brother.

B. Content and structure

The letter is an example of Paul not exercising his authority coercively. The apostle forgoes his right to command (8–9), seeking instead Philemon's voluntary consent (14), and allows him the freedom to express his love as he sees fit (5, 7). Paul effectively hopes to persuade Philemon to think through the implications of there being no slave or free person in Christ (Gal. 3:28). He may even be hinting that Onesimus should be released, in order to become a colleague of Paul.

vv. 1–3	Opening greeting
vv. 4–22	Request
vv. 23–25	Closing greetings

C. Reading Philemon today

Philemon reveals Paul's attitude to the institution of slavery. Although on face value he accepts its legitimacy, his championing of the individual slave undermines the practice. Paul emphasizes Onesimus' true identity as a brother in Christ. His appeal echoes the gospel in urging Philemon to welcome his slave and give him a new status (16–17) and in offering to pay his debt in his stead (18).

HEBREWS

The thirteen chapters of the book of Hebrews form a tightly reasoned argument designed to encourage faithfulness and bolster confidence. This argument forms the NT's longest explanation of the significance of Jesus' person, ministry and death. The explanation is given in terms of priesthood, sacrifice, covenant and ritual purity, and reminds us that early Christianity was a movement within Judaism.

A. Author and origin

Hebrews nowhere identifies its author or recipients. Nonetheless, there are several things we can say about them. The Greek style of the book is eloquent and precise, and the argument rhetorically sophisticated. The author displays an intimate knowledge of the OT, and close familiarity with Jewish interpretative techniques. This points to both Greek and Jewish education. The author had long known the readers and planned to visit them soon (13:23). He knew Timothy and hoped to travel with him (13:23). This indicates that he was part of the early missionary circle which included Paul and his associates. While Hebrews nowhere claims Pauline authorship, ancient manuscripts always include Hebrews among Paul's letters. However, from ancient times readers have observed significant stylistic differences between Paul's letters and Hebrews. The differences are so great that nearly all modern scholars conclude that Paul did not write Hebrews. Who did? We don't know. We cannot be certain that the author is even a person named in the NT. Nevertheless, we can credit him for being a creative and pastorally wise theologian.

Heb. 13:24 contains greetings sent by 'those from Italy' (13:24). If this refers to Italian ex-patriots sending greetings home, then the recipients lived somewhere in Italy. However, the idiom 'those from (place name)' usually identified people living at the named location. Further, several ancient manuscripts allude to the greeting in longer versions of the letter's title, so their scribes took Italy to be the place of composition. Thus we should conclude that Hebrews was written from Italy, and in 13:24 local Italians convey their greeting to Christians elsewhere.

B. Occasion and purpose

The readers had been believers for some time (5:11–14). Heb. 2:3 implies that they had been evangelized by those who had heard Jesus in person. In the past they had endured persecution because of their confession of Christ (10:32–34). Now they found themselves facing hardship again, but this time their faithfulness waned. Some grew lax in doing good works (10:24; 13:1–3). They were perplexed that God was permitting hardship (12:3–17). Some even stopped meeting with other believers altogether (10:25). Others continued to meet, but apostasy was a foreseeable possibility which the author sought to pre-empt.

The book's preoccupation with sacrifice and priesthood would have had particular relevance for Christians living near the temple, so the traditional title 'to the Hebrews' probably refers to Christians in Palestine. Some discount the title as speculation, noting that the book's argument depends on descriptions of sacrifice and priesthood found in the Mosaic law, and that it consistently refers to the tabernacle (or tent of meeting) rather than the temple. This is thought problematic for a Palestinian destination. Recent discoveries, however, support the traditional view.

A Dead Sea letter known as 4QMMT protests against the policies of Jerusalem's leaders regarding the sacrificial cult and Levitical priesthood. This dispute centred on the proper application of OT laws originally formulated for the wilderness camp and the tabernacle. The author of 4QMMT insists that 'the temple is the place of the tent of meeting, and Jerusalem is the camp; and outside the camp is outside Jerusalem'. Thus 4QMMT defines 'tabernacle/tent of meeting', 'camp' and 'outside the camp' very specifically.

These definitions are helpful for understanding Hebrews. First, the book expresses significant concern about the law's status (7:12; 10:1), the basis in it for Jesus' priesthood and sacrifice (e.g. 5:1–10; 7:11 – 8:13; 9:15–24), and other related matters. As with 4QMMT, our author apparently referred to the tabernacle rather than the temple because for him the temple is the tabernacle.

Secondly, the book's climax refers to 'the camp' (13:11–14). This is often presumed to indicate Judaism in general, but there is no precedent for this in contemporary sources. By contrast, the definitions of 4QMMT fit the context perfectly. Jesus suffered 'outside the city gate' (13:12), i.e. outside Jerusalem. The readers are to 'go outside the camp' (13:13) because 'here we do not have an enduring city...' (13:14), i.e. earthly Jerusalem (cf. 12:22; Gal. 4:25–26), '...but we are looking for the city that is to come', i.e. the heavenly Jerusalem (cf. Rev. 21:10). The parallel structure of the passage supports identifying 'the camp' with Jerusalem, in line with 4QMMT. Corroborating this, Jerusalem is referred to elsewhere in the NT as 'the camp of God's people, the city he loves' (Rev. 20:9).

According to early traditions, the Jerusalem church received prophetic warning to leave Jerusalem before its destruction. The call to 'go outside the camp' (13:13) may be advice to obey that warning (cf. 11:13–15; 12:26–28). Even if not, 'the camp' appears to designate Jerusalem. Thus the recipients probably lived in Jerusalem before AD 70, and their concerns with sacrifice, priesthood and ritual purity were real, not theoretical.

C. Structure and genre

1:1 – 10:18	The superiority of Jesus, and exhortations for faith
1:1–4	God's revelation through his Son
1:5 – 2:18	Jesus' superiority to angels
3:1 – 4:13	Jesus' superiority to Moses and Joshua
4:14 – 10:18	Jesus' superiority as high priest and sacrifice
10:19 – 13:25	Exhortations for faithful living

Typical Greek letters begin by identifying their author and recipients. Because Hebrews does not, some interpreters suggest that it is not really a letter. Many classify it instead as a sermon, because it supposedly calls itself a 'word of exhortation' (13:22). The same Greek phrase is used in

Acts 13:15 to refer to a message Paul delivered in the synagogue at Antioch. However, there is good reason to believe that the normal synagogue sermon would have been completed before Paul gave his 'word of exhortation'. Further, the close association between exhortation and prophecy in Acts and Paul's letters suggests that Paul delivered a prophetic exhortation in Antioch (cf. Acts 4:36; 15:32; 1 Cor. 14:3, 31). So here in Hebrews, 'the word of exhortation' may refer to a prophetic warning the community had already received (12:25; cf. 11:7).

In any case, Heb. 1 – 12 contains a handful of features characteristically found in the body of ancient letters. And the book clearly ends like a letter (13:20–25), e.g. 13:24 (see above) and 13:22, where the author uses a Greek word for 'write' (*epistello*) that often means 'write an epistle/letter' (*epistole*). So the author apparently considered himself to be writing an epistle.

D. Reading Hebrews today

1. Jesus' supremacy

The earliest Christians were zealous to obey God's law (cf. Acts 21:20), and saw no tension between the gospel and the sacrificial system (cf. Acts 2:46; 3:1; 5:25; 6:13–14; 21:17–26). For the readers of Hebrews, however, there was a tension between obeying Jesus and obeying the law. Further, the law seemed to have more in its favour, as God's word to Israel mediated by angels (2:2; cf. Gal. 3:19) and delivered by Moses.

The author tackles this concern head-on. The word spoken by God's Son is superior to the word spoken by the prophets (1:1–2). Jesus himself is superior to the angels who mediated the Law (1:3 – 2:18). He is also superior to Moses who received the law (3:1–6). This implies that the message first declared by Jesus (2:1–4) has greater authority than the law. In these arguments Jesus is unhesitatingly identified with Israel's creator God (1:2, 10; cf. 11:3), and deserves worship from the mightiest angelic beings (1:6). In fact, he is nothing less than God (1:8).

2. Contrasting covenants

Several times Hebrews contrasts the old and new covenants. These covenants do not represent two religions, as often assumed, but rather the stages in God's redemptive work. They are contrasted to demonstrate primarily two things. First, by its very nature the old covenant could not fully sanctify the worshipper or put sin away once and for all (cf. 9:9–10). Jesus' new covenant ministry does accomplish this (9:11–28), and the new covenant contains better promises (8:6). Second, the old covenant was never intended to be permanent, but only applied 'until the time of the new order' when things would be set right (9:10). Now the messiah has come. The institutions of the old covenant have fulfilled their purposes, are obsolete, and will soon disappear (8:13). So Christians may leave them behind, and are no longer obligated to follow OT laws governing sacrifice, priesthood and ritual purity.

3. Examples of faithfulness

The readers faced a crisis that shook their confession of faith in Christ. God was speaking to them (cf. 12:25), but they found it difficult to obey. The author encourages them 'to imitate those who through faith and patience inherit what has been promised' (6:12). They should 'believe and [be] saved' (10:39), like 'the great cloud of witnesses' (12:1). These are the heroes of Israel's past (11:1–40) who endured hardship and death as they faithfully obeyed God. Similarly, the community's former leaders displayed faithfulness worthy of imitation (13:7). Lastly, Jesus endured much for his people. He exemplifies what it means to be a faithful son of God who obeys even in hardship (5:7–10). Jesus did this in order to bring 'many sons and daughters to glory' (2:10). As children of God destined for glory (2:17), the readers should imitate their brother's example (12:1–2; 13:12–13). We likewise should imitate the faithful obedience of the Bible's heroes, Christian leaders and, above all, Jesus himself.

JAMES

The letter of James was famously denounced by Luther as 'an epistle of straw'. Yet it remains a favourite letter of the NT for many Christians, and its call to integrity of living is strikingly relevant to both the contemporary church and contemporary society.

A. Occasion and purpose

Although English derives the author's name from Latin, his name in Greek is 'Jacob', like Israel's patriarch (Gen. 25 – 35). Of the Jacobs/ Jameses mentioned in the NT, the only serious contender for authorship is James the brother of Jesus (Mark 6:3; Gal. 1:19), who became a believer after the resurrection (1 Cor. 15:7) and went on to be a leading figure in the church in Jerusalem (Acts 12:17; 15:13). One tradition says he was known as 'camel knees' because of his habit of praying in the temple!

If this authorship is correct, then the letter must have been written before AD 62, since we are told by Josephus that James was stoned to death by order of High Priest Ananus prior to the arrival of a new governor of Judea that year (Josephus *Antiquities of the Jews* 20.197–203). The lack of reference to the fall of Jerusalem in AD 70 and the assumption that the church is led by elders (5:14) both fit with this early date.

Commentators have speculated about the possible situations that the letter is addressing. But the general title and the general nature of the comments make defining the situation of the intended audience difficult – and in fact this does not affect interpretation.

The language and rhetorical style of James compares very well with other Greek literature, and this has made some question whether it could really be written by an Aramaic-speaking Jew from Galilee. However, we know of other competent writers in Greek from the region, so this is not as unlikely as it may at first sound. Other objections to James as author are based on the few references to Jesus, and on the relation between the teaching here on faith and works and the teaching of Paul – and to these we now turn.

B. Content and genre

In contrast to some of Paul's letters (especially Romans), James does not appear to present a developed argument of any kind. The most obvious division of the letter is into three sections:

1:2–27	Introduction to the letter's themes
2:1 – 5:6	Development of these themes
5:7–20	Conclusion, with final appeals

Although the themes in ch. 1 are not developed in the same order in the body of the letter, there are striking correspondences between the two sections:

1:2–27		**2:1 – 5:6**	
2–4	Endure testing with joy		
5–8	Ask God for wisdom	3:13–18	The nature of the wisdom from above
9–11	Rich and poor are equal in the face of mortality	4:13–17	Plans to prosper come to nothing in the face of mortality
12–16	Endure testing, which comes from inner desires not God	4:1–10	Disputes arise from our worldly desires

1:2–27 (*cont.*)		**2:1 – 5:6** (*cont.*)	
17–18	God the giver		
19–21	Be quick to listen, slow to speak and slow to anger	3:1–12	The powers and peril of speech
		4:11–12	Don't judge one another
22–25	Be doers of the word, not merely hearers	2:14–26	Verbal assent is worth nothing without action
26–27	True religion means helping the poor	2:1–13	Don't show favouritism to the rich
		5:1–6	Judgment on rich oppressors

Although the opening greeting styles this book as a letter, James has a distinctive feel compared to other NT letters. The main reason is that about half the verses in James have verbs in the imperative form, that is, they are commands or encouragements to do something (e.g. 'consider it pure joy', 1:2; 'don't be deceived', 1:16; 'take note of this', 1:19). Other NT letters have sections written in this style, but no other consists only of this kind of writing.

This has made some commentators argue that James is a particular kind of literature labelled *paraenesis* (Greek for 'encouragement'), which consists of collections of sayings, unconnected with one another, and without reference to a particular author or situation. However, we shall see that James does not fall so neatly into this category.

James' ethical perspective and use of practical examples and general sayings, along with the reference to 'wisdom', have suggested to some that it sits within Israel's 'wisdom' tradition, represented chiefly in the OT by Proverbs and Ecclesiastes. Despite these common features, James has more emphasis on eschatology (God's end-times judgment of all) than does other wisdom literature. And James offers a much more radical ethic in relation to wealth and poverty than we find in (for example) Proverbs.

The opening greeting 'To the twelve tribes scattered among the nations' is very general, and it is perhaps difficult to imagine this actually being sent as a letter. In comparison with Paul's letters, which have much more detailed introductions and conclusions, following the usual conventions of ancient letter writing (see section above), James looks rather sparse. But we do have examples of circular letters which have a very similar form, e.g. in the intertestamental book 1 Maccabees 10:25–45. We also know that the Pauline letters were circulated beyond the churches to which particular letters were addressed, and in the case of Ephesians we have a letter probably intended to be a circular from the beginning.

So James may well have been written as a circular letter, but with a particular focus on encouragement, drawing on Jewish wisdom traditions and elsewhere.

C. James, Jesus and Paul

There are only two references to Jesus, in 1:1 and 2:1, and these are made almost in passing. There is no reference to the major events of Jesus' life, and in particular his death and resurrection, and no reference to the Holy Spirit.

Closer inspection, however, shows that there are many links to the teaching of Jesus as recorded in the Gospels, and especially the Gospel of Matthew, which is often understood to be addressing Jewish concerns. The closest is in 5:12 ('All you need to say is a simple "Yes" or "No"') which looks like a quotation of Matt. 5:37 – but there are many other similarities in wording and theme. The ethic of James looks as though it has been closely shaped by the teaching of Jesus.

At first sight, James' statement that 'people are justified by what they do and not by faith alone' (2:24) looks like the opposite of Paul's comment in Rom. 3:28 that 'a person is justified by faith apart from observing the law'. Further, both Paul and James appeal to the example of Abraham, but apparently to prove opposite ideas. This has been one of the main reasons for the neglect of James – but it is something of a false dichotomy.

The idea that Paul is only interested in what we believe, not what we do, is at best a poor parody. For instance, the failure to act aright highlights humanity's need of God in Rom. 3; the struggle to act right in Rom. 7 is answered by the gift of the Spirit in Rom. 8; and Rom. 12 is all about how we live out in action what God has done for us in Christ. On the other hand, James is clearly not interested in action alone; for Abraham, 'his faith and his actions were working together' (2:22). James' concern is that our trust in God should be seen clearly in how we live our lives. Paul and James would agree that the problem of human sin is *both* a spiritual one (our standing before a holy God) *and* a practical one (our inability to live aright).

D. Reading James today

Perhaps a helpful key to understanding James' concerns, and putting the discussion about faith and works into context, is to notice the importance for James of integrity, wholeness or oneness. The confession of the oneness of God in Deut. 6:4 ('Hear O Israel: the LORD our God, the LORD is one') was central to Jewish belief. Although sometimes understood as emphasizing that there is only one God, it is at least as important in affirming the single nature of God. James cites this confession near the middle of his letter, at 2:19, but the idea permeates his reflection about the nature of God and the nature of discipleship.

- There is no changing in God; he is not fickle, showing a dark side one minute and light another, tempting then accusing (2:17).
- We are to treat others with integrity, rather than paying attention to their outward appearance (the Greek for 'favouritism' in 2:1, 9 means literally 'looking upon the face') and ignoring their inner reality.
- Our speech should be marked by integrity, not saying one thing at one time and another at another, letting our 'yes' be 'yes' and our 'no' be 'no'.
- We must have integrity within ourselves, so that what we believe in our hearts is matched by the actions of our lives.
- We need to live in communities of integrity, seeking together God's wisdom rather than be broken up by disputes arising from our own desires.
- We need to integrate how we see the present and how we see the future, living now in the light of the coming judgment of God.

Living in a broken world – where the church appears (in public at least) to do nothing but fight with itself, when the most persistent question about faith is whether you can believe in a good God in the face of human suffering, and when nothing hinders mission more than lack of integrity amongst believers – this is a message we need to hear more than ever.

1 PETER

Unlike the letter of James, the first letter of Peter has many more of the features of a NT letter. It also has a clearer sense of progress and developing argument, and, like many of the Pauline letters, has a general pattern of moving from exploration of theological truths to the working out of these truths in daily living.

A. Occasion and purpose

1. The apostle

The letter claims to be from Peter, 'apostle of Jesus Christ'. Although the term 'apostle' may have been applied more widely, it is usually understood in the NT to refer to the Twelve. The style of the letter borrows some elements from classical Greek, and this might be seen as odd for something written by an 'unschooled' fisherman (Acts 4:13).

However, Galilee was on a major trade route, and it would not be unusual for ordinary people to be multilingual. Moreover, the letter cites Silas (Silvanus) as Peter's *amanuensis* or letter-writing 'secretary', and from Silas' extensive travels with Paul it is clear that he was a skilled Greek speaker.

2. The dispersed

The letter is addressed to 'God's elect' who are 'scattered'. The word used here is *diaspora*, a standard term for the Jews living outside Palestine following the exile to Babylon in 587/6 BC. (Some versions translate this term 'the Dispersion'.) Along with Peter's use of the OT, this might suggest that he is addressing a primarily Jewish audience. However, the language about the believers' former way of living in 4:3 echoes typical Jewish criticism of pagan living, so Peter is in fact carrying language about the Jews over to the mixed Jewish/Gentile Christian community. (The use of 'Christian' in 4:16 is the only occurrence of the term outside Acts in the NT.) What is particularly interesting is that Peter applies the promises of God and identity of God's OT people to this mixed Christian community *without exception*. There are no promises which this community will not inherit, no aspects of identity from the OT which are not true of them.

3. Foreigners and aliens

Peter also addresses his readers as 'exiles' and 'foreigners' (1:1, 17; 2:11). In the Greek OT (the Septuagint) these words were applied to Abraham in Canaan (Gen. 26:23; 23:4) and Israel in Egypt (Gen. 15:13) and later to Judah in exile in Babylon and the Jewish community in Egypt. In the Greco-Roman world, these terms referred to resident aliens who ranked above foreign visitors and slaves, but below full citizens, and were often viewed with some suspicion. Peter is not using the term to suggest that his audience belong to this actual social class – after all, they are viewed with mistrust because of changed lifestyles, not social standing (4:4). Rather, this term shows the severe social pressures they were under, treated as strangers in their own land and paying the price for standing out as different from the surrounding culture.

4. Persecution

Pliny was governor of Pontus-Bithynia in the early second century, and took specific measures against Christians in this area. We know of this from a letter he wrote to Emperor Trajan in AD 111–112. Some of the language he uses has echoes in 1 Peter, which might suggest that our letter is of a similar date. However, Pliny talks of executing Christians, which Peter does not mention. In fact, Peter comments that the suffering of his readers is no different from what other Christians are suffering (5:9), and he uses the general Greek word for suffering (*pascho*, 12 times, more than any other NT book) rather than the word for persecution.

5. Babylon

The use of 'Babylon' as a symbol for Rome is found in a number of Jewish and Christian documents. This would be a natural association to make, especially after the destruction of Jerusalem by Rome in AD 70 – and most of the references come from this later period. If Peter, whom tradition strongly associates with Rome and who died c. AD 65, is indeed the author of this letter, this makes 5:13 one of the earliest such references.

B. Content and structure

1:1–2	Opening greeting in standard letter format
1:3–12	Praise to God ('doxology', similar to many Pauline letters)
1:13 – 2:3	Response to God's grace in holy living
2:4–10	Jesus, the living stone, and his chosen people
2:11 – 3:7	Live godly lives: everyone, slaves, wives, husbands
3:8–22	Live well together, and accept suffering
4:1–11	Live changed lives, alert and sober
4:12–19	Suffering as sharing in the suffering of Christ
5:1–11	Appeals to elders, young men, and all
5:12–14	Greetings from Peter, Silas and the church in 'Babylon'

The letter is notable for its extensive use of the OT, not only in direct quotations (usually indicated in English Bibles) but also in phrases and sayings throughout the letter. Especially notable are its references to Isa. 53, e.g. 2:22 quotes a verse, and 2:24–25 quotes three other phrases. Although this passage is not cited very frequently in the NT, it probably stands behind much of its understanding of Jesus' death, including Jesus' own predictions of his being rejected and killed (see Mark 8:31; 9:13; 10:33 and parallels), and perhaps Paul's description of Jesus dying for our sins 'according to the Scriptures' (1 Cor. 15:3).

C. Reading 1 Peter today

1. Community

1 Peter is full of very strong language about the communal identity of believers, mostly rooted in the OT but also echoing Paul (cf. 4:8–11 with Rom. 12:4–8). This is a powerful challenge to individualized ideas of 'personal' faith in Western society today, which prizes individual freedom of choice.

2. Witness

Our engagement with society will involve affirming the positive alongside bearing witness to God by living good lives (2:12) and speaking out (3:15). And we might not always realize how radical this is. The simple command to 'honour everyone' (2:17, literally) flew in the face of hierarchical Roman society, where honour was accorded in proportion to someone's power and influence. In our society, which values appearance above everything, to imitate God in not judging by outward appearance would be radical indeed.

3. Submission

In making sense of how, exactly, we 'live well' before others, we need to think carefully about the nature of the various submissions that Peter mentions.

- He words the commands carefully (cf. his distinction between *fearing* God and *honouring* the king/emperor in 2:17). Wives should 'submit' to their husbands, the word used elsewhere of the attitude all believers should have to one another (the NT never uses the word 'obey' for wives, though it does use this word for children to their parents). As in Eph. 5:22, wives should submit to *their own* husbands.
- The three commands to submit must be read in the wider context of the NT. The respect due to authorities (Rom. 13) does not ignore their potential as agents of the enemy (Rev. 13). The apparent acceptance of slave/master relationships must be held in tension with the radical equality of all in Christ. And the ordering of family relations needs to take account of the radical involvement of women in the worshipping life of the Christian community.
- How we live out the radical challenge of the gospel today in a context where there is still a legacy of respect for Christian belief, and where all have a democratic right to speak out, will be very different from

living it out as a small and threatened minority in the autocratic and hierarchical society of the first century.

4. Jesus descending to hell?

1 Pet. 3:19 ('the imprisoned spirits') and 4:6 ('gospel preached to those who are now dead') have been understood to mean that Jesus 'descended into hell' (as found in the Apostle's Creed) to preach to those who died before his coming. But there is now widespread agreement that these difficult verses do not support this interpretation. The first is best read in the context of Jewish belief about 'fallen angels' awaiting final judgment, to whom Jesus' victory is proclaimed. The second refers to those who have been evangelized but who have now died, as can be seen by the reference to the dead in the preceding verse.

2 PETER AND JUDE

2 Peter and Jude are often treated together in commentaries because of the large overlap in material between Jude and 2 Pet. 2. This in itself is not a problem; after all, there is considerable overlap between the three 'synoptic' Gospels, while Isa. 36 – 39 is reproduced almost word for word in 2 Kgs 18 – 20. But it does raise the question of the relation between the two texts. The close similarity in wording implies some literary dependence. So either both used a common source – but then more than half of Jude consists of this source, and its writer simply repeated what was written elsewhere; or Jude drew on 2 Peter – but strangely used only the middle part; or 2 Peter used Jude – the view of most commentators, supported by close study of the relevant passages.

A. Occasion and purpose

The author of Jude identifies himself as 'a servant of Jesus Christ and a brother of James' (v. 1). It was unusual to identify oneself as a brother rather than a son, so this probably relates the author to Jesus' brother James, who was prominent in the leadership of the church in Jerusalem. Like James (Jas 1:1), Jude now sees Jesus' position as 'Master and Lord' as more significant than his relation as brother, not least because, again like James, he was not a disciple during Jesus' earthly ministry (Mark 6:3).

The authorship of 2 Peter is probably the most hotly contested in NT studies. The clear claim of the letter is that it is written by the apostle Peter (see 1:1 and 3:1) and there are comments about being an eyewitness to Jesus to back this up (1:16–18). However, the style of writing appears quite different from 1 Peter; the letter incorporates Greek religious and philosophical ideas that might be surprising for a Galilean fisherman (such as 'participating in the divine nature', 1:4; and the list of virtues in 1:5–9); and the tense shifts between present and future in describing the threat of false teachers (compare 2:1–3 with 2:10–12).

So some scholars conclude that 2 Peter is a form of Jewish 'testament', where a later author writes in the name of a famous leader as if giving his last words. However, while some features of 2 Peter fit this theory, others do not. Computer linguistic analysis shows 2 Peter to be significantly closer to 1 Peter than to the rest of the NT, and there is always a danger in assuming a limited understanding for a 'simple' Galilean fisherman. So the case against Peter as author is not as strong as it might be – though puzzles, especially those concerning tense, remain.

Some claim that Jude and 2 Peter mark the beginnings of an early 'catholicism', which would make them late. However, both show expectation of Christ's return and neither show interest in sacramentalism or church offices, which argues against this.

A letter written by Jude would most naturally be dated to the 50s. If 2 Peter is written by Peter, it must be no later than the 60s; if by someone else, it must be no later than around 100, when other writings appear which seem to be dependent on it.

B. Content and structure

Jude's style of argument is evident from its structure.

1–4	Opening greeting and purpose
5–13	Six OT examples, applied to false teachers
14–16	A prophecy from 1 Enoch 1:9, applied to false teachers
17–19	A prophecy from the apostles, applied to false teachers
20–25	Closing exhortations and doxology

2 Peter includes different styles of writing, but the shape of its argument is clear.

1:1–2	Address and greeting
1:3–15	Summary of message and reason for writing
1:16–21	Apostolic witness and prophecy is from God
2:1–22	Future false teachers and God's certain judgment
3:1–10	Future scoffers and Christ's certain return
3:11–18	Exhortation to holy living and doxology

C. Reading 2 Peter and Jude today

These two letters contain some of the most obscure verses in the NT (Jude 6, 9, 14–15; 2 Pet. 2:4) and others that have caused considerable disagreement as to their interpretation (such as 2 Pet. 3:10). But there are also some key verses, not least the acknowledgment of the importance of Paul's writings in 2 Pet. 3:15–16. These have been perhaps the most neglected books of the NT and need to be taken seriously – but we need to be careful how we interpret and use them.

Much of the language, particularly in Jude and the parallel sections in 2 Peter, is highly polemical, and makes sharp distinctions between true and false teachers. These texts have at times been used to justify a confrontational approach to relations with other Christians, or a retreat into a 'faithful remnant' detached from others. So it is important to notice these features of the text:

- The sections about false teachers are not simply outbursts of animosity, but are reasoned arguments based on texts of Scripture that would have been recognized as such within first-century Judaism.
- The consistent appeal is not to separation but to a shared communal inheritance in the OT Scriptures and in the apostolic witness prior to its being formalized within the canon of the NT.
- Jude's warnings appear to be against rejecting traditional Jewish and Christian teaching on morality (i.e. 'antinomianism'). 2 Pet. 2:7–9 adds to this a focus on the security of the godly; whenever we talk of the judgment of others, we must also face the reality of judgment ourselves.
- We need to read these calls to purity of life and doctrine in the light of Jesus' ministry: both his own call to holiness and warnings of judgment, and his radical inclusion of the unholy and the marginalized.
- In all this, grace remains central. Jude's letter closes with an injunction to be 'merciful to those who doubt' (22) and a wonderful doxology to God, who alone guarantees our security and fashions in us his perfection. 2 Peter places a list of virtues in the context of the forgiveness of sins (1:5–9) and of receiving the inheritance God has given us (1:10–11). Moreover, many of these ideas, originally expressed in Jewish terms, are re-expressed in a way that is accessible to a Greek audience. Grace is always mission-hearted.

1, 2 & 3 JOHN

The three Johannine letters have a style distinct from other NT letters, and some clear connections with the Gospel of John. These connections are most evident in 1 John, though there are phrases in the other two letters that in turn connect them with 1 John.

A. *The letters and the Gospel*

It is not immediately clear that 1 John is in fact a letter. It has no mention of author or audience, no opening or closing greetings, and no obvious structure, unlike the Pauline letters. At first reading it feels rather repetitive, or at least has a circular, reflective shape to it.

There are many connections with John's Gospel both in vocabulary and ideas. Many of them are found in the opening verses, but in most cases they are repeated throughout:

- The opening of the letter talks of 'the beginning' (1:1; cf. John 1:1).
- The place of testimony to what has been seen and heard (1:2–3; cf. John 1:14).
- The ideas of light and life, closely related to one another (1:2; cf. John 1:4; 8:12).
- Eternal life (1:2; cf. John 1:4; 3:16).
- Jesus as God's son (1:7, 9–10; cf. John 1:14, 18; 5:17–18).
- Joy being made complete (1:4; cf. John 3:29; 15:11; 16:24).
- The new commandment (2:7–8; cf. John 13:34–35).
- Contrast between light and darkness (2:8–10; cf. John 1:5).
- The hostility of the world (2:15–17; cf. John 1:10–11).
- Living in the truth (2:21; 3:18–19; cf. John 3:21).
- Remaining (abiding) in God (2:24–27; cf. John 15:4–10).
- Jesus laying down his life for us (3:16; cf. John 10:11; 15:13).

By contrast, there are three areas which might set the letter apart from the Gospel. First, the letter appears still to expect the coming of Jesus in the near future (e.g. 2:28), in contrast to the 'realized eschatology' of the Gospel which suggests that the full reality of Christ has come in his death and resurrection. However, the Gospel does still retain a future perspective (e.g. John 6:39–40), and conversely the letter sees the reality of the final victory already anticipated in the present (2:13–14).

Secondly, the letter describes Jesus' death as an 'atoning sacrifice' (2:2) which rather contrasts the Gospel's idea of the Son being 'lifted up' (John 12:32–34). However, the Gospel also talks of Jesus as the sacrificial lamb (John 1:29), and both Gospel and letter refer to Jesus laying down his life.

Thirdly, the letter's references to the Holy Spirit do not match the highly personalized language of the Gospel (John 14 – 16). However, the letter does identify the 'anointing' of the Spirit as leading into truth (2:20, 27) in a way that is strikingly reminiscent of the Gospel (John 16:13).

2 & 3 John share some phraseology with 1 John: a new command, loving one another, obedience, Jesus coming in the flesh and joy being complete (2 John); and doing what is good and having true testimony (3 John). But they are more obviously written as letters, in the one case to a church, in the other to an individual church leader.

With so much overlap in vocabulary and theme, it is hard to resist the conclusion that 1 John was written by the same person who wrote John's Gospel – or at least someone who was very familiar with and influenced by the Gospel.

Papias, writing in the second century, adds a possible confusion to the question of authorship. He refers to 'elders', including John, who were disciples of the Lord, but then also refers to 'the elder John'. It is unclear whether he is referring here to one person or to two separate people. If there was a 'John the elder' as distinct from John the apostle, then he may have been the author of 2 and 3 John. And 1 John may then have been written by either of the two.

B. Content and structure

Rather than having a typical letter structure, 1 John moves in a particular shape, often making general statements from which conclusions about Christian living and behaviour are then drawn.

1:1–4	Prologue (similar to John 1:1–18)
1:5 – 2:14	We must walk in the light, obeying God's commands
2:15–17	We must not love the world
2:18–27	We have the anointing of the Spirit, to know the truth
2:28 – 3:10	As God's children, we cannot continue in sin
3:11–24	We must love each other in action, as Jesus loved us
4:1–6	Spirits from God acknowledge Jesus' incarnation
4:7–21	God's love for us prompts our love for each other
5:1–12	We overcome the world through obedience and faith
5:13–21	Conclusion: our confidence in approaching God

Like other early Christian writings, 1 John appears to be addressing concerns raised when Christian belief encountered Greek philosophical ideas, especially those that gave rise to Gnosticism in the second century. There is a strong emphasis on Jesus' true humanity, the reality of sin, and the need for practical ethical change in response to knowing God. There is also a clear focus that so-called 'special knowledge' is actually the privilege of all who follow Christ, and is in fact the open secret of transformed relationships.

2 John and 3 John are brief letters, with encouragement and warning:

2 John		3 John	
1–3	Opening greetings	1–2	Opening greetings
4–6	Love one another	3–8	Love visiting believers
7–11	Watch out for deceivers	9–12	Diotrephes and Demetrius
12–13	Closing greetings	13–14	Closing greetings

C. Reading 1, 2 & 3 John today

1 John offers us an integration between truth and love, so often separated in our modern concerns. It also holds together the work of the Spirit with the affirmation of tradition, at least in some form – again, issues which are often set against each other today. The letter at times has an inward-looking feel with its focus on loving relationships within the believing community. But alongside that is the emphasis on the importance of testimony, and a recognition that claims to know God are vacuous without the evidence of transformed relationships.

With 2 & 3 John it is important to note that the discussion of welcome occurs in the context of offering hospitality to wandering teachers. The refusal of hospitality (2 John 10–11) is not about being mean, but about being careful not to give approval to their teaching.

JUDE

See under 2 Peter.

Further reading (see **Introduction** for good commentary series)

Howard Marshall, Steven Travis and Ian Paul, *Exploring the New Testament 2. The Letters and Revelation* (SPCK 2002) – excellent introduction, with panels highlighting themes and points to ponder.
Tom Wright, *What Saint Paul Really Said* (Lion, 1997) – very readable summary of Paul's main themes across his letters.
F. F. Bruce, *Paul: Apostle of the Free Spirit* (Paternoster, 1981) – great combination of Paul's story and his teaching.
Craig Blomberg, *From Pentecost to Patmos: An Introduction and Survey* (IVP 2006) – well-written guide to the key issues.

12. Revelation

Carl Mosser

Revelation is the most misunderstood, abused and maligned book of the Bible. It is also a book of singular importance when properly understood.

A. Authorship and date

Four times the author indicates that his name is John (1:1, 4, 9; 22:8). He refers to himself as a 'servant' of God (1:1) as well as a 'brother and companion' in suffering (1:9). An angel classifies him among a group of Christian prophets (22:9), a designation consistent with John's awareness of writing a prophecy (1:3; 10:11; 22:7, 10, 18–19).

Traditionally the author has been identified with John the son of Zebedee, one of the twelve apostles. There is clear Semitic influence on the book's Greek grammar, indicating that he was a native of Palestine whose first language was Aramaic or Hebrew. This is consistent with authorship by John the son of Zebedee.

However, John was an extremely common name among Palestinian Jews, and we know that at least one other prominent first-century Christian bore the name. John the son of Zebedee became an apostle, but little in Revelation supports identifying its author with one of the apostles. He never calls himself an apostle, and gives no indication that he is among the twelve apostles written on the New Jerusalem's foundations (21:14), or is among the twenty-four enthroned elders, probably the twelve patriarchs and twelve apostles (4:4, 10; 5:8; 11:16;

19:4). So it seems unlikely that the author was John the son of Zebedee but we cannot determine his identity any more than that.

Since the second century most have thought that Revelation was written late in the reign of the emperor Domitian (AD 81–96), though some have argued for the reigns of either Nero earlier (AD 54–68) or Trajan later (AD 98–117). None of the proposals easily accounts for all the internal evidence, but a date near the end of the first century faces the fewest difficulties.

B. What is Revelation?

Misinterpreting Revelation usually begins with misunderstanding the kind of book it is. So we need to consider its genre very carefully.

1. Revelation, not revelations

Revelation is commonly but erroneously referred to as 'the Book of Revelations' (plural). This stems from the widespread assumption that it is a series of esoteric revelations about end-time events. Readers then treat its imagery and symbolism as a kind of code, and attempt to decipher it to reveal literal descriptions of the near future. For example, some have 'discovered' that the locusts with human faces, breastplates and stings in their tails (9:7–10) are really Apache attack helicopters, or that the 'mark of the beast' (13:16–17) is really a microchip placed under the skin or on product barcodes. And every few years someone claims to have deciphered the precise date of Jesus' return. But numerous predicted dates have now passed, and Jesus has yet to return.

Does the Bible really conclude with a book of cryptic revelations, undecipherable until long after it was written? The book itself refutes this view. It begins by declaring itself a 'revelation [singular] from Jesus Christ' (1:1). This revelation was written for churches in the first-century Roman province of Asia (1:11; 22:16), what today is western Turkey. Church members were told to read and listen attentively, because the time was near (1:3). So they would have had to understand the book in order to comply with it. Moreover, the author was told not to seal up the book's prophecy due to the nearness of its fulfilment (22:10). This contrasts markedly with Daniel in the OT, for whom 'the words are closed up and sealed until the time of the end' (Dan. 12:9). All this entails that Revelation's symbolism and imagery would have been meaningful to the first recipients. So the context for properly under-standing the book's message must be their historical situation, not ours. Nevertheless, as with the rest of the NT, the message of Revelation transcends the circumstances of its original readers to speak to Christians in all times.

2. Revelation the letter

After a brief prologue (1:1–3), the formal beginning of Revelation (1:4–6) is that of a typical letter. It identifies the author, John, and the recipients, the seven churches in Asia. This is followed by a wish of grace and peace, a common feature of early Christian letters. The book also concludes with a grace wish (22:21), another characteristic of early Christian letters. In this way the entire book is framed as a letter to seven churches. So it is a serious mistake to divorce chs. 1 – 3 from chs. 4 – 22, as if only the first part of the book was really intended for those named as the addressees.

John informs us about a visionary experience he had while exiled on the island of Patmos. He is instructed to record his vision and send the written scroll to the churches (1:9–11). Each church is discussed specifically (2:1 – 3:22), but the letter as a whole is addressed to all seven. This means that the visions were intended to be applied in practical ways to the specific circumstances of these churches. We must therefore take their first-century historical context seriously in the interpretation of every part of the letter.

3. Revelation the apocalypse

The book's opening line refers to 'the revelation [Greek: *apokalypsis*] from Jesus Christ' (1:1). It is not clear whether this is intended as a technical literary classification. Nonetheless, the word revelation and the book's subsequent content suggest that it should be regarded as an 'apocalypse'. Modern scholars classify a number of early Jewish and Christian texts as apocalypses, though Revelation is the only NT example.

Apocalypses centre on a first-person narrative in which a supernatural agent mediates revelatory visions to the narrator, who then records them for the benefit of others. These visions employ rich imagery, symbolism and other literary devices to communicate a transcendent perspective on human experience, especially that of the readers, and to encourage conformity to this perspective in thinking and behaviour. But the visions are *not* encoded instructions. Whereas code must be deciphered and translated into plain language to be understood, symbolic imagery is an irreducible part of the message being communicated in the apocalypse. The symbolism conveys something about reality that is otherwise impossible to articulate.

Revelation's symbolic visions are not encoded descriptions of events either. Even less are they John's attempts to describe technologies of the far distant future. Instead, the symbols would have communicated transcendent truths in a meaningful way to the immediate addressees. They were meant to give the original recipients insight into their own situation and its place in God's plan of salvation, and to inspire confidence in God's promise.

4. Revelation the prophecy

In addition to being a letter and an apocalypse, Revelation also identifies itself as a prophecy to be read in the context of Christian worship (1:3). Like OT prophetic texts, its primary purpose was not foretelling the future. Rather, as a prophecy, it contains God's rebuke of the sinful compromises of his people (e.g. 2:4–5, 14–16, 20–25; 3:1–3, 15–18) and his critique of a corrupt society's rampant injustice and immorality (see esp. 17:1–4; 18:2–24; 21:8, 27). It calls the people of God to respond in repentant obedience (cf. 22:7).

To the degree that future events are predicted, they chiefly declare two certainties. The first is the certainty of God's coming judgment against unrighteousness. The second is the certainty of his promise to make a world that reflects his untarnished goodness and glory. Both aspects encourage repentance and faithful perseverance. Those who hear the prophecy are expected to heed its warnings, and will be blessed if they do. By contrast, judgment awaits anyone who attempts to alter the prophecy and its implications, whether by subtraction or addition (22:18–19).

C. Structure

1:1–8	Prologue and epistolary introduction
1:9 – 3:22	Initial vision of Jesus and messages to the seven churches
4:1 – 5:14	Vision of heaven and the Lamb worthy to open God's scroll
6:1 – 8:5	Opening the scroll's seven seals
8:6 – 11:19	Blowing the seven trumpets
12:1 – 14:20	Conflict between the saints and the powers of evil
15:1 – 16:21	The seven bowls of plague
17:1 – 19:10	Babylon the Great and her downfall
19:11 – 20:15	The world's conquest and judgment
22:1 – 22:5	The New Jerusalem and renewal of the cosmos
22:6–21	Epilogue and epistolary closing

D. Content

Revelation opens with a prologue that describes the book and its basic purpose (1:1–3). Then comes the formal beginning of the letter (1:4–8). This epistolary introduction leads into a vision of the glorified Jesus and his messages to the churches in Ephesus, Smyrna, Pergamum, Thyatira, Sardis, Philadelphia and Laodicea (1:9 – 3:22). Each message follows the same basic pattern: address to the church's angel or messenger; Jesus' self-description drawn from the vision in ch. 1; commendation for the church's good qualities and critique for its faults; warning to heed the message; and finally promise for the victorious. Within this pattern, nothing good is said about the churches in Sardis and Laodicea, and nothing bad about those in Smyrna and Philadelphia.

Next, John is taken up to the throne room of heaven by the Spirit (4:1–11). God is on the throne, holding a sealed scroll with his decree of judgment and redemption for the world. A voice asks, 'Who is worthy to break the seals and open the scroll?' (5:2). But no one worthy is found anywhere in the created order, so John weeps (5:4). Then the Lamb of God enters and is declared worthy to open the scroll, because he shed his blood to purchase people for God from 'every tribe and language and people and nation' (5:9).

After receiving praise from every kind of created being (5:13), the Lamb proceeds to open each of the scroll's seals in turn. For the first six seals this is accompanied by momentous events: conquest (6:1–2), the removal of peace (6:3–4), famine (6:5–6), death (6:7–8), the cry of the martyrs for justice (6:9–11), an earthquake and cosmic signs of doom (6:12–14). Then, before the final seal's opening, John has two visions of groups of people, first 144,000, consisting of 12,000 from each of the twelve tribes of Israel (7:1–8), and then a vast multitude (7:9–12).

The identity of the 144,000 has often been misunderstood. They are mentioned again later, where they are identified as the human 'first-fruits' offered to God and the Lamb (14:4), and described as those who 'did not defile themselves with women', truthful and blameless (14:4–5). This does *not* intend to idealize ascetic celibacy or imply that women are somehow tainted! Rather, 'blameless' refers to the OT requirement that priests and sacrificial animals be free from physical defect, and that soldiers on duty be free from ritual impurity caused by seminal emission (Deut. 23:9–14; 1 Sam. 21:5–6). The 144,000 are a contingent of physically whole, ritually pure, morally upstanding individuals qualified to serve as warriors in a holy war. In other words, the 144,000 represent the armies from heaven that the Messiah leads to victory over the forces of evil (cf. 19:11–14).

The opening of the seventh seal is followed by a long silence and the distribution of trumpets to seven angels (8:1–5). As with the opening of each seal, the blowing of each trumpet leads to disaster on the earth (8:6 – 11:19). Prior to the seventh trumpet, John again has two visions (10:1 – 11:14). In one he eats a little scroll, and in the other he sees two witnesses who prophesy, are killed and rise up again. The seventh trumpet is then blown, leading to hymns praising God for his righteous judgments (11:15–19).

At 12:1 the book takes a new direction. John's vision shifts from God's outpoured judgment to a series of 'signs' which depict God's people in conflict with evil (12:1 – 15:4). The theme of divine judgment is picked up again with an even greater 'sign'. John sees 'seven angels with the seven last plagues' (15:1) representing 'God's wrath on the earth' (16:1). As with the plagues on Egypt in Exodus, the angels pour out the full force of God's holy anger against the wickedness embodied by Rome. We then see Rome, called 'Babylon the Great, the Mother of Prostitutes', destroyed and lamented (17:1 – 19:10).

The vision reaches its climactic section with the arrival of the rider on a white horse along with the armies of heaven (19:11–16). They prove victorious in their battle against the kings of the earth. This ushers in a millennium in which the righteous reign with Christ on the earth (20:1–6). After the thousand years Satan is released and prepares for one final battle, but fire from heaven devours his forces (20:7–10). This sets the stage for the resurrection and last judgment (20:11–15). John's vision – as well as the entire biblical drama – then reaches its climax as he sees 'a new heaven and a new earth', in which God dwells with his people for ever (21:1 – 22:5).

E. Symbolism

The imagery of Revelation is intentionally evocative and suggestive. While depicting both transcendent and earthly realities, it does not always correspond with literal events. Moreover, it often alludes to the experiences and fears of people living in the Roman Empire at the end of the first century, including popular myths, rumours and expectations. For example, it alludes to popular fears about a Parthian invasion from the east (9:13–19; 16:12), and to the contemporary myth that Nero, though long dead, would one day return (13:3; 17:8) – 'the number of the Beast', 666, is also 'the number of a man' (13:18), probably Nero. He was the 'head' of the Roman Empire that violently persecuted Christians, one of the chief sins for which Rome would be judged (cf. 16:6; 17:6; 18:24; 19:2).

This kind of imagery engages the imagination and provokes consideration of the divine judgment that awaits Rome and the world. Christians have long debated whether it also predicts specific future events. Similarly, they have long debated whether the evocative description of the saints' millennial reign on earth is meant to be fulfilled literally. These are important questions, but they should not be allowed to eclipse the book's central message. Even if this symbolism is meant to find fulfilment in future events, that is not its primary purpose. Rather, Revelation seeks to influence present behaviour by a profound vision of God, his judgment, the vindication of the righteous, and the renewal of creation.

F. Canonical function and contemporary significance

John sees himself as standing in the tradition of the OT prophets, and his prophetic commission (10:8–11) clearly recalls Ezekiel's (Ezek. 2:8 – 3:3). But he goes beyond them in declaring 'the mystery of God ... announced to his servants the prophets' (10:7). They foretold the coming Day of the Lord, while John proclaims its fulfilment in God's final judgment and re-creation of the earth. Like them, he is someone to whom the Lord reveals his secrets (cf. Amos 3:7; 1 Pet. 1:10).

Revelation is saturated with the terminology and imagery of the OT, especially the prophetic books. Yet, John never quotes any specific passages. Instead he appropriates prophecies and applies them in new ways. They provide him with building material for a prophetic vision that brings the entire prophetic tradition to a stunning climax. Regardless of their original application, John interprets their ultimate fulfilment in the events he foretells. For example, Isaiah and Jeremiah deliver a number of oracles against Babylon (Isa. 13:1 – 14:23; 21:1–10; 47; Jer. 25:12–38; 50 – 51), and John echoes these in his own oracle against Babylon (18:1 – 19:8). But whereas Isaiah's and Jeremiah's oracles were directed against the Neo-Babylonian empire, John's is directed at Rome, giving the ancient oracles new currency. This one example illustrates the way in which John's prophecy serves as the culmination of the Bible's entire prophetic tradition. His prophetic critique continues to apply whenever injustice, tyranny and wickedness are recapitulated within human history.

As the climax of biblical prophecy, Revelation also brings the biblical drama of creation and redemption to a close. It gives readers a glimpse of the reality that lies behind world history. While evil may seem unstoppable in our fallen world, this is mere appearance. Reality is found in the promise of the almighty Creator. Revelation reveals that promise by portraying the drama's final act: the enemies of the Lamb are defeated, his followers are vindicated, and the kingdom of the world becomes the kingdom of God and the Lamb. The God who created the world triumphs over evil, renews the cosmos, and comes down to dwell with humanity in the New Jerusalem. The purposes for which the cosmos and humanity were originally created are now fulfilled. The biblical drama is brought full circle.

This brings the canon of Scripture to a close with a solemn promise – God obligates himself to complete the salvation that he revealed in Jesus Christ. He binds himself to consummating the new creation begun in Jesus' resurrection and the regeneration of his followers (cf. 1 Pet. 1:3–5; 2 Cor. 5:17). This promise is intended to bolster confidence and hope in God's people, as they contend with the powers of this age.

With John we are able to penetrate heaven and see what is really going on in the world. There we see that the views of reality perpetuated by every tyrannical regime and power are false, that the façades and illusions created by evil powers like Rome are lies. We discover that the Creator has intentions for the world that transcend anything rebellious creatures might concoct for themselves. And the Creator's intentions will be fulfilled, whereas those of rebels will be brought to naught. The here-and-now can be depressing and hopeless when viewed only from within. But when seen from a transcendent perspective, it looks quite different. And this vision has a powerful effect on how one lives in the eager anticipation of the revealing of Jesus Christ.

Further reading (see **Introduction** for good commentary series)

Howard Marshall, Steven Travis and Ian Paul, *Exploring the New Testament 2. The Letters and Revelation* (SPCK, 2002) – excellent introduction, with panels highlighting themes and points to ponder.

Marvin Pate (editor), *Four Views on the Book of Revelation* (Zondervan, 1998) – good summary of different interpretations.

Richard Bauckham, *The Theology of the Book of Revelation* (CUP, 1993) – careful, readable study.

Craig Blomberg, *From Pentecost to Patmos: An Introduction and Survey* (IVP, 2006) – well-written guide to the key issues.

Reading the Bible

Suppose that you are sitting down with your Bible for the first time. How then do you best approach the job of reading it?

From start to finish

This is certainly a valid approach: begin with Genesis and work your way through to Revelation. It will give you a comprehensive idea of what is in the Bible, and you will avoid the danger of spending all your time in certain books and ignoring others. You will also be beginning where Jesus and the apostles began: the only Bible they had was the OT. A variation on this theme is to read the OT and the NT side by side, taking a chapter or two from each every day. This gives you a more varied diet.

The major problem with reading the Bible in this way is that some of the earlier books of the OT are not easy to understand, especially for new Christians. If you start at the beginning and quickly arrive at some difficult material, you may get stuck. For more established Christians, however, this method could well yield surprising and fruitful discoveries. But be aware that unless you can tackle large chunks of the Bible every day, you will take a long time to read from cover to cover.

A book at a time

Although individual Bible texts can mean a great deal to us, the authors wrote whole books, which have various themes running through them. This means that a logical way to read a Bible book is from beginning to end. In doing this we see how the author has developed the themes, and get an idea of how the readers were meant to respond. We see isolated verses and events in their wider context. As we go along, we begin to understand the sequence of the story or argument.

Some people prefer to start with the big picture and fit all the details into it; others would rather begin with the details and use them to put the picture together. If you are a big picture person, you will want to try to take in a whole book before going on to look at shorter passages and separate verses. But whatever your point of departure, remember that the parts need to be set in the context of the whole, or you may interpret them in ways that the authors never intended.

Small sections

At some point we will want to begin asking what the individual passages, sentences and words of the Bible meant to the authors, and what they mean for us. This approach means reading much shorter portions than whole books, and for this we will need some sort of plan. You can make your own, by reading to the most natural break in the story or argument, or reading one or two of the sub-sections into which many Bible translations divide the text. Most daily Bible reading notes also take you through a book by short steps.

Because you are dealing only with short sections, you have more time to ask detailed questions about the meaning of the passage. It is at this point that many of the books in the Further Reading sections will be most useful, helping you to understand the background issues, illuminating the difficult words and phrases, and applying the text to your own life. You may also like to make notes as you go along, especially if one reason for studying the Bible is to teach it to others. In your preparation you can then go back to what you have discovered yourself.

Themes

This is a more challenging method of Bible study, but it repays the effort. We may want to know what the whole Bible teaches about 'the kingdom of God', or what Paul meant by 'righteousness'. If so, we will need to look at all the major passages that deal with the theme, collecting their teaching and building up the picture for ourselves. The possibilities are numerous and varied, and a Bible dictionary or other study aid will give you some ideas and help you pursue them.

But notice the reference above to 'passages'. When studying a Bible topic it is tempting to get out a concordance and look up every verse in which the term is mentioned. Although this exercise has some value, you run the risk of seeing individual verses in isolation from their context, and so of misunderstanding them. It is much better to find the longer sections in which the subject is discussed and study these one by one. When you put their teachings together you will have a much more coherent view of the theme.

Reading for pleasure

Some people like to sit down in comfort, pick up their Bible and just read it. We can relax into the world of Scripture and simply let it speak to us. Or we can read it more slowly and prayerfully until we find it addressing our current circumstances. Often we will discover a new command or promise, or some aspect of God's purpose that strengthens or challenges us. But if you like to use this method, don't neglect to do some detailed study as well, so that it is God's voice that you hear in the Bible and not just your own!

Studying with others

Although it is good to read the Bible for yourself, it is also useful to come to it with other Christians. Some people have the gift of teaching, and can make the Bible clear to a whole group of people. In our churches we have an opportunity week by week to explore God's Word together through the ministry of our leaders. We may like to use the church Bibles or take one of our own to follow the readings and look up the references.

Another popular and helpful way of looking at the Bible is in small groups. The particular value of this approach is that, although the group leader will have prepared the study, it gives an opportunity for each person to share their understandings with the others. Also the leader is able to put right any obvious *mis*understandings!

To get the most out of a small group study, have a look at the passage and any notes beforehand, and come prepared to share what you have found, as well as to listen to others and ask questions. The best small group studies are very practical, so expect to learn together how the passage you are studying can apply to your lives.

Memorization

One well-tried way of retaining what you have read is to commit it to memory. With our convenient chapter and verse divisions, it is fairly easy for us to memorize verses from the Bible, and we can learn the references too. But as we have already seen, single verses can too easily be taken out of their context and be made to mean less – or more! – than they should. So it is often more helpful to learn chapters or passages.

In your studies you will come across sections that mean a great deal to you. Note these, reread them several times, try writing them from memory, and you will find that learning a passage is not so hard. But make sure that you have first tried to understand them and apply them to your own life. Repeating Bible passages parrot-fashion is no use at all!

Meditation

Meditation is something we can do at any time of the day, and not just in special times that we set apart. If we have spent time studying the Bible, trying to understand and apply it, and perhaps committing it to memory, then through the day, when our minds would otherwise be idle, it can come back to us. Sometimes we realize how the passages we have been reading apply to particular situations at home or at work.

But meditation is something more than just casually remembering what we have read; it is taking time to ponder it. We have worked hard to understand what it means in its setting; now we let it run through our minds. As we do so, we begin to use our imagination as well as our reason to explore the implications of the truth under review. Sometimes it is good to sit down quietly and close your eyes, shutting out the world. Some people find it helpful to jot down their thoughts as these arise.

You don't have to be very knowledgeable to meditate. You need only a Bible verse to start, and then a little mental discipline so that your mind doesn't wander. Meditation is an art, so you will find it getting easier the more you do it.

Prayer

As Christian believers we come to the Bible with faith, expectancy, and willingness to submit to God's will as he reveals it to us. That is why it is most natural to ask God for his help as we read it. This principle applies whether we study it privately, or whether we listen to its exposition in public.

Not only should we move into our Bible study with prayer; we should also move from it in the same way. We may turn the themes, promises and commands that we have read into praise, confession, petition and intercession for others. To surround our Bible study with prayer is to approach it in the right way, as God's written Word to us.

Index of Scripture References